HISTORICAL ATLAS
OF MORMONISM

Edited by

S. Kent Brown
Donald Q. Cannon
Richard H. Jackson

D0004430

SIMON & SCHUSTER

A Paramount Communications Company

New York   London   Toronto   Sydney   Tokyo   Singapore

Copyright © 1994 by Simon & Schuster Inc.

All rights reserved. No part of this book may be
reprinted or reproduced or utilized in any form or by any
electronic, mechanical, or other means, now known or
hereafter invented, including photocopying and recording,
or in any information storage or retrieval system, without
permission in writing from the publisher.

Simon & Schuster
Academic Reference Division
15 Columbus Circle
New York, New York 10023

Printed in the United States of America

printing number

1 2 3 4 5 6 7 8 9 10

Library of Congress Cataloging-in-Publication Data

Historical atlas of Mormonism / edited by S. Kent Brown, Donald Q.
    Cannon, Richard H. Jackson.
        p.   cm.
    Includes index.
    ISBN 0-13-045147-9 (alk. paper)
    1. Mormon Church—History—Maps.   2. Mormons—History—Maps.
I. Brown, S. Kent.   II. Cannon, Donald Q., 1936– .   III. Jackson,
Richard H., 1941–
G1021.E42H5   1994   <G&M>
289.3'022'3—dc20
                                                94-21912
                                                CIP
                                                MAP

This paper meets the requirements of ANSI/NISO Z39.48-1992
(Permanence of Paper).

CONTENTS

INTRODUCTION

The experience of the Church of Jesus Christ of Latter-day Saints is a unique one in the annals of American history and geography. Organized in upstate New York on April 6, 1830, with only six charter members, the Church—known popularly as the Mormon Church—had grown to over 8 million members by the beginning of 1994. The 164 years of its existence have been characterized by persecution, migration, expansion, and growth.

The Church itself is a uniquely American institution, emphasizing puritanical virtues of industry, thrift, community cooperation, grassroots democracy, patriotism, and abstinence and moderation in a context of striving for individual spiritual perfection. Founded under the direction of Joseph Smith, Jr., who recorded in his history of the Church that he had seen God in a vision, the Mormon Church alienated other religions by its claim to be the only true Christian church. Its earliest converts were from the northeastern United States, but the American penchant for westward movement was paralleled by the Mormon movement to Ohio in 1831. Locating at Kirtland, Ohio, the nascent movement sent out missionaries to other parts of the United States and Canada. The frontier spirit of America was manifested as Joseph Smith proclaimed that Jackson County, Missouri, was the new promised land for the Latter-day Saints. By the mid 1830s the Church was concentrated in and around Kirtland and in Missouri.

The population of the new faith soared in the latter half of the 1830s as missionaries went to Europe and found fertile ground for the Latter-day Saints' message of hope. As new converts gathered to join the main body of the Saints, growing conflict with other frontier settlers repeatedly interrupted the Mormons' community-building efforts. Persecutions forced Mormons to move from Missouri to Illinois, where the Prophet Joseph Smith, Jr., was martyred in 1844. Leaving behind their city of Nauvoo, which had been one of the largest settlements in Illinois, the Mormons, beginning in 1846, fled to the arid Great Basin of the American West.

That the Mormons colonized the West is well known, but less known is the fact that as with their eastern experience, the western settlement was marked by hardship and persecution. Arriving in the Salt Lake valley in 1847, Mormons established hundreds of communities from Canada to Mexico. Under the direction of Brigham Young they created a far-flung empire whose impact on the geography of the West persists today. Mormon exploration and colonization helped lay the framework for the 20th-century growth of the West, a framework reinforced by continued immigration of converts from the East and from Europe.

The 20th century brought ever increasing growth to the Mormon Church, which has begun the transition from an American institution to a worldwide one. The flow of immigrants that characterized the Great Basin Mormon communities for a century has been diverted as new converts have been encouraged to gather in their own homelands. The growth of the Church has transformed it into a worldwide multicultural organization whose membership remains committed to the doctrines and beliefs espoused by the Prophet Joseph Smith, Jr.

The Mormon experience has been unevenly associated with local and national geographies. In some places, such as Kirtland, Ohio; Nauvoo, Illinois; or the communities of the Intermountain West, the Mormon experience was central to both the local history and geography. Some places have the impact of the Mormon experience deeply imprinted upon their geography today, while in others only a few relics remain to speak mutely of the past role of the Mormons. The Mormon role in some local and national geographies is recent, and the evidence of the Mormon presence is but a small piece of the larger geographic mosaic of such places. Regardless of the evidence of the Mormon experience in a specific place, the growth and spread of the Church is tied to the history and geography of that locale.

The maps in this volume introduce the reader to the geographic relationships associated with the history of the Mormons. Each map attempts to answer geographic questions concerning the who, where, when, and how of events important in Mormon history. The essay associated with each map provides the detail necessary to move beyond the map to understanding the people and events whose actions shaped the Mormon experience. Bibliographies direct readers to sources of more information. We hope that the combination of map and written explanation will be useful to all who have any level of interest in the rise and spread of this American religious institution.

As editors, we accept responsibility for any errors herein. We also acknowledge that the authors of each essay and map are largely responsible for whatever merit the volume may contain. Suggestions for corrections or improvements will be graciously accepted.

S. Kent Brown
Donald Q. Cannon
Richard H. Jackson

Provo, Utah
May 1994

PREFACE

Undertaking the task of mapping the local, regional, and global aspects of any group is demanding. When that group's growth over a century and a half corresponds with diffusion across America and into numerous foreign countries, it creates an even greater challenge in simply defining what is important enough to map. This volume was undertaken to help users understand where and how the events of Mormon history relate to specific places or regions. This atlas is not intended to be exhaustive, but it is hoped that the maps and subjects included will enlighten readers about the places affected by the unique American religion commonly referred to as Mormon.

The actual maps and topics included are the result of discussion by the editors with numerous scholars of the Mormon experience over the last three decades. Some maps the editors' personal interest in Mormon history; others were suggested by colleagues. We are particularly indebted to the numerous contributors who freely devoted their time to prepare each essay and provide the data necessary to design each map. They shared years of research willingly, and without complaint condensed hundreds of pages of scholarship into the one page we allotted for each essay.

The maps reflect the diligent work of the contributors and the cartography laboratory of the Geography Department of Brigham Young University. Jeffry S. Bird, cartographic technician for the Geography Department, and his assistants Gaiping Li, Kim Young-Sook, and Jeffery N. Jarvis provided yeoman service in data entry and cartographic design through many phases of development. Jeff Bird was particularly instrumental in helping design the maps and in making all the final cartographic changes.

The idea for this work was suggested to us by Charles E. Smith, President of the Academic Reference Division of Simon & Schuster, when he visited Brigham Young University in June 1992. His enthusiasm helped the editors persist in their task. Paul Bernabeo, Editorial Director of the Academic Reference Division, brought the project to fruition. Paul shepherded the editors through the numerous details associated with editing a multiauthor volume and encouraged the prompting of dilatory contributors to complete their tasks.

Mary V. Dearborn served as manuscript editor. Her careful editing of each essay clarified ambiguities, reduced redundancy, and focused the authors' prose. Debra H. Alpern and Sara E. Simon have been responsible for map review and day-to-day management of the project. Their work has ensured that logistics of the project did not overwhelm the editors and provided a professional overview of the maps. To each of these individuals and to all others of Simon & Schuster who made this volume possible, we extend our heartfelt thanks.

We would also like to thank the Dean of Religious Education and the Chair of the Department of Geography at Brigham Young University for their encouragement and support. Deans and department chairs assisted graciously when requested, and their willingness to allow us to devote time to this project made it possible for us to complete it.

Finally, we want to recognize the unstinting efforts of Barbara Newell Crawley, secretary of the Religious Studies Center of Brigham Young University. She willingly added service as secretary and general factotum for the editors to her already heavy load. Moreover, she provided keen insight as we reviewed each essay and map, catching errors we otherwise would have missed. For her assistance and enthusiasm we dedicate this volume to her.

DIRECTORY OF CONTRIBUTORS

A. Gary Anderson
Associate Professor of Church History and Doctrine,
Brigham Young University
Migration Routes to the West

Karl Ricks Anderson
Retired Consultant, Instructor for LDS Church Education
System, Lyndhurst, Ohio
Northern Ohio Settlements

Lavina Fielding Anderson
Editing Inc., Salt Lake City
David O. McKay's Worldwide Travels

Richard Lloyd Anderson
Professor of Ancient Scripture, Brigham Young University
Joseph Smith's Ancestors

Leonard J. Arrington
Professor Emeritus of History; Professor Emeritus, Charles
Redd Center for Western Studies; Brigham Young University
Economic Development in Early Utah

Milton V. Backman
Professor Emeritus of Church History and Doctrine,
Brigham Young University
Nauvoo Tourist Sites

Maureen Ursenbach Beecher
Professor of English, Research Professor, Joseph Fielding Smith
Institute for Church History, Brigham Young University
Relief Society (1884)
Eliza R. Snow's Relief Society Travels (1880–1881)

Richard E. Bennett
Head, Archives and Special Collections,
University of Manitoba
Canada

Lowell C. Bennion
Professor of Geography, Humboldt State University
Saints of the Western States (1990)

Susan Easton Black
Professor of Church History and Doctrine,
Brigham Young University
Early Missionary Journeys
Earliest Congregations (1828–1831)
The Mormon Battalion

Alma R. Blair
Professor of History, Graceland College
Conflict in Missouri

David F. Boone
Assistant Professor of Church History and Doctrine,
Brigham Young University
Missions
Missionary Training Centers

Martha S. Bradley
Visiting Assistant Professor of Architecture, University of Utah
Polygamy

S. Kent Brown
Professor of Ancient Scripture, Brigham Young University
Birthplaces of Church Leaders (1830–1840)

Brian Q. Cannon
Assistant Professor of History, Brigham Young University
Salt Lake City (1847)
Salt Lake Valley (1848–1870)

Donald Q. Cannon
Professor of Church History and Doctrine,
Brigham Young University
Commerce, Illinois
Nauvoo (1842)
Hancock County, Illinois

Sean J. Cannon
Captain, U.S. Army, Ft. Leonard Wood, Missouri
Expulsion from Missouri

Howard A. Christy
Senior Editor, Scholarly Publications,
Brigham Young University
Indian Farms

Richard O. Cowan
Professor of Church History and Doctrine,
Brigham Young University
Temples

Jessie L. Embry
Instructor, Department of History; Director, Oral History
Program, Charles Redd Center for Western Studies;
Brigham Young University
Ethnic Makeup in the 20th Century

Donald L. Enders
Senior Curator, LDS Museum of Church History and Art, Salt Lake City
Palmyra, New York
New York State

Ronald K. Esplin
Director and Research Associate Professor, Joseph Fielding Smith Institute for Church History, Brigham Young University
Brigham Young's Travels in the West

Arnold K. Garr
Professor of Church History and Doctrine, Brigham Young University
Early Missionary Journeys in North America

Audrey M. Godfrey
Logan, Utah
Relations with the U.S. Military

Kenneth W. Godfrey
Institute Director, LDS Logan Institute of Religion, Utah State University
Illinois
Immigration to Nauvoo

Fred R. Gowans
Professor of History, Brigham Young University
Exploring the West before 1847
Exploring the West after 1847

Leon R. Hartshorn
Professor of Church History and Doctrine, Brigham Young University
Educational Institutions

Gail Geo. Holmes
Omaha, Nebraska
The Missouri River Valley

Richard Neitzel Holzapfel
Assistant Professor of Church History and Doctrine, Brigham Young University
The Church on the Early 19th-Century Frontier
Pennsylvania

Lloyd E. Hudman
Professor of Geography, Brigham Young University
Historic Sites and Tourism

Richard H. Jackson
Professor of Geography, Brigham Young University
Hill Cumorah
First Gathering to Zion
The City of Zion Plat
Nauvoo: Frontier City

Clark V. Johnson
Professor of Church History and Doctrine, Brigham Young University
Northern Missouri

James L. Kimball , Jr.
LDS Church Historical Department, Salt Lake City
Land Ownership in Nauvoo and Vicinity

Stanley B. Kimball
Professor of History, Southern Illinois University
Eastern Iowa
Rail Routes (1831–1869)
From Nauvoo to Council Bluffs

Glen M. Leonard
Director, LDS Church Museum of Church History and Art, Salt Lake City
Pioneer Property in Salt Lake City

Garth L. Mangum
McGraw Professor of Economics, Professor of Management, University of Utah
Welfare Projects

Dean L. May
Professor of History, University of Utah
Expansion along the Wasatch Front
The State of Deseret

Philip F. Notarianni
Coordinator of Public Programs, Utah Historical Society, Magna, Utah
Gentiles in Utah

Max H Parkin
Instructor, Salt Lake University Institute of Religion, University of Utah
Jackson County and Vicinity
Independence, Missouri

Keith W. Perkins
Professor of Church History and Doctrine, Brigham Young University
Kirtland and Vicinity
Land Ownership in Kirtland

Paul H. Peterson
Associate Professor of Church History and Doctrine, Brigham Young University
Sam Brannan and the *Brooklyn* Saints

Lynn A. Rosenvall
Chair, Department of Geography, University of Calgary
Expansion outside the Wasatch Front
Abandoned Settlements in the West

Steven L. Shields
RLDS Minister, El Segundo, California
Divergent Paths from Nauvoo

Jan Shipps
Professor of History and Religious Studies, Indiana University–Purdue University at Indianapolis
Emergence of Mormonism on the American Landscape (1950–1965)

J. Matthew Shumway
Assistant Professor of Geography, Brigham Young University
Membership Growth by States and Countries
Distribution of World Membership (1992)

Dale J. Stevens
Professor of Geography, Brigham Young University
Doctrine and Covenants
Growth of Stakes

Vivian Linford Talbot
Bountiful, Utah
Exploring the West after 1847

LaMond Tullis
Professor of Political Science, Brigham Young University
Mormon Colonies in Mexico

Bruce A. Van Orden
Associate Professor of Church History and Doctrine, Brigham Young University
From Kirtland to Missouri
Expeditions from Kirtland

Wayne L. Wahlquist
Professor of Geography, Weber State University
Mormon Trail

Jean Bickmore White
Professor Emeritus of Political Science, Weber State University
Utah Voting Patterns in the 20th Century

David J. Whittaker
Associate Professor of History; Senior Librarian, Harold B. Lee Library; Brigham Young University
Missionary Journeys to Foreign Countries

HISTORICAL ATLAS
OF MORMONISM

BIRTHPLACES OF CHURCH LEADERS (1830–1840)

S. Kent Brown

The early Latter-day Saint movement centered chiefly in New York and Ohio, and initial missionary activity focused on the northeastern United States. Consequently, most early Mormon leaders resided in this region. Moreover, when they heard the missionaries' message, many lived no farther than a few hundred miles from their places of birth.

The Prophet Joseph Smith was born December 23, 1805, in Sharon, Vermont, the third son of Joseph Smith, Sr., and Lucy Mack. Emma Hale, wife of the Prophet, was born July 10, 1804, in Harmony (now Oakland), Pennsylvania, the seventh of nine children of Isaac and Elizabeth Lewis Hale. She and Joseph married January 18, 1827.

The Three Witnesses to the Book of Mormon became prominent in ecclesiastical affairs at an early date. In June 1829 they received a divine charge to choose twelve apostles, a task finally completed on February 14, 1835. Of the Three Witnesses, Martin Harris was the first to have contact with Joseph Smith—in Palmyra, New York, where the Smith family had moved in 1816. Harris was born May 18, 1783, in Easton, New York. Oliver Cowdery, another of the witnesses, met Joseph Smith on April 5, 1829, and became the chief scribe for the Book of Mormon. Cowdery was born in Wells, Vermont, on October 3, 1806. The last, David Whitmer, came to know the Prophet when he and Oliver Cowdery moved to the Whitmer farm in Fayette, New York, to finish translating the Book of Mormon (June 1829). Whitmer was born near Harrisburg, Pennsylvania, on January 7, 1805.

The initial First Presidency of the Church was organized in March 1832. It included Joseph Smith as president, and Sidney Rigdon and Jesse Gause as counselors. After the excommunication of Gause later that year, Frederick G. Williams was selected as second counselor. Rigdon was born February 19, 1793, in St. Clair Township, near Pittsburgh, Pennsylvania. In August 1844, following the martyrdom of Joseph Smith, Rigdon tried to convince church members to select him as guardian of the Church, holding the slain Joseph Smith as the only Prophet. While little is known about Gause's birth, it is certain that he was born to William and Mary Beverly Gause about 1785 in Pennsylvania. Williams was born October 28, 1787, in Suffield, Connecticut. He turned against the Prophet and the Church in 1838 during the period of rising tensions in Missouri.

The original Quorum of Twelve Apostles was organized February 14, 1835, in Kirtland, Ohio. The quorum's first president was Thomas B. Marsh, who was born in Acton, Massachusetts, on November 1, 1799 (some sources say 1800). He apostatized from the Church in 1839, but rejoined in 1857. The second member of the quorum was David W. Patten, born November 14, 1799, in Theresa, New York. He was killed at the Battle of Crooked River in a clash with Missouri settlers on October 25, 1838. Brigham Young followed David Patten in seniority, and was the senior apostle when Joseph Smith was killed on June 27, 1844. Young was born on June 1, 1801, at Whitingham, Vermont.

Heber C. Kimball, the fourth member, was born June 14, 1801, in Sheldon, Vermont. He served as first counselor to Brigham Young from December 1847 until his death on June 22, 1868. The fifth person in the quorum was Orson Hyde, born January 8, 1805, in Oxford, Connecticut. His best-known act was the dedication of the Holy Land for the return of the Jews (1841). William E. McLellin, born January 18, 1806, in Smith County, Tennessee, was the sixth original apostle. He was excommunicated from the Church less than four years after his apostolic calling.

Parley P. Pratt became the seventh apostle. Born April 12, 1807, in Burlington, New York, he was assassinated May 13, 1857, in Arkansas while returning from a mission. The next apostle was Luke S. Johnson, who was born November 2, 1807, in Pomfret, Vermont. Excommunicated in 1838, he was rebaptized in 1846. William B. Smith, brother of Joseph Smith, was the ninth. Born March 13, 1811, in Royalton, Vermont, William was excommunicated October 19, 1845, more than a year after the martyrdoms of his older brothers Joseph and Hyrum.

The tenth member of the quorum was Orson Pratt, younger brother of Parley. Orson was born September 19, 1811, in Hartford, New York. He became known as an important theologian of the Church. John F. Boynton, born September 20, 1811, in Bradford, Massachusetts, stood in eleventh place. He was excommunicated in 1837 during the economic turmoil in Kirtland, Ohio. The final member of the quorum was Lyman E. Johnson, who was born October 24, 1811, in Pomfret, Vermont, and was a younger brother of Luke. He was excommunicated in April 1838, three years after his call to the apostleship.

In 1838 and 1839 four men were called to be apostles to replace those who had been killed (Patten) or excommunicated (Boynton, Marsh, McLellin, and Luke and Lyman Johnson). Of those four, two became presidents of the Church. John Taylor was the only president born outside the United States, in Milnthorpe, England, on November 1, 1808. He joined the Church in 1836 in Toronto, Canada. Wilford Woodruff, the fourth president of the Church, was born March 1, 1807, in a part of Farmington, Connecticut, that is now Avon. He is known as the president who abolished plural marriage (1890).

Lyndon W. Cook, *The Revelations of the Prophet Joseph Smith* (1981); Andrew Jenson, *Latter-day Saint Biographical Encyclopedia* (1901).

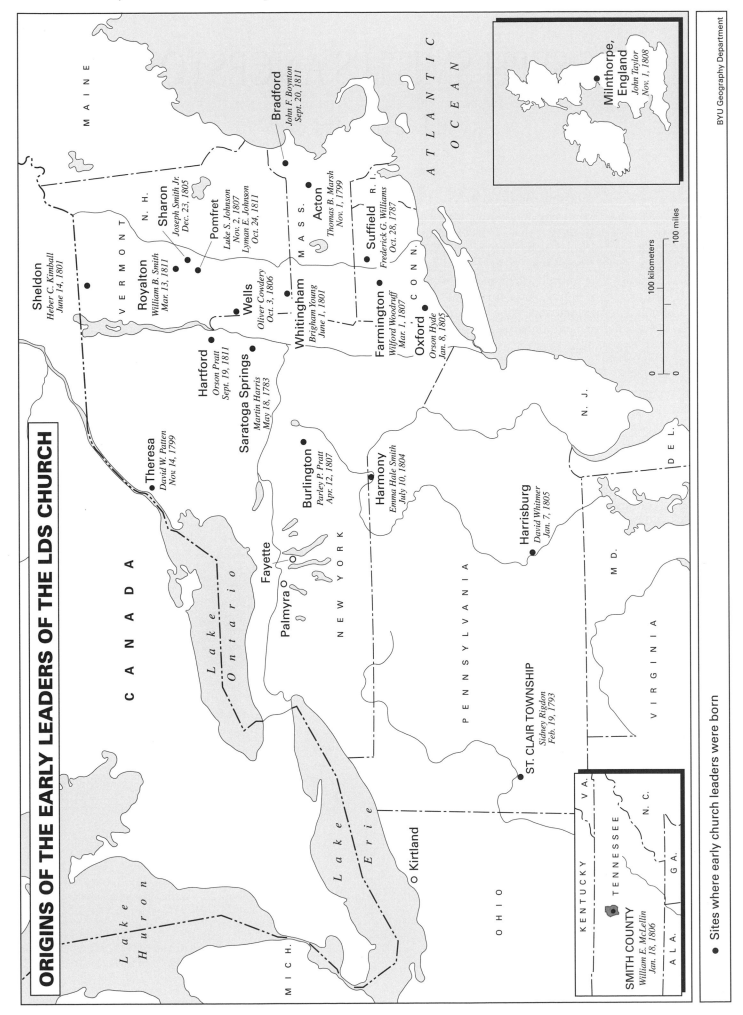

ORIGINS OF THE EARLY LEADERS OF THE LDS CHURCH

Bradford
John F. Boynton
Sept. 20, 1811

Sharon
Joseph Smith Jr.
Dec. 23, 1805

Pomfret
Lake S. Johnson
Nov. 2, 1807
Lyman E. Johnson
Oct. 24, 1811

Acton
Thomas B. Marsh
Nov. 1, 1799

Suffield
Frederick G. Williams
Oct. 28, 1787

Royalton
William B. Smith
Mar. 13, 1811

Wells
Oliver Cowdery
Oct. 3, 1806

Whitingham
Brigham Young
June 1, 1801

Farmington
Wilford Woodruff
Mar. 1, 1807

Oxford
Orson Hyde
Jan. 8, 1805

Sheldon
Heber C. Kimball
June 14, 1801

Hartford
Orson Pratt
Sept. 19, 1811

Saratoga Springs
Martin Harris
May 18, 1783

Theresa
David W. Patten
Nov. 14, 1799

Burlington
Parley P. Pratt
Apr. 12, 1807

Harmony
Emma Hale Smith
July 10, 1804

Harrisburg
David Whitmer
Jan. 7, 1805

Fayette

Palmyra

Kirtland

ST. CLAIR TOWNSHIP
Sidney Rigdon
Feb. 19, 1793

Milnthorpe,
England
John Taylor
Nov. 1, 1808

SMITH COUNTY
William E. McLellin
Jan. 18, 1806

ATLANTIC OCEAN

CANADA

MAINE

N. H.

VERMONT

MASS.

R. I.

CONN.

N. Y.

NEW YORK

PENNSYLVANIA

N. J.

DEL.

MD.

VIRGINIA

OHIO

MICH.

Lake Huron

Lake Erie

Lake Ontario

KENTUCKY

TENNESSEE

N. C.

GA.

ALA.

V. A.

100 miles

100 kilometers

● Sites where early church leaders were born

BYU Geography Department

JOSEPH SMITH'S ANCESTORS

Richard Lloyd Anderson

Joseph Smith's family lines all run through New England, where ancestors were typically community leaders in various locations. Progenitors several steps from Joseph Smith closely fit Christine Leigh Heyrman's profile of the New England norm: "their lives [were] defined by the seasonal rhythms of agriculture, the bonds of family, church, and local community, and a fundamentally religious outlook" (in Eric Foner and John A. Garraty, editors, *Reader's Companion to American History*, 789). The family predecessors of the Prophet were generally active in church and in the New England towns, the self-governing area units that do not appear on ordinary maps unless a municipality of the same name developed.

The roots of Joseph Smith's father were north of Boston. His grandfather was Samuel Smith, Jr., born in Topsfield, Massachusetts, to a family living there since ancestor Robert Smith came from England during the Puritan "great migration." The younger Samuel Smith was a revolutionary patriot and active Congregationalist who regularly represented Topsfield in the state legislature and in local positions as selectman or town clerk. He married Priscilla Gould, of a family going back to the town's founding which produced many prominent public servants.

The second son of this couple was the Prophet's grandfather, Asael Smith. He married Mary Duty, born in the nearby town of Rowley, Massachusetts. Her parents, Moses Duty and Mary Palmer, had generational roots there—records show religious involvement and revolutionary patriotism. Mary and Asael Smith lived for a time at Topsfield, but the second son did not normally inherit, so the couple settled for years in southern New Hampshire, mainly in the towns of Windham and Derryfield, now the town of Manchester. After service in the Revolutionary War, Asael was elected seven times as town clerk at Derryfield, but he returned to Topsfield to salvage his father's honor by settling a complicated estate in difficult economic times. Two main residences followed. Asael first pioneered uncleared land and developed family farms at Tunbridge, Vermont, continuing his pattern of prominence in town and church affairs, though he was a dissenter. He served three terms as selectman, one of the three town managers.

Asael and Mary Smith moved once again in their older age, leaving Vermont for the New York lands that beckoned their children. They were at the town of Stockholm, in upper New York, during the censuses of 1820 and 1830. In 1830, Asael Smith died after receiving a visit from his son Joseph Smith, Sr., and believing the Book of Mormon. Widow Mary Duty Smith also believed, and applied for baptism after migrating to Kirtland, Ohio, before her death in 1836.

The Prophet's maternal ancestors also have familiar New England origins. His mother's mother was Lydia Gates Mack, a teacher with profound Christian faith, born and raised in East Haddam, Connecticut. Her father was Daniel Gates, sometime selectman of the town and also deacon. He married Lydia Fuller, born at East Haddam to a family prominent in the area.

Lydia Gates married Joseph Smith's grandfather, Solomon Mack, whose venturesome life included placement in youth with another family because of the financial misfortune of his parents. Solomon's father was Ebenezer Mack, born in Lyme, Connecticut, and named by his father's will to inherit the family property. Ebenezer married Hannah Huntley, a lifetime schoolteacher who was also from Lyme.

Solomon Mack's quest for success encompassed New England and the Maritime Provinces. He was a colonial and revolutionary soldier, farmer, merchant, shipmaster, millwright, and builder. His main residences later in life were in Marlow and Gilsum in New Hampshire, and then Montague, Massachusetts, and Sharon, Vermont. He published a pamphlet about his legendary life, crediting his wife with educating their family and leading him to Christ late in life.

Lucy Mack, one of the vigorous children of this couple, was the Prophet's mother. She met Joseph Smith, Sr., on a visit to Tunbridge, Vermont, where the couple were married in 1796. Through the father's farming and schoolteaching, and Lucy's crafts, they built assets in the adjoining White River towns of Tunbridge, Randolph, Royalton, and Sharon, the birthplace of the Prophet in 1805. Then they moved down the Connecticut River to the village of West Lebanon, New Hampshire, where in semiretirement they began to give their children formal education.

But sickness depleted their savings, and the Smiths started over, first farming in the nearby town of Norwich, New Hampshire. After three crop failures, in 1816 the family struck out for the village of Palmyra, in western New York. The Smiths' exodus ended two miles south, in the town of Manchester, New York. Here they contracted for land near the Hill Cumorah, where the buried plates were about to be revealed.

Mary Audentia Smith Anderson, *Ancestry and Posterity of Joseph Smith and Emma Hale* (1929); A. Gary Anderson, "Smith Family Ancestors," in *Encyclopedia of Mormonism*, Daniel H. Ludlow, editor (1992) 3:1361–1363; Richard Lloyd Anderson, *Joseph Smith's New England Heritage* (1971); Lucy Mack Smith, *Biographical Sketches of Joseph Smith the Prophet and His Progenitors for Many Generations* (1853) [an accessible reprint, lightly edited by Preston Nibley, is available under the following title: *History of Joseph Smith by His Mother* (1979)].

Genealogy of Joseph Smith, Jr.

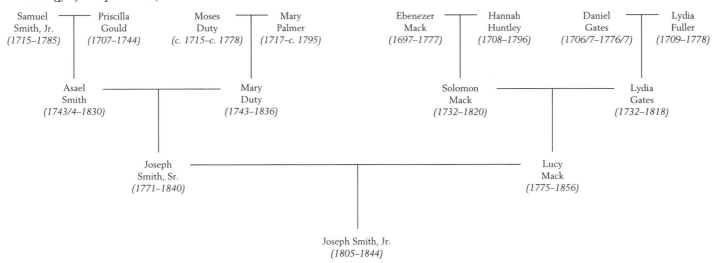

Samuel Smith, Jr. (1715–1785) ⎯ Priscilla Gould (1707–1744)

Moses Duty (c. 1715–c. 1778) ⎯ Mary Palmer (1717–c. 1795)

Ebenezer Mack (1697–1777) ⎯ Hannah Huntley (1708–1796)

Daniel Gates (1706/7–1776/7) ⎯ Lydia Fuller (1709–1778)

Asael Smith (1743/4–1830) ⎯ Mary Duty (1743–1836)

Solomon Mack (1732–1820) ⎯ Lydia Gates (1732–1818)

Joseph Smith, Sr. (1771–1840) ⎯ Lucy Mack (1775–1856)

Joseph Smith, Jr. (1805–1844)

Double dates occur because of the changeover
from the Julian calendar to the Gregorian calendar.

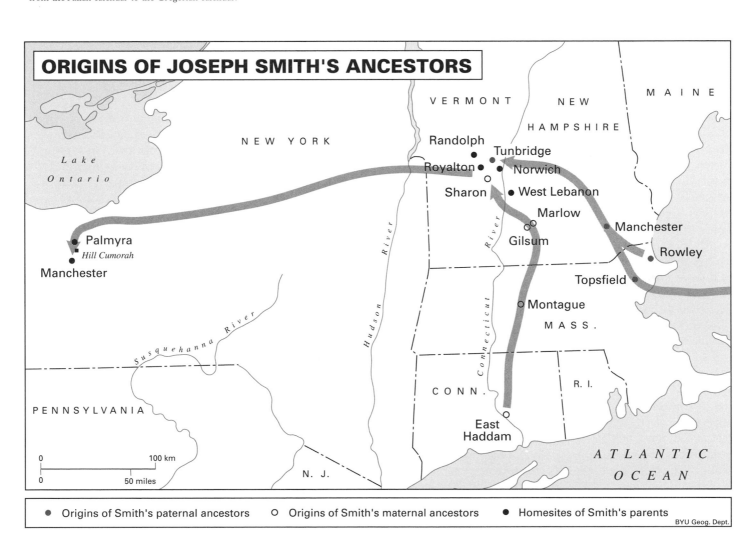

ORIGINS OF JOSEPH SMITH'S ANCESTORS

- ● Origins of Smith's paternal ancestors   ○ Origins of Smith's maternal ancestors   ● Homesites of Smith's parents

BYU Geog. Dept.

THE CHURCH ON THE EARLY 19TH-CENTURY FRONTIER

Richard Neitzel Holzapfel

The Latter-day Saint movement began with one family, that of Joseph Smith, Sr., and Lucy Mack. Migration to the advancing American frontier was one of the dominant forces shaping their social world. Westward expansion, social change, and religious ferment were the principal features of this new world. Economic necessity, war, and migration by their parents and themselves separated the family from central aspects of New England society: extended family members living in close geographical proximity, well-established town hierarchies, and the hegemony of the established Congregationalist Church. Their physical and social separation from New England played a fundamental role in circumstantial preparations for the establishment of the LDS Church. The western frontier of the new nation dramatically expanded in the postrevolutionary period. Immigrants flooded the new wilderness opening up before them; most came hoping to find inexpensive land and a new beginning. By the first American census (1790), nearly one million African Americans and four million European Americans resided in the United States, an area of 891,364 square miles. Internal migration opened up new territories in Pennsylvania, New York, the Ohio River valley, and Tennessee before the end of the 18th century.

By 1800 the fringe of settlement had formed an arc from western New York south through the new states of Kentucky and Tennessee to Georgia. U.S. territory nearly doubled with the 1803 Louisiana Purchase. The War of 1812 had disastrous results for most Indian peoples, who occupied much of the frontier. With the loss of their strongest ally, Great Britain, they were unable to resist U.S. expansion. By 1820 the frontier had shifted to Ohio, Indiana, and Illinois in the north. The natural orientation of the 1800 frontier (Ohio, Kentucky, and Tennessee) was south—along the southward-flowing Ohio and Mississippi rivers, which were the lifelines of early western settlement. The canal fever of the 1820s and 1830s and the railroad fever of the 1830s and thereafter changed the orientation to east-west travel.

The Smith family followed the patterns of western settlement, moving several times by the time the younger Joseph Smith was 12 years of age. His parents were married in Tunbridge, Vermont, on January 24, 1796. They remained near their extended family for six years on their own farm before they made their first move in 1802 to Randolph, a neighboring village seven miles to the west, to open a store. They were forced to sell their Tunbridge farm to pay the debts of their unsuccessful business venture, and as a result the family, like other propertyless individuals, was required to move frequently (at least seven times during the next 14 years).

Between 1803 and 1811 all of the Smith family moves were in a tiny circle around Tunbridge, Randolph, Royalton, and Sharon (the birthplace of Joseph Smith, Jr., in 1805). The circle then enlarged when they relocated 20 miles across the Connecticut River to Lebanon, New Hampshire, in 1811. The family returned to Vermont and moved to a rented farm in Norwich in 1814. Finally, they separated themselves in 1816 from family and friends and removed to Palmyra, New York, some 300 miles west.

When they arrived in western New York, the area had been settled for nearly 25 years. The growth and prosperity of the region were influenced by the construction of the Erie Canal (the Palmyra section was finished in 1822), which, when completed in 1825, connected Albany and Buffalo, a distance of 363 miles. The combination of western New York's flourishing economy, the significant labor contributed by the two oldest Smith sons, and the family's own industry put them in a better economic position than they had enjoyed in nearly 15 years. They purchased a heavily forested tract less than two miles south of Palmyra village on Stafford Street, just over the town line in Farmington (later Manchester) Township.

When the Smith family arrived in western New York, the great religious revival of 1816 and 1817 was in progress—a period of social change and religious ferment in the so-called Burned-over District. During this time Joseph Smith, Jr., became concerned about his personal salvation and religion in general. Beginning in the early spring of 1820 and throughout the decade, the major founding events of the Restoration—the restoration of the Church and gospel of Jesus Christ—transpired, culminating in the organization of the Church on April 6, 1830, in Fayette, New York.

Several small Church branches were organized in the area, but as a result of increased persecution and a desire to find their own "promised land," the faithful removed to the Western Reserve in Ohio. Within a short time, many continued on to Jackson County, Missouri, the site designated for the latter-day Zion, which was at the very edge of the 1831 American frontier.

Ray Allen Billington and Martin Ridge, *Westward Expansion: A History of the American Frontier* (1982), pp. 203–266; Richard L. Bushman, *Joseph Smith and the Beginnings of Mormonism* (1984); Richard Neitzel Holzapfel and T. Jeffery Cottle, *Old Mormon Palmyra and New England: Historic Photographs and Guide* (1991); Larry C. Porter, "A Study of the Origin of the Church of Jesus Christ of Latter-day Saints in the States of New York and Pennsylvania, 1816–1831" (Ph.D. diss., Brigham Young University, 1971).

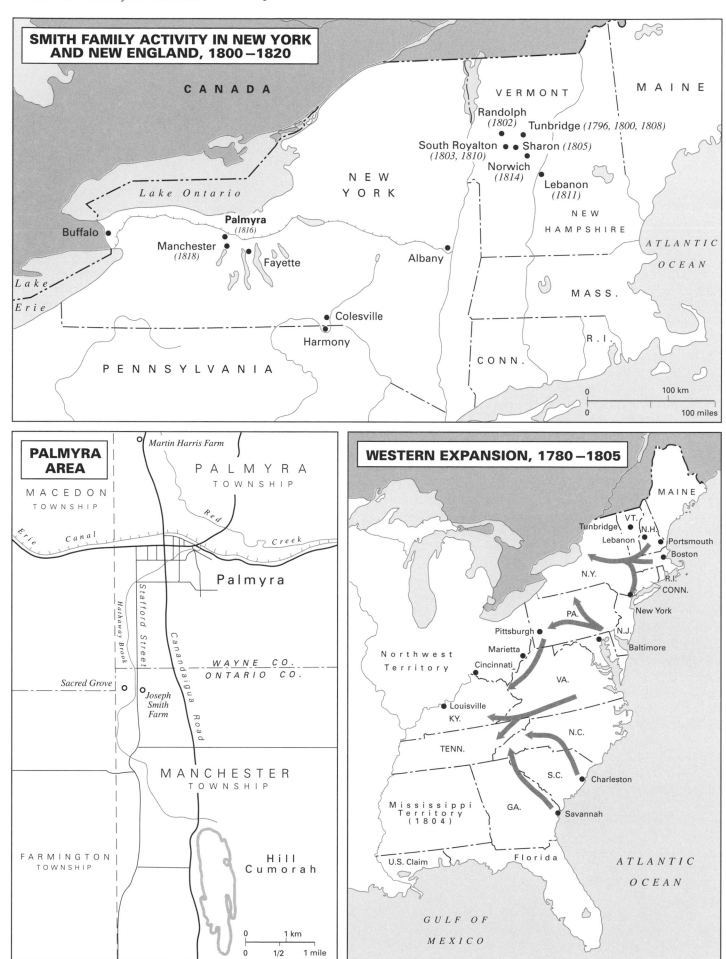

SMITH FAMILY ACTIVITY IN NEW YORK AND NEW ENGLAND, 1800–1820

CANADA

VERMONT

MAINE

Randolph *(1802)*

Tunbridge *(1796, 1800, 1808)*

South Royalton *(1803, 1810)*   Sharon *(1805)*

NEW YORK

Norwich *(1814)*

Lebanon *(1811)*

NEW HAMPSHIRE

Lake Ontario

Palmyra *(1816)*

Buffalo

Manchester *(1818)*   Fayette

ATLANTIC OCEAN

Albany

Lake Erie

MASS.

R.I.

Colesville

Harmony

CONN.

PENNSYLVANIA

0 — 100 km
0 — 100 miles

PALMYRA AREA

Martin Harris Farm

PALMYRA TOWNSHIP

MACEDON TOWNSHIP

Red

Erie   Canal

Creek

Palmyra

Hathaway Brook

Stafford Street

Canandaigua Road

WAYNE CO.
ONTARIO CO.

Sacred Grove

Joseph Smith Farm

MANCHESTER TOWNSHIP

FARMINGTON TOWNSHIP

Hill Cumorah

0 — 1 km
0 — 1/2 — 1 mile

WESTERN EXPANSION, 1780–1805

MAINE

VT.   N.H.

Tunbridge

Lebanon   Portsmouth

Boston

N.Y.

R.I.   CONN.

PA.

New York

Pittsburgh

N.J.

Northwest Territory

Marietta

Baltimore

Cincinnati

VA.

Louisville

KY.

N.C.

TENN.

S.C.

Charleston

Mississippi Territory *(1804)*

GA.

Savannah

U.S. Claim   Florida

ATLANTIC OCEAN

GULF OF MEXICO

o LDS historic site   Direction of U.S. migration   Dates in italics indicate period of Smith family residence.

BYU Geography Dept.

HILL CUMORAH

Richard H. Jackson

The Hill Cumorah is an important feature in Mormon geography and history. Located in Manchester Township, New York, it is four miles southeast of the town of Palmyra and three miles south of the farm of the Prophet Joseph Smith's father. On the night of September 21, 1823, the young Joseph was visited by the Angel Moroni, who showed him in a vision a place on the west side of the hill where were hidden the gold plates from which the Book of Mormon was to be translated. For four years Smith returned each September to that site to be instructed by the Angel Moroni. The combination of historical and sacred events associated with the Hill Cumorah makes it one of the most important places for Mormons.

The Hill Cumorah was created by the great ice age in North America. Technically it is a drumlin, a natural feature created by the deposition of clay, gravel, and rocks as the slowly advancing ice passed over some small obstruction. This process created landforms that are linear in form, with their axes paralleling the direction of movement of the ice. The Hill Cumorah drumlin is one of a number of north-south oriented drumlins south of Lake Ontario. The Hill Cumorah rises approximately 110 feet above the surrounding land, with relatively gentle slopes.

The writings of the prophet Joseph Smith generally refer to the Hill Cumorah as simply "the hill." An 1842 revelation (D&C 128:20), referring to "glad tidings from Cumorah," is his only reference to it by name. Other early leaders, however, used the term, apparently beginning with Oliver Cowdery in 1829 and 1830. Other early members also used this name, but it was referred to as Mormon Hill on U.S. topographic maps from 1898 to 1952, when it was changed to Hill Cumorah.

The westward movement of the Mormons in the 1830s and 1840s did not lessen their interest in the Hill Cumorah area, but settlement of the Great Basin and related persecution and poverty occupied the Church until the 20th century. In the early part of 1907, the Apostle George Albert Smith purchased the Joseph Smith, Sr., farm, and in 1914 a caretaker was sent to live on the farm. The caretaker soon purchased a 98-acre farm on the western side of the Hill Cumorah, and in 1928 the Church purchased the 283 acres comprising the rest of the hill.

At the time of its purchase the Hill Cumorah had been part of a farming system that included grazing sheep, cattle, and horses. Most of the hill was, therefore, covered with grass, and trees occupied only the rougher areas. Beginning with the first farm purchase, Mormons began a process of landscaping the hill that continues to the present. The first improvement was limited, consisting of a parking place by the road for visitors on the first 98 acres purchased by the Church. After the rest of the hill was acquired in 1928, two paths and a gravel road leading to the top of the hill were provided. In 1935, a 40-foot shaft of Vermont granite crowned by a nine-foot bronze statue of the Angel Moroni was placed on the highest point of the hill. In 1936 a bureau of information and floodlights to illuminate the monument were placed at the base of the hill. The most important changes to the landscape of the Hill Cumorah are related to the development of the Hill Cumorah Pageant held each July. Attracting some 100,000 visitors annually, the pageant owes its origins to missionaries who began celebrating July 24—the date of the Mormon entry into Salt Lake Valley in 1847—at the site in 1917. In 1936, plans were announced to hold an annual pageant. Entitled "America's Witness for Christ," it was performed with only occasional revisions until 1988, when an entirely new pageant with the same title was commissioned.

Performance of the pageant has been associated with additional changes in the Hill Cumorah. Twenty-five stages, an expanded visitors' center, and a two-story administrative building were constructed by 1988. Additional changes included recontouring to provide lighting, walkways, trees, and shrubs. In 1988, the Church completely overhauled the landscape of the Hill Cumorah, providing new stages, seating, and special effects for the pageant.

The recontoured and landscaped Hill Cumorah remains one of the most important attractions in the Mormon Church. For members and nonmembers, the pageant—with its volunteer performers—is a singular experience emphasizing the divinity of Jesus Christ and his mission. The rest of the year the Hill Cumorah presents an opportunity to visitors to reflect on the significance of the events that occurred here in September 1823 and the subsequent establishment and growth of the Mormon Church.

Gerald S. Argetsinger, "Cumorah Pageant," in *Encyclopedia of Mormonism*, Daniel H. Ludlow, editor (1992), 1:347; David A. Palmer, "Cumorah," in *Encyclopedia of Mormonism*, Daniel H. Ludlow, editor (1992)1:346–347; Rex C. Reeve, Jr., and Richard O. Cowan, "The Hill Called Cumorah," in *Regional Studies in Latter-day Saint Church History*, Larry C. Porter et al., editors (1992), pp. 70–91.

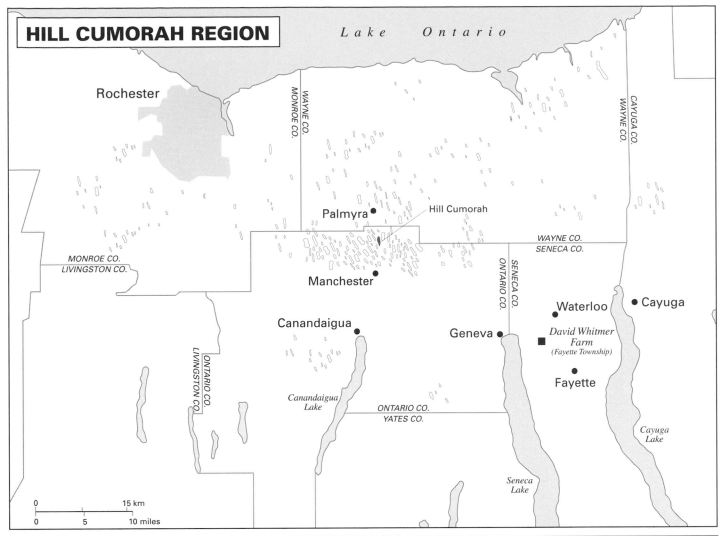

HILL CUMORAH REGION

Lake Ontario

Rochester

WAYNE CO.
MONROE CO.

CAYUGA CO.
WAYNE CO.

Palmyra ●

Hill Cumorah

WAYNE CO.
SENECA CO.

MONROE CO.
LIVINGSTON CO.

Manchester ●

ONTARIO CO.
SENECA CO.

Waterloo ●

● Cayuga

Canandaigua ●

Geneva ●

■ *David Whitmer Farm*
(Fayette Township)

LIVINGSTON CO.
ONTARIO CO.

● Fayette

Canandaigua Lake

ONTARIO CO.
YATES CO.

Cayuga Lake

Seneca Lake

| 0 | | 15 km |
| 0 | 5 | 10 miles |

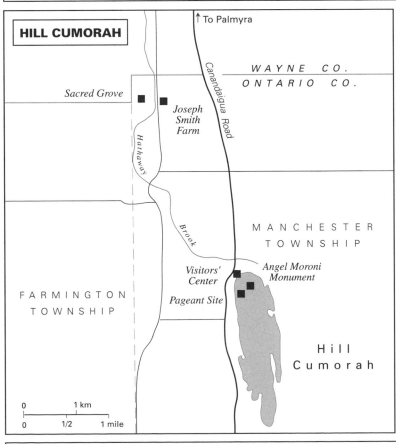

HILL CUMORAH

↑ To Palmyra

Sacred Grove ■

WAYNE CO.
ONTARIO CO.

■ *Joseph Smith Farm*

Canandaigua Road

Hathaway

Brook

MANCHESTER
TOWNSHIP

Visitors' Center

Angel Moroni Monument

Pageant Site

FARMINGTON
TOWNSHIP

Hill
Cumorah

| 0 | | 1 km |
| 0 | 1/2 | 1 mile |

HILL CUMORAH c. 1900

■ LDS historic site   Drumlins

BYU Geography Department

PALMYRA, NEW YORK

Donald L. Enders

In 1816 the family of Joseph Smith, Sr., moved from Vermont to western New York and settled at Palmyra, a promising village located on the proposed route of the Erie Canal.

The Smith Farm. About 1818 the Smiths moved into a log home two miles south of Palmyra Village down Stafford Road toward Manchester. Two years later they purchased 100 acres of heavily forested land just over the line in Manchester Township. During the next decade they fenced the land, cleared 60 acres, built a barn, a cooper's shop, and animal shelters, planted a garden, started a large apple orchard, and developed meadows and fields. They also built a one-and-one-half-story frame home, which was sufficiently finished to occupy during the spring of 1825.

Unable to make the last payment on the farm, the Smiths lost title to the land in late 1825, but remained on it as renters until spring 1829, when they returned to their log home. The Smiths moved from the Palmyra-Manchester area in late 1830, leaving a farm known for its "good order and industry" and assessed in tax records one of the better farms in Manchester Township.

The Sacred Grove and the First Vision. This farm was the setting for the experiences of Joseph Smith, Jr., that Latter-day Saints accept as the divine manifestations that inaugurated the restoration of the gospel. In early spring 1820, while prayerfully seeking forgiveness and divine direction, fourteen-year-old Joseph received a visitation from God the Father and Jesus Christ wherein he was told to join no existing church. This vision occurred in a wood near the Smiths' log home. A beautiful woodland of substantial age at the west end of the farm is reverenced as this site. For almost a century, it has been known among Latter-day Saints as the Sacred Grove.

The Smith Log Home and the Angel Moroni Visitations. On the evening of September 21–22, 1823, seventeen-year-old Joseph received an angelic visitation in the garret of his family's log home. The messenger, named Moroni, first described a record of ancient America that contained "the fulness of Christ's gospel," instructed him to obtain it, and then promised that he would translate the record. In published form this record is the Book of Mormon. It was also in this house that the printer's copy of the Book of Mormon was copied, in 1829 and 1830, and where early preaching and worship services were held before the formal organization of the Church in 1830.

Hill Cumorah. The ancient record lay buried on the west slope of a wooded hill three miles southeast of the Smith farm, along the main road leading from Palmyra to Manchester. Called Cumorah by early Mormons, this hill, or drumlin, formed during the retreat of the Ice Age glaciers, rises 110 feet above the valley floor. Joseph visited this site and conferred with the messenger annually until September 22, 1827, when he was permitted to take the record.

Martin Harris Farm. Martin Harris, a prosperous farmer, religious man, and respected citizen of Palmyra, lived with his wife, Lucy, and their children on a productive and well-developed 300-acre farm a mile and a half north of the town. Their residence was a one-and-one-half-story white frame home surrounded by farm buildings, an orchard, and fields.

Harris, who became acquainted with the Smiths about 1824, assisted Joseph Smith, Jr., as scribe in the early days of the translation of the Book of Mormon, but lost the first 116 pages of dictated manuscript. He no longer acted as scribe but became one of the Three Witnesses to see the ancient record and thereafter mortgaged 150 acres of his farm to pay for printing the first edition of the Book of Mormon.

E. B. Grandin Printing Office. In June 1829, Joseph Smith, Jr., and Martin Harris contracted with Egbert Grandin, a youthful newspaper editor in Palmyra, to print 5,000 copies of the Book of Mormon for $3,000. Grandin used a hand-lever press and worked on the project from early August 1829 to March 1830. One of few printers in western New York with the capability of producing such a large volume of work, he employed a staff of at least 16 people during this period to print his weekly newspaper, his job-work, and the Book of Mormon. The printing office was located at the west end of the upper level of the recently constructed three-story brick building called Exchange Row on Palmyra's Main Street.

Milton V. Backman, Jr., *Joseph Smith's First Vision* (1980); Richard L. Bushman, *Joseph Smith and the Beginnings of Mormonism* (1984).

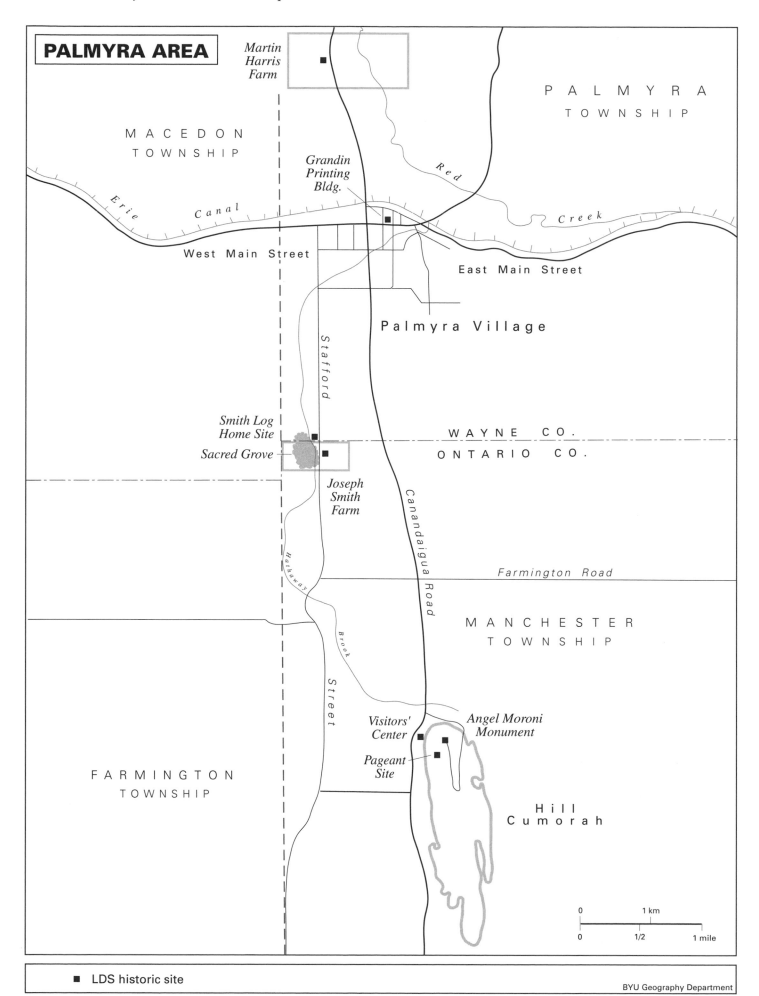

PALMYRA AREA

Martin
Harris
Farm

P A L M Y R A
T O W N S H I P

M A C E D O N
T O W N S H I P

Erie   *Canal*

Red

Grandin
Printing
Bldg.

Creek

West Main Street

East Main Street

P a l m y r a   V i l l a g e

Stafford

Smith Log
Home Site

Sacred Grove

W A Y N E   C O.

O N T A R I O   C O.

Joseph
Smith
Farm

Canandaigua Road

Hathaway

Farmington Road

M A N C H E S T E R
T O W N S H I P

Brook

Street

Visitors'
Center

Angel Moroni
Monument

Pageant
Site

F A R M I N G T O N
T O W N S H I P

H i l l
C u m o r a h

| 0 | | 1 km |
| 0 | 1/2 | 1 mile |

■   LDS historic site

BYU Geography Department

NEW YORK STATE

Donald L. Enders

Significant events in the restoration of the gospel and in the life of Joseph Smith occurred in New York State well beyond the Smith farm and Palmyra village. These included Joseph's translation of the Book of Mormon, his restoration of Christ's church, and his marriage to Emma Hale.

South Bainbridge, Chenango County, is the marriage place of Joseph Smith and Emma Hale. In October 1825, Smith left the family farm at Manchester to work for Josiah Stowell about 130 miles southeast at Bainbridge, near the Pennsylvania border. Laboring for Stowell at Harmony (now Oakland), Pennsylvania, Smith met Emma Hale, a schoolteacher and daughter of the respected farm family of Isaac and Elizabeth Hale.

Their eventual courtship displeased Emma's parents, whose traditional Christian beliefs hardened them against Smith's spiritual claims. Hale's parents refused to consent to the marriage, so the couple eloped to South Bainbridge, 30 miles north of Harmony, to the home of Squire Tarbell, justice of the peace. They were married there January 18, 1827. After the Church was organized, Smith, for preaching the Book of Mormon, stood trial for disorderly conduct at this small farming village on the Susquehanna River, but he was acquitted and released.

Colesville, Broome County, was the home of faithful early converts to the Church. While working for Josiah Stowell, Smith became acquainted with the kindly Joseph Knight, Sr., his wife, Polly, and their family. The Knights were longtime residents of Colesville, a village about 20 miles north of the residence of Emma Hale's parents. In November 1826, Smith began working for Joseph Knight.

Smith impressed the Knights with his steady labor and quiet but friendly manner, and more particularly, the conviction of his prophetic call. Joseph Knight, Sr., and a son, Newel, sought and obtained a spiritual witness of young Joseph's divine appointment. Joseph Knight assisted Joseph and Emma at the time of their elopement and again after they set up housekeeping at the Hale farm, but especially during the season of translation at Harmony. The Knights and their extended family, friends, and acquaintances were among the first to embrace the restored gospel and formed one of the three original congregations (or branches) of the Church. In 1831 these Colesville Saints emigrated together to the Church's new gathering place at Kirtland, Ohio.

Fayette, Seneca County, is the location of the translation of the Book of Mormon, the Three Witnesses' experience, and the organization of the Church. The Peter and Mary Whitmer family lived about 100 miles northwest of Colesville in Fayette Township. Since 1809 they had owned a good farm. Members of the family held public responsibility and worshiped in the German Reformed Church. A son, David, became aware of Joseph Smith's translation of the gold plates in 1828 from Oliver Cowdery. He manifested a sincere interest in Smith's work, which was soon shared by his family.

When it became impossible for the young prophet to continue the work of translation at Harmony, the Whitmers offered the peace and security of their home. Joseph gratefully accepted, and by June 1, 1829, he and his scribe Oliver Cowdery renewed their sacred labor at the Whitmer Farm, where they completed translation of the Book of Mormon one month later.

As translation neared completion, Smith confided that the Spirit of the Lord impressed him to show the ancient plates to three others. Oliver Cowdery, David Whitmer, and Martin Harris experienced a remarkable heavenly visitation in a grove on the farm, in which the Angel Moroni appeared and showed them the plates and other sacred artifacts. The Three Witnesses heard the voice of God declare the truthfulness of the translation and were commanded to bear record of its divinity to the world.

Even before the Book of Mormon went to press, Smith revealed that a church was to be established. April 6, 1830, was the date prescribed by revelation. On that Tuesday morning six charter members—Joseph, Hyrum, and Samuel Smith, Oliver Cowdery, and David and Peter Whitmer, Jr.—organized the Church and baptized new members. Some 50 faithful from the areas of Fayette, Manchester, and Colesville were in attendance and witnessed the formal organization of "The Church of Christ" (The Church of Jesus Christ of Latter-day Saints).

According to revelation, the Church was to meet regularly in conferences so that its members might be spiritually instructed and fellowshiped. The first two conferences were held at the Whitmer farm on June 9 and September 26, 1830. A revelation (D&C 20) titled "The Articles and Covenants of the Church of Christ" was read aloud at the first conference and unanimously accepted by the congregation as God's affirmation that his kingdom was again established on earth.

Beginning in 1831, the Whitmer family and other members of the Church in the Fayette branch left western New York, as did Saints from the Manchester and Colesville branches, to gather at Kirtland, Ohio.

James B. Allen and Glen M. Leonard, *The Story of the Latter-day Saints* (1976); Richard L. Bushman, *Joseph Smith and the Beginnings of Mormonism* (1984).

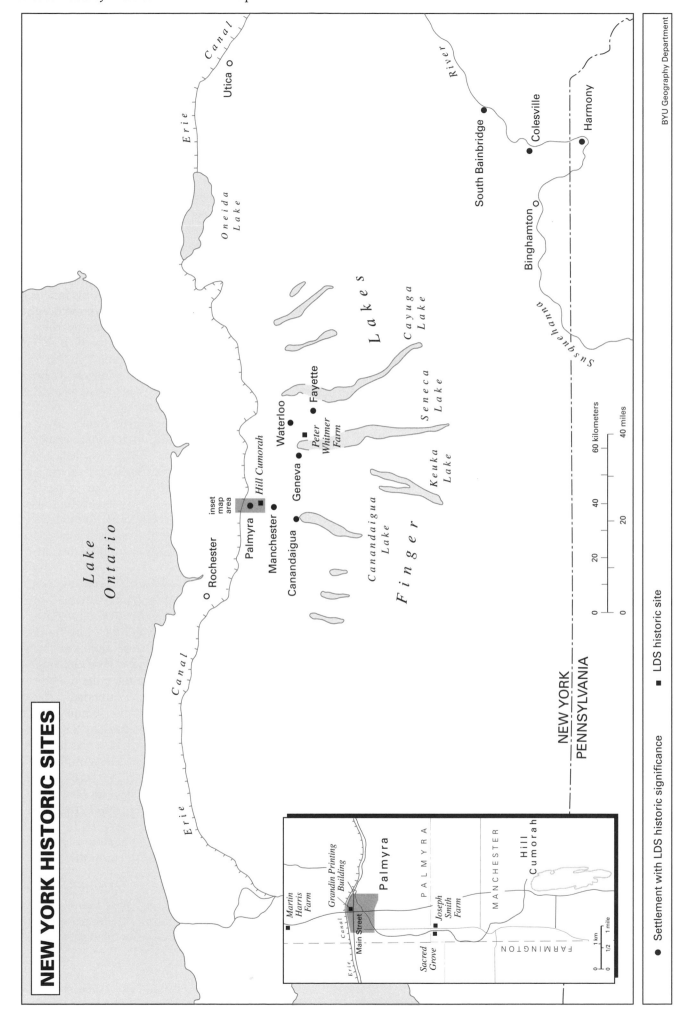

NEW YORK HISTORIC SITES

Lake Ontario

Erie Canal

Rochester ○

Palmyra ●

Manchester ●

Canandaigua ●

inset map area

Hill Cumorah

Waterloo ●

Geneva ●

Fayette ●

Peter Whitmer Farm

Canandaigua Lake

Keuka Lake

Seneca Lake

Cayuga Lake

Finger Lakes

Erie Canal

Oneida Lake

Utica ○

Erie Canal

River

South Bainbridge ●

Colesville ●

Binghamton ○

Harmony ●

Susquehanna

NEW YORK
PENNSYLVANIA

0   20   40   60 kilometers
0   20   40 miles

● Settlement with LDS historic significance   ■ LDS historic site

Palmyra inset:

Martin Harris Farm

Grandin Printing Building

Main Street

Erie Canal

Palmyra

PALMYRA

MANCHESTER

Sacred Grove

Joseph Smith Farm

FARMINGTON

Hill Cumorah

0   1/2   1 mile
0   1   1 km

BYU Geography Department

EARLY MISSIONARY JOURNEYS

Susan Easton Black

Before the Book of Mormon was fully printed and bound, missionaries carried excerpts hundreds of miles and shared them with relatives and friends. Thomas B. Marsh carried 16 of these loose pages to Charlestown, Massachusetts, to read with his family. Solomon Chamberlain took 64 pages to Canada. After traveling 800 miles through the Canadian wilderness, he stated, "I exhorted all people to prepare for the great work of God that was now about to come forth" (Chamberlain, 362). Such enthusiasm for the Book of Mormon led one historian to pen, "It was not uncommon, in the earliest days of the movement, for a man to hear Mormonism preached one day, be baptized the next, be ordained an elder on the following day and the day after that to be out preaching Mormonism" (Williams, 10).

Samuel Harrison Smith was the first missionary set apart by the Prophet Joseph Smith, his brother. On June 30, 1830, he left on his mission with copies of the Book of Mormon filling his knapsack. After traveling 30 miles the first day he slept under an apple tree, having "been turned out of doors that day" for the fifth time (Smith, 169). The next day he journeyed eight miles to Bloomington, New York, where he met John P. Greene, a Methodist preacher. Although Greene did not initially accept the Book of Mormon, he consented to take a book on his next preaching tour. Later Smith returned to the home of Reverend Greene. His persistence eventually led to the baptisms of John P. Greene, Brigham Young, and Heber C. Kimball.

During the following 15 months Smith traveled over 4,000 miles, preaching from Maine to Missouri. He journeyed with Orson Pratt from New York to Kirtland, Ohio, a distance of 250 miles. By spring of 1831 he was preaching 50 miles west of Kirtland in Amherst. From June 1831 through August he preached with Reynolds Cahoon from Ohio to Missouri. The remainder of 1831 he served missions in eastern Ohio. He and Orson Hyde were called to the northern states on January 25, 1832. They journeyed from Salem, Ohio, to Springfield, Pennsylvania. They then walked to Erie, Pennsylvania, and continued north until they reached western New York. The missionaries also traveled to Boston and Providence, Rhode Island. Continuing north, they journeyed through New Hampshire to York County, Maine. During this 11-month mission Samuel Smith helped organize four branches of the Church.

While Samuel was the first and foremost missionary in the Smith family, other family members also served missions. Joseph Smith, Sr., and Joseph Jr.'s brother Don Carlos Smith traveled to St. Lawrence County, New York, in August 1830 to share the Book of Mormon with relatives. Another of Joseph Jr.'s brothers, Hyrum Smith, strengthened and exhorted the Saints in Palmyra, Colesville, and Fayette, New York.

The most arduous early mission was served by Oliver Cowdery, Peter Whitmer, Ziba Peterson, and Parley P. Pratt. In October 1830 they began their journey to the edge of the frontier to share the Book of Mormon with Indian tribes, known among Mormons as *Lamanites*. Near Buffalo, New York, they preached to the Cattaraugus Indians. From Buffalo they traveled to Mentor, Ohio, where they converted the Reverend Sidney Rigdon and many of his congregation. They then journeyed to Sandusky, Ohio, to preach to the Wyandot Indians. From Sandusky they traveled to Cincinnati and then 200 miles to St. Louis. For the last 300 miles they trudged through trackless wastes of snow to Independence, Missouri, about 1,500 miles from where they had started.

Parley P. Pratt claimed that they had "preached the gospel to tens of thousands of Gentiles and two nations of Indians; baptizing, confirming, and organizing many hundreds of people into churches" (Pratt, 52). Near Independence, Oliver Cowdery explained to the Delaware Indian chief, "We have traveled a long distance from towards the rising sun to bring you glad news [of] great knowledge which has lately come to our ears and hearts" (Pratt, 54). After listening to Cowdery's discourse the chief replied, "We feel truly thankful to our white friends who have come so far, and been at such pains to tell us good news, and especially this new news concerning the Book of our forefathers" (Pratt, 56).

While these missionaries were traveling to the Indians, other missionaries also accepted calls to serve. Jared Carter preached from Ohio to Chenango, New York, and then to Benson, Vermont. From Vermont he traveled to Galien, New York, to share the Book of Mormon with his family. He then journeyed to Springfield, Pennsylvania, before returning to Ohio. Ebenezer Page also journeyed to Chenango, New York, and shared the truths of the gospel. It was their conviction about the truth of the Book of Mormon that led these missionaries to testify equally to friends, relatives, and strangers.

Solomon Chamberlain, "A Short Sketch of the Life of Solomon Chamberlain," cited by Larry C. Porter in "A Study of the Origins of The Church of Jesus Christ of Latter-day Saints in the States of New York and Pennsylvania, 1816–1831" (Ph.D. diss., Brigham Young University, 1971); Samuel George Ellsworth, "A History of Mormon Missions in the United States and Canada, 1830–1860" (Ph.D. diss., University of California, 1952); Dean Jarman, "The Life and Contributions of Samuel Harrison Smith" (Master's thesis, Brigham Young University, 1961); Parley P. Pratt, *Autobiography of Parley Parker Pratt* (1980); Lucy Mack Smith, *History of Joseph Smith by his Mother* (1956); Richard Shelton Williams, "The Missionary Movements of the LDS Church in New England, 1830–1850" (Master's thesis, Brigham Young University, 1969).

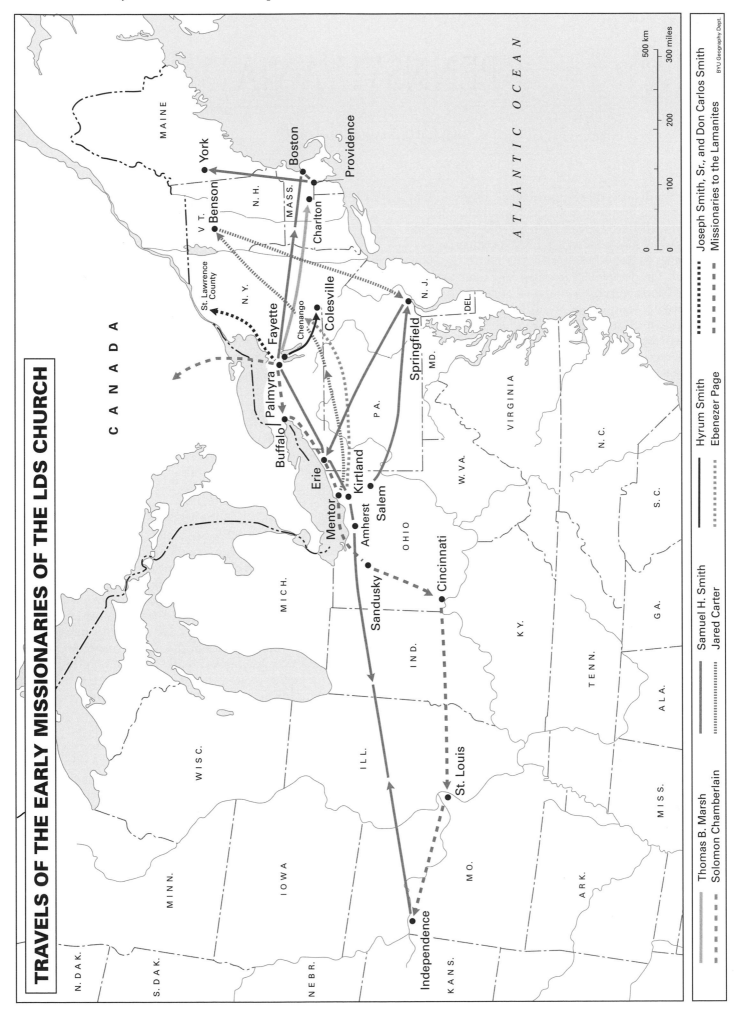

TRAVELS OF THE EARLY MISSIONARIES OF THE LDS CHURCH

ATLANTIC OCEAN

500 km
300 miles
0   100   200

BYU Geography Dept.

Joseph Smith, Sr., and Don Carlos Smith
Missionaries to the Lamanites
Hyrum Smith
Ebenezer Page
Samuel H. Smith
Jared Carter
Thomas B. Marsh
Solomon Chamberlain

CANADA

MAINE
N. H.
VT.
MASS.
N. Y.
PA.
N. J.
DEL.
MD.
VIRGINIA
W. VA.
N. C.
S. C.
OHIO
IND.
KY.
TENN.
GA.
ALA.
MICH.
WISC.
ILL.
IOWA
MINN.
N. DAK.
S. DAK.
NEBR.
KANS.
MO.
ARK.
MISS.

York
Boston
Providence
Benson
Charlton
St. Lawrence County
Fayette
Chenango
Colesville
Springfield
Palmyra
Buffalo
Erie
Mentor
Kirtland
Amherst
Salem
Sandusky
Cincinnati
St. Louis
Independence

PENNSYLVANIA

Richard Neitzel Holzapfel

Joseph Smith arrived in Susquehanna County, Pennsylvania, for the first time in November 1825. He boarded with Isaac Hale in Harmony Township while employed by Josiah Stowell, who was at that time attempting to find a lost Spanish gold mine. Smith's brief stay had considerable influence on him and on the beginnings of Mormonism.

Four important events occurred in or near Harmony. Smith met his future wife, Emma Hale (Isaac's daughter); he completed much of the Book of Mormon translation; he received several divine revelations and visitations; and he had early associations with individuals in the area that would prove important for the infant Church.

After Joseph Smith and Emma Hale were married in January 1827, they moved to his father's farm in Manchester, New York. Smith obtained the gold plates from a hill nearby in September 1827. Joseph and Emma Smith were forced to find safe refuge from the storm of opposition mounting against his effort to translate the plates. Though not entirely happy about the reason for their return, Isaac Hale welcomed the young couple back to Harmony.

The translation process then commenced in earnest, but with several major interruptions. Eventually, in May 1829, Smith and his scribe, Oliver Cowdery, reached a section in the Book of Mormon that discussed baptism. As they prayed for guidance on the subject, an angel (John the Baptist) appeared and gave them the authority to baptize.

Prejudice in the area increased, and Smith sought another place to finish translating. With Cowdery, the Smiths moved to the Peter Whitmer farm in Fayette, New York, in June 1829 to complete the work. The Smiths returned temporarily to Harmony in October 1829, but in the early spring of 1830 returned to New York. Soon thereafter they gathered at the Whitmer farm and organized the Church of Christ on April 6. In 1831, they and the other faithful Saints removed themselves entirely from the region to the Western Reserve and established a Church center in Kirtland, Ohio, and another in Jackson County, Missouri.

As the message of the Restoration spread from the new Church center in Ohio, it was inevitable that missionaries would arrive in Pennsylvania. Within a year of the organization of the Church, its membership numbered nearly 2,000, with 125 members living in Pennsylvania, more than in any other states except Ohio and Missouri.

Church branches were first established in the northern counties of the state. Most of the membership lived in Bradford and Tioga counties, which bordered New York State. Recent converts often were sent back to their homes to proselyte family and friends. During the summer of 1831 branches of the infant Church were organized in Columbia and Rutland townships, respectively located in Bradford and Tioga counties. Later, missionaries from Columbia set out to proselyte in the Mendon, New York, area. Among those eventually converted from this missionary activity were Brigham Young and Heber C. Kimball. Young, along with family and friends, traveled the 120 miles to the Columbia branch to investigate news about the Church more thoroughly. Over the next several months other family members visited the small branch and were baptized. Erie County, in the northwestern corner of the state, was another early field of missionary labor because of its geographic proximity to Kirtland (40 miles away) and its location as a bridge for Kirtland missionaries' efforts to the east. Two branches were organized in the county (Springfield and Elk Creek). Among those converts who would become prominent in the Church was Jedediah M. Grant, baptized at Elk Creek in 1833.

In the latter half of the 1830s, missionary efforts shifted from the northern counties to western and southern counties. In 1839, missionary labors resulted in the establishment of branches in southeastern Chester and Philadelphia counties. Three Pennsylvania converts, Jedediah M. Grant, Joshua Grant, Jr., and Benjamin Winchester, may have been the first missionaries to visit Philadelphia. By 1839, there were approximately 40 members within 60 miles of the city. A branch was organized there by Joseph Smith on December 23, 1839.

During the 1830s as many as 14 branches were organized, mostly in sparsely settled counties. Missionary successes were tempered by the doctrine of gathering as local Saints moved to Church headquarters farther west. Most branches followed a fluctuating pattern: first, missionary activity; second, branch organization; third, a growth period; fourth, loss of membership due primarily to the gathering to Ohio; and finally, the stabilization of a branch or its disorganization. As a result only three units, Brandywine, Philadelphia, and Leechburg, continued to function from 1830 until 1840.

Richard L. Bushman, *Joseph Smith and the Beginnings of Mormonism* (1984), pp. 79–113; Richard Neitzel Holzapfel and T. Jeffery Cottle, "Pennsylvania," in *Old Mormon Palmyra and New England: Historic Photographs and Guide* (1991), pp. 140–163; Larry C. Porter, "A Study of the Origins of The Church of Jesus Christ in the States of New York and Pennsylvania, 1816–1831" (Ph.D. diss., Brigham Young University, 1971); Zilch Rosenbaum, "The Church of Jesus Christ of Latter-day Saints in Pennsylvania (1830–1854)" (Master's thesis, East Stroudsburg State College, 1982).

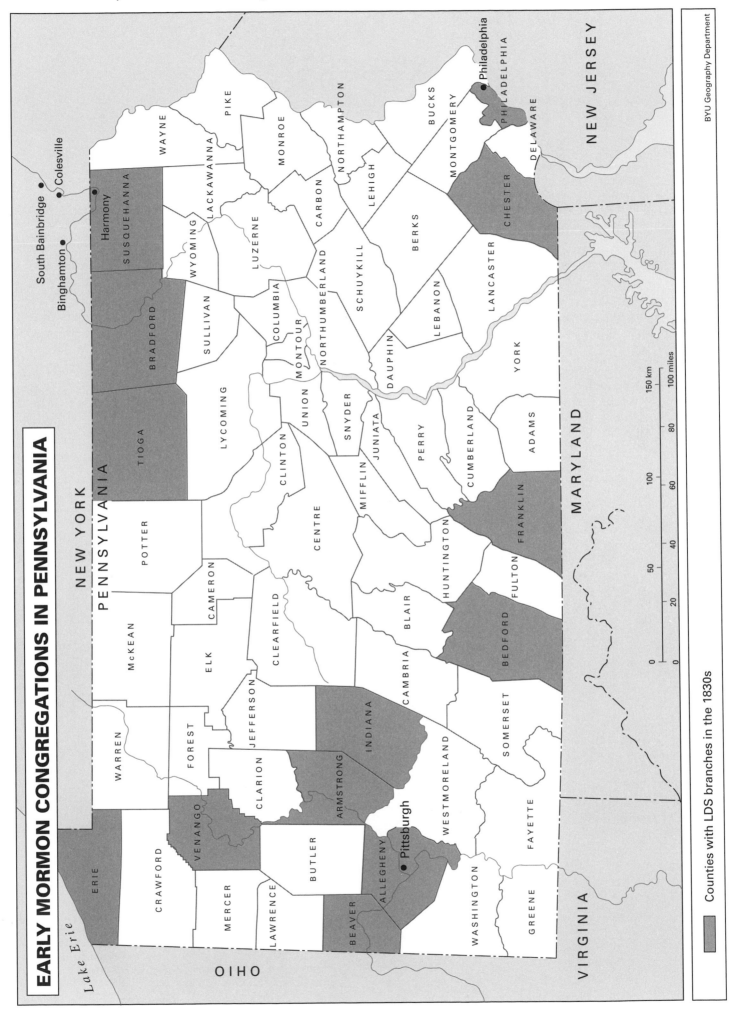

EARLY MORMON CONGREGATIONS IN PENNSYLVANIA

NEW YORK

PENNSYLVANIA

NEW JERSEY

MARYLAND

VIRGINIA

OHIO

Lake Erie

Colesville

South Bainbridge

Binghamton

Harmony

Philadelphia

Pittsburgh

ERIE
WARREN
McKEAN
POTTER
TIOGA
BRADFORD
SUSQUEHANNA
WAYNE
PIKE
MONROE
WYOMING
LACKAWANNA
SULLIVAN
LYCOMING
CRAWFORD
FOREST
JEFFERSON
CLEARFIELD
CAMERON
ELK
CLINTON
CENTRE
UNION
COLUMBIA
MONTOUR
NORTHUMBERLAND
SNYDER
MIFFLIN
JUNIATA
LUZERNE
CARBON
NORTHAMPTON
LEHIGH
SCHUYLKILL
BERKS
BUCKS
MONTGOMERY
DELAWARE
CHESTER
LANCASTER
LEBANON
DAUPHIN
PERRY
CUMBERLAND
YORK
ADAMS
FRANKLIN
FULTON
BEDFORD
HUNTINGTON
BLAIR
CAMBRIA
SOMERSET
WESTMORELAND
FAYETTE
GREENE
WASHINGTON
ALLEGHENY
BEAVER
BUTLER
ARMSTRONG
INDIANA
VENANGO
CLARION
MERCER
LAWRENCE

150 km
100 miles
0   50   100   150
0   20   40   60   80   100

BYU Geography Department

Counties with LDS branches in the 1830s

17

EARLIEST CONGREGATIONS (1828–1831)

Susan Easton Black

Announcements in the early 1800s of land "well-timbered, well-watered, easily accessible, and undeniably fertile—all to be had on long term payments for only two or three dollars an acre," piqued interest and propelled the American populace to press against the frontier from Maine to Kentucky (Stilwell, 135). The lure of superior soil and the promise of the Erie Canal extending water transport to the Great Lakes led many of the adventurous and the hopeful to western New York. Among those joining the pioneering quest for a better life were future prominent Latter-day Saints, including Joseph Smith, Sr., Hiram Page, Hezekiah Peck, Benjamin Slade, and Oliver Cowdery, all former residents of Vermont. They ventured west with many contemporaries seeking a new beginning in the New York wilderness.

The explosive growth of small villages and townships in western New York was paralleled by the religious fervor among the new inhabitants. Itinerant preachers from the East moved west with the hope of instilling religion in the pioneers. Early revivals, dating from 1799, ignited townsfolk from one village to another in a spiritual awakening. Congregations often doubled as enthusiasm for old-time religion rekindled. Lucy Mack Smith penned, "There was a great revival in religion, which extended to all the denominations of Christendom in the surrounding country in which we resided. Many of the world's people concerned about the salvation of their souls came forward and presented themselves as seekers after religion" (Smith, 74).

During this revival era, young Joseph Smith labored "under the extreme difficulties" occasioned by contesting religionists (Pearl of Great Price, Joseph Smith—History 1:11). Seeking to unravel the prevailing religious confusion, he sought the Lord in prayer in the spring of 1820. His heavenly answer included "a promise that the fulness of the gospel should at some future time be made known unto [him]" (The Wentworth Letter, cited in Backman, 169).

As this promise was fulfilled, the young Prophet shared his revelations with early believers in the small New York communities of Palmyra, Colesville, and Fayette. These three towns became the destination for some of the earliest converts. Learning of the gospel at the Smith home in Manchester were Oliver Cowdery, a native of Rutland County, Vermont; Solomon Humphrey, originally from Hartford County, Connecticut; Thomas B. Marsh, from Middlesex County, Massachusetts; Solomon Chamberlain, from Litchfield County, Connecticut; and Martin Harris, from Saratoga County, New York. From the Prophet and his family they learned of angelic visitations and the coming forth of the Book of Mormon. This small but faithful congregation produced the earliest stalwarts of Mormonism.

Those who anchored the first branch of the Church in Fayette traced their awareness of the Prophet to David Whitmer, who had heard of young Joseph Smith in Palmyra. He shared his insights with Oliver Cowdery, who later promised Whitmer that he would write to him about Smith. It was Cowdery's letter to Whitmer in May 1829 that precipitated Smith's important move—while translating the Book of Mormon—from his home in Harmony, Pennsylvania, to the Whitmer farm, 4.7 miles northeast of Fayette. The Whitmers embraced the gospel and four family members testified, "We have seen and hefted, and we know of a surety that the said Smith has got the plates" (The Testimony of the Eight Witnesses). Forming the nucleus of the branch in Fayette were the families of Peter Whitmer, formerly from Dauphin County, Pennsylvania; Hiram Page, a native of Vermont; Phillip Burroughs, originating from New Hampshire; and William Jolly, a lifelong resident of Seneca County, New York.

The Colesville branch traced their awareness of Joseph Smith's religious experiences to Joseph Knight, a native of Worcester County, Massachusetts. He, like Whitmer, became acquainted with the Smiths in Palmyra. Knight lent encouragement to young Smith by employing him in his carding mill and on his farm. He was privileged to be in the Smith home the morning that Joseph entered with the original gold plates of the Book of Mormon in his possession. Joining the Knight family in the Colesville branch were Freeborn DeMill, originally from Ulster County, New York; Ira Willes, formerly from Albany County, New York; Hezekiah Peck, from Windham County, Vermont; William Stringham, from Queens County, New York; and Benjamin Slade, from Windham County, Vermont.

The Saints in these small communities strengthened and encouraged each other as they met in worship. It was these early meetings in western New York that became the basis of the first branches of the Church, whose membership knew and professed Joseph Smith to be a prophet of God.

Milton V. Backman, Jr., *Joseph Smith's First Vision: The First Vision in Its Historical Context* (1971); Larry C. Porter, "A Study of the Origins of The Church of Jesus Christ of Latter-day Saints in the States of New York and Pennsylvania, 1816–1831" (Ph.D. diss., Brigham Young University, 1971); Lucy Mack Smith, *Biographical Sketches of Joseph Smith the Prophet, and His Progenitors for Many Generations* (1853); Lewis D. Stilwell, *Migration from Vermont* (1948).

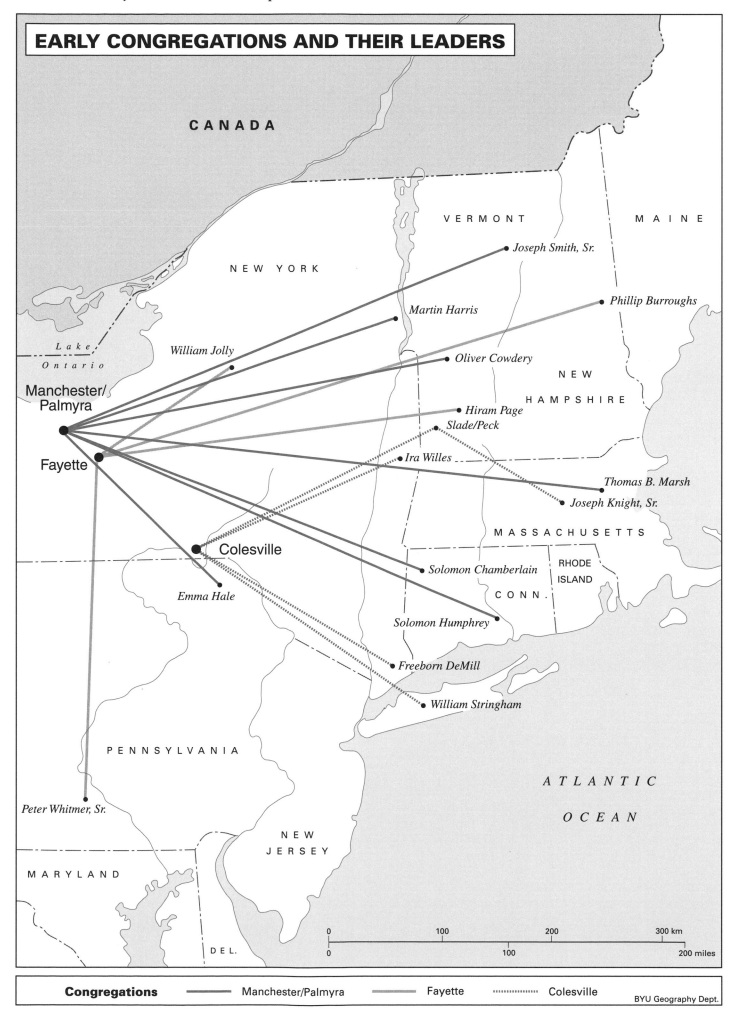

EARLY CONGREGATIONS AND THEIR LEADERS

CANADA

VERMONT

MAINE

NEW YORK

• Joseph Smith, Sr.

• Martin Harris

Phillip Burroughs •

Lake
Ontario

William Jolly •

• Oliver Cowdery

NEW

HAMPSHIRE

Manchester/
Palmyra

• Hiram Page
Slade/Peck

Fayette

• Ira Willes

Thomas B. Marsh •

Joseph Knight, Sr. •

Colesville

MASSACHUSETTS

Solomon Chamberlain •

RHODE
ISLAND

Emma Hale •

CONN.

Solomon Humphrey •

Freeborn DeMill •

William Stringham •

PENNSYLVANIA

ATLANTIC

OCEAN

Peter Whitmer, Sr. •

NEW
JERSEY

MARYLAND

| | 0 | | 100 | | 200 | | 300 km |
| 0 | | | 100 | | | 200 miles |

DEL.

Congregations ——— Manchester/Palmyra ——— Fayette ·········· Colesville

BYU Geography Dept.

NORTHERN OHIO SETTLEMENTS

Karl Ricks Anderson

Latter-day Saints populated northern Ohio in the 1830s barely 30 years after the first surveyors and pioneer settlers arrived, primarily from Connecticut. Populated by the Indians prior to 1800, northeastern Ohio, known as the Western Reserve, consisted of land owned by the state of Connecticut for western expansion. This accounts for the dominance of New England culture and heritage in the area.

The Latter-day Saint population resulted from missionary conversions in the area and from Saints gathering from other areas of the United States and Canada. Most sailed across Lake Erie, arriving at Fairport Harbor. They then walked the 12 miles to Kirtland, Church headquarters from 1831 to 1838, and settled either in or near Kirtland. Missionary conversions in northern Ohio were augmented significantly by Sidney Rigdon, a Reformed Baptist minister who had much to do with Church settlement and growth in northern Ohio. Rigdon, of whom the Lord said, "thou wast sent . . . to prepare the way before me . . . and thou knewest it not" (D&C 35:4), preached throughout northern Ohio from 1826 to 1830, establishing congregations in Mentor, Mantua, Kirtland, Florence, Elyria, and Mayfield. Following his November 1830 conversion in Mentor, hundreds were baptized from his contacts in these areas.

Centers of Church population and activity included the following:

Kirtland was the primary settlement in Ohio; however, Latter-day Saint population and activity spilled over into surrounding towns such as Mentor, Willoughby (known as Chagrin prior to 1834), Chesterland (known as Chester), and Mayfield.

Hiram served essentially as Church headquarters for the year that Joseph Smith and his family lived with John Johnson's family. Sixteen sections of the Doctrine and Covenants were received here. It was the site of many Church conferences. Intense missionary activity surrounded Hiram, and many converts came from Parkman, Nelson, and Shalersville, which all became Church branches. Others were converted in Ravenna, Streetsboro, Shalersville, and Mantua; in Mantua, Lorenzo Snow was born, and there Eliza Snow and other members of their family first heard the gospel. Joseph Smith and Sidney Rigdon were called on a local preaching mission in December 1831 (D&C 71) to counter the effects of nine anti-Mormon newspaper articles published in the Ravenna newspaper by Ezra Booth. (Booth was apparently the first apostate publicly to attack the Church in writing.)

Painesville was the home of Edward Partridge, first bishop of the Church, who operated a hatter's shop near the town square. Joseph Smith made many trips to Painesville. He was often arrested on what he called "malicious and vexatious lawsuits" and put on trial here. A hotbed of anti-Mormon sentiment, Painesville produced the first anti-Mormon publication, *Mormonism Unvailed*. The Church was built up in surrounding towns such as Perry, Madison, and Thompson. It was in Thompson that the Colesville Saints first settled, the Law of Consecration was first attempted, and section 51 of the Doctrine and Covenants was revealed.

Chardon was the county seat for Kirtland prior to 1840. Leaders, including Joseph Smith, traveled frequently to Chardon for preaching, visiting members, and attending to legal and court business. Joseph Smith's sisters, Sophronia and Katherine, lived here.

Amherst, site of a Church conference and the reception of Doctrine and Covenants section 66, was one of the first areas of significance to the Church. Parley P. Pratt settled here in 1826, four years before his conversion in New York. Sidney Rigdon recruited Pratt to preach the Campbellite faith here and later appointed Orson Hyde as a minister in this same area. After their conversion to Mormonism, working with others, they built up branches of the Church in and surrounding Amherst in Brownhelm, Florence, Elyria, New London, and Ridgeville.

Orange and Warrensville were adjoining townships and sites of successful missionary activity and Church branches. An 1831 Church conference was held in Orange. Joseph and Emma Smith's twins, adopted from John and Julia Murdock, were born here.

Barberton (known as New Portage prior to 1890), at the headwaters of the Tuscarawas River, was the site of one of the largest branches of the Church in Ohio. A plague, thought to have been typhus, almost wiped out the town in 1828. Barberton served as a rendezvous point for Zion's Camp and also for members of the Smith family as they left Ohio for Missouri in 1838. It was a Church center for missionaries and members surrounding Akron. Such members of the Church as Pratt, Don Carlos Smith, and Hyrum Smith lived here for a short time.

Karl Ricks Anderson, *Joseph Smith's Kirtland* (1989); Milton V. Backman, Jr., *The Heavens Resound: A History of the Latter-day Saints in Ohio, 1830–1838* (1983).

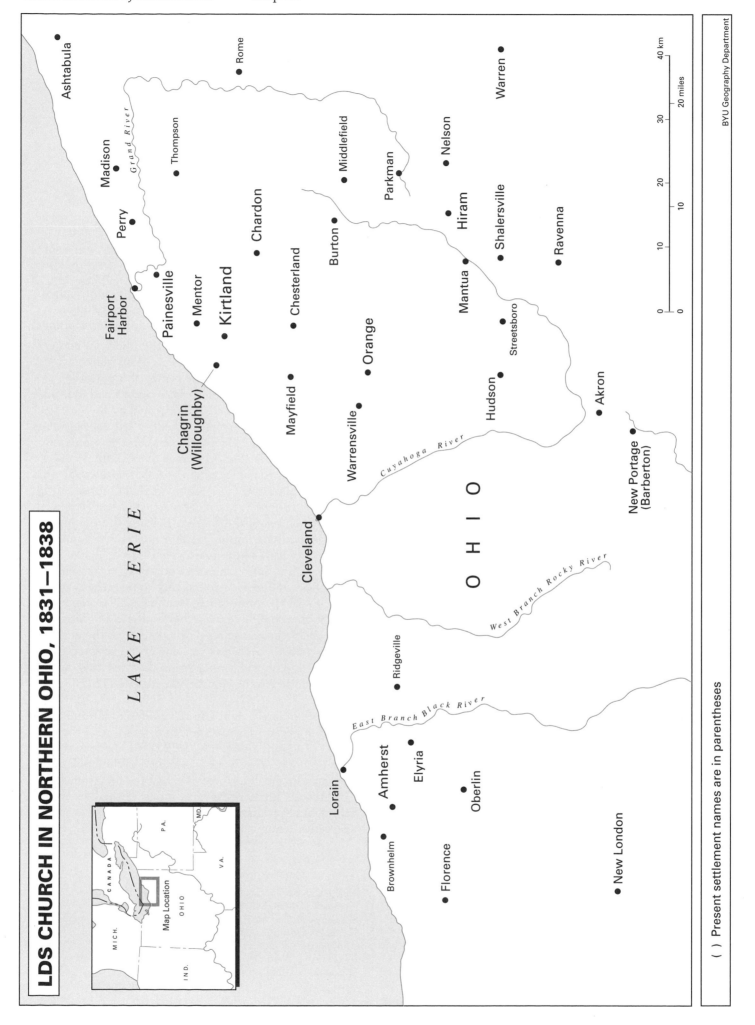

LDS CHURCH IN NORTHERN OHIO, 1831–1838

BYU Geography Department

( ) Present settlement names are in parentheses

KIRTLAND AND VICINITY

Keith W. Perkins

The first white settlers of northeastern Ohio were the French, followed by the English. After the Revolutionary War, a group of land speculators known as the Connecticut Land Company gained possession of this portion of Ohio and sold sections of it to settlers. One of these speculators, Judge Turhand Kirtland, left his name with Kirtland town. When four LDS missionaries arrived from New York and converted many local citizens, the town began to be a Latter-day Saint community.

There are many spots significant to the LDS Church that can be visited in northeastern Ohio, but three are most prominent.

Newel K. Whitney and Company Store. The Newel K. Whitney store opened in a log cabin in 1823. The present frame structure was built in Kirtland, Ohio, by 1827. Operating as a mercantile establishment and as a post office, this building played a major role in the history of the Latter-day Saints in Kirtland, Ohio, during the years 1831–1838. The Prophet Joseph Smith arrived in Kirtland on February 1, 1831.

The Prophet later worked on the Joseph Smith translation of the Bible in an upstairs room. He also received a number of significant revelations in the Whitney store, including the Word of Wisdom (D&C 89) and two important revelations on priesthood (D&C 84, 88).

In the winter of 1833, in accord with revelation (D&C 88:127–141), the School of the Prophets, whose purpose was to prepare missionaries to take the gospel to the world, was begun in the store. The United Order, the predecessor of the current welfare system of the Church, also had its beginning in the store, which was used as the bishop's storehouse (D&C 72:8–10; 78:3). Today the building has been restored to its 1830s state and is operated by The Church of Jesus Christ of Latter-day Saints as a historic site open to visitors.

Kirtland Temple. The most prominent Kirtland structure is the stately House of the Lord, the first Latter-day Saint temple. It overlooks the city from the top of the hill. The design, measurements, and functions of the Kirtland Temple were given in revelation by the Lord. Its interior was to be 55 feet wide and 65 feet long and to have a lower and a higher court. The lower part of the inner court was to be dedicated "for your Sacrament offering, and for your preaching, and your fasting, and your praying, and the offering up of your most holy desires unto me, saith your Lord." The higher part of the inner court was to be "dedicated unto me for the school of mine apostles" (D&C 95:13–17).

The external design of the Kirtland Temple is typical of other contemporary houses of worship at that time, but the arrangement of the interior is unique. On each of the two main floors are two series of four-tiered pulpits, one on the west side, the other on the east. These are symbolic of the offices of the Melchizedek and Aaronic priesthoods and accommodated their presidencies.

The Saints completed the temple in less than three years. The cornerstone was laid at the southeast corner on July 23, 1833, and it was dedicated on March 17, 1836. The temple became the center of life for the Saints, housing the School of the Prophets and Elders. The temple is now owned and operated by the Reorganized Church of Jesus Christ of Latter Day Saints.

The John Johnson Home, Hiram, Ohio. A prominent church family, the John Johnsons, lived about 30 miles southeast of Kirtland. Two of their sons, Luke and Lyman, became members of the original Quorum of the Twelve. A daughter, Marinda, married Orson Hyde, another member of the Twelve. Because their home served not only to house Joseph Smith and his family, but also as Church headquarters and site of a large branch of the Church in 1831 and 1832, many significant events occurred in and around this home (*History of the Church* 1:215). For instance, Joseph Smith worked on his translation of the Bible while he resided in the Johnson home and received the revelation known as the degrees of glory (D&C 76). Moreover, one of the adopted twin babies of Joseph and Emma Smith died in Hiram and was perhaps buried in the cemetery there in 1832 (*HC* 1:265).

Approximately eight Church conferences were conducted in Hiram. The decision to print some of the revelations of Joseph Smith (*HC* 1:222) was made in the Johnson home. This work was known as the Book of Commandments, but today is called the Doctrine and Covenants. Currently the farm is part of the Latter-day Saint Church welfare services system and has been restored as a home and visitors' center.

Karl Ricks Anderson, *Joseph Smith's Kirtland: Eyewitness Accounts* (1989); Milton V. Backman, Jr., *The Heavens Resound: A History of the Latter-day Saints in Ohio, 1830–1838* (1983); Keith W. Perkins, "Kirtland Temple," in *Encyclopedia of Mormonism*, Daniel H. Ludlow, editor (1992) 2:798–799; Keith W. Perkins, "Whitney Store," in *Encyclopedia of Mormonism*, Daniel H. Ludlow, editor (1992) 4:1566–1567.

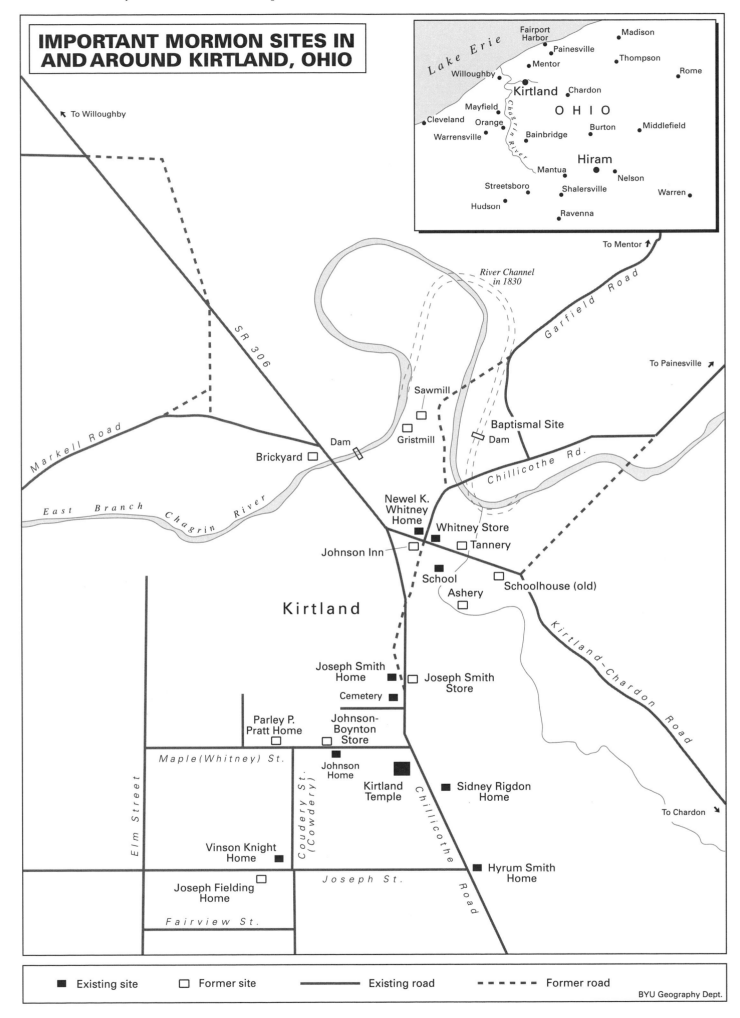

IMPORTANT MORMON SITES IN AND AROUND KIRTLAND, OHIO

To Willoughby

SR 306

Markell Road

To Mentor

Garfield Road

To Painesville

River Channel in 1830

Sawmill

Baptismal Site

Dam

Gristmill

Dam

Chillicothe Rd.

Brickyard

Dam

East Branch Chagrin River

Newel K. Whitney Home

Whitney Store

Tannery

Johnson Inn

School

Schoolhouse (old)

Ashery

Kirtland

Joseph Smith Home

Joseph Smith Store

Cemetery

Kirtland-Chardon Road

Parley P. Pratt Home

Johnson-Boynton Store

Maple (Whitney) St.

Johnson Home

Coudery St. (Cowdery)

Kirtland Temple

Sidney Rigdon Home

Elm Street

To Chardon

Chillicothe Road

Vinson Knight Home

Joseph St.

Hyrum Smith Home

Joseph Fielding Home

Fairview St.

Inset map (Ohio):

Lake Erie

Fairport Harbor

Madison

Painesville

Thompson

Mentor

Rome

Willoughby

Kirtland

Chardon

OHIO

Mayfield

Chagrin River

Cleveland

Orange

Burton

Middlefield

Warrensville

Bainbridge

Hiram

Mantua

Nelson

Streetsboro

Shalersville

Warren

Hudson

Ravenna

Legend:

■ Existing site   □ Former site   —— Existing road   - - - - Former road

BYU Geography Dept.

23

LAND OWNERSHIP IN KIRTLAND

Keith W. Perkins

The original Latter-day Saint landowners in Kirtland, Ohio, were residents of Kirtland who had been converted to the Church in 1830 and 1831. Some of the most prominent converts were Newel K. Whitney, A. Sidney Gilbert, and Isaac Morley. Newel K. Whitney and his partner Sidney Gilbert owned the N. K. Whitney and Company Store, which played a major role in providing for the numerous Latter-day Saints who later moved to Kirtland. They paid taxes on $2,500 worth of merchandise, making this one of the largest mercantile stores in northeastern Ohio at the time. Isaac Morley owned a large farm consisting of 130 acres. It was to his farm that most of the Saints gathered when they immigrated to Kirtland in 1831.

As the Saints began to gather to Ohio, the amount of property owned and managed by Church leaders in Kirtland significantly increased. In April 1832, Frederick G. Williams purchased 144 acres for $2,000. On May 3, 1834, this property was conveyed without monetary remuneration to Joseph Smith, as agent for the Church. In April 1833, Joseph Coe and Ezra Thayre purchased, for the Church, the Peter French farm of 103 acres for $5,000. It was on a small portion of this property that the Kirtland Temple was later built. Much of the money for this purchase must have been donated by John Johnson from the sale of his farm in Hiram, Ohio, since most of this property was later deeded to him. On October 5, 1836, another large farm, consisting of 239 acres, was purchased by the Church for $11,777.50.

The Church also purchased a tannery, an ashery, a printing office, and later a steam sawmill under the United Order. This order was an organization that managed the economic affairs of the Church, presided over by nine of the leading Brethren. Four of these Brethren were residents of Kirtland: Joseph Smith, Sidney Rigdon, Jesse Gause, and Newel K. Whitney. Five lived in Missouri: Oliver Cowdery, Edward Partridge, Sidney Gilbert, John Whitmer, and William W. Phelps (D&C 82:11–12). When Jesse Gause was excommunicated in Kirtland, Frederick G. Williams replaced him not only as a member of the United Order, but also as a member of the First Presidency of the Church (D&C 81; 92:1–2). Later, John Johnson was added to the Order, apparently because of his major financial contribution to the Church (D&C 96:6–9). When Oliver Cowdery and Martin Harris moved back from Missouri they also became a part of the United Order. These 12 men held properties in trust and cared for the poor by supervising the Bishop's Storehouse. They also purchased land and assisted in the construction of the Kirtland Temple.

A major change in the United Order came on April 23, 1834, when it was divided up into two orders, the United Order of the Stake of Zion, the City of Kirtland, and the United Order of the City of Zion (D&C 104:48). This was necessary because the Latter-day Saints had been driven out of Jackson County, Missouri, a few months earlier. At this time individual stewardships were assigned to various leaders of the United Order. Sidney Rigdon not only received responsibility for his place of residence, but also the tannery as his stewardship (D&C 104:20). Oliver Cowdery and Frederick G. Williams received the printing office as their stewardship (D&C 104:29). Newel K. Whitney received the mercantile store and the ashery for his stewardship (D&C 104:39, 41). Joseph Smith, Jr., received for his stewardship the property where the temple was later built (D&C 104:43). John Johnson received most of the French farm that had been purchased a year earlier (D&C 104:34–37). The land from the Johnson stewardship was later divided up into lots that were "laid off for the building up of the city of the saints" (D&C 104:36) and form part of the city of Kirtland today.

Milton V. Backman, Jr., *The Heavens Resound: A History of the Latter-day Saints in Ohio 1830–1838* (1983); Marvin S. Hill, C. Keith Rooker, and Larry T. Wimmer, "The Kirtland Economy Revisited: A Market Critique of Sectarian Economics," *BYU Studies* 17 (Summer 1977): 389–475. For reference to Jesse Gause, who is not listed in D&C 82:11–12, see *Far West Record: Minutes of the Church of Jesus Christ of Latter-day Saints, 1830–1844*, Donald Q. Cannon and Lyndon W. Cook, editors (1983).

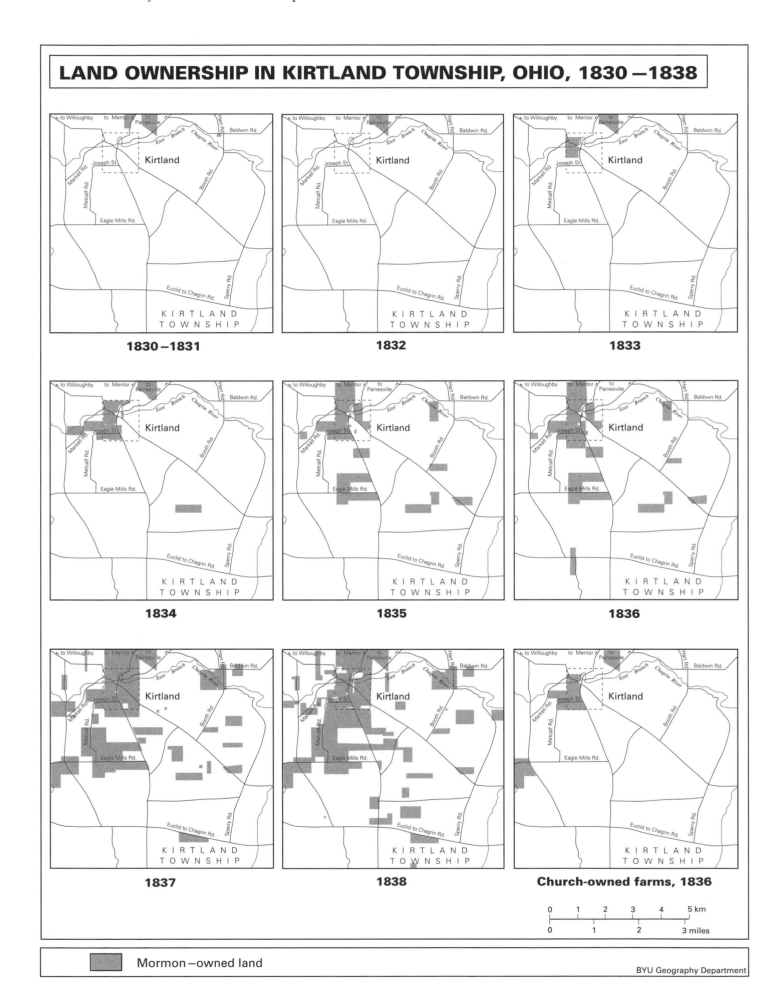

LAND OWNERSHIP IN KIRTLAND TOWNSHIP, OHIO, 1830 – 1838

1830 – 1831

1832

1833

1834

1835

1836

1837

1838

Church-owned farms, 1836

Mormon – owned land

BYU Geography Department

FROM KIRTLAND TO MISSOURI

Bruce A. Van Orden

Between 1830 and 1838, thousands of Latter-day Saints made the 900-mile trek from northeastern Ohio to Missouri. They utilized the common modes of travel of that day: wagons, canal boats, stages, and steamboats. Or they simply walked on the National Road or on other trails. Some journeyed as missionaries; others joined with Joseph Smith because they were specifically commanded to do so; 200 or so served as paramilitary personnel because they intended to escort fellow members back to their homes in Jackson County, Missouri; hundreds went because they simply wanted to "gather to Zion"; and still others were fleeing difficulties in Kirtland in 1838 to join the body of the Church in northern Missouri.

The so-called Lamanite missionaries were the first group to journey in this direction. In the fall of 1830, Joseph Smith received a revelation in New York designating Oliver Cowdery, Parley P. Pratt, and two others to preach to the Lamanites—a Book of Mormon term for Native Americans—on the border with Missouri (D&C 28, 30, 32). En route to Missouri these missionaries tarried near Kirtland, Ohio, while Pratt introduced the gospel to his friend, the noted Reformed Baptist minister Sidney Rigdon. The missionaries converted not only Rigdon, but also approximately 130 others in the Kirtland area. The missionaries then took passage down the Ohio River toward St. Louis until they encountered ice near Cairo, Illinois, which forced them to trudge through deep snow the rest of the way. From St. Louis they followed the Boonslick and Santa Fe trails to Independence, seat of Jackson County. Independence lay only 12 miles from the western Missouri border. A number of Native American tribes had settled on the other side of the border, having been relocated there under direction of the U.S. government.

These missionaries did not convert many Native Americans, but their mission led to the coming of Joseph Smith to Jackson County. He had received a series of revelations indicating that the New Jerusalem would be located in Missouri "on the borders by the Lamanites" (D&C 28:9; 42:35; 45:64-71; 52:2-5, 42; 54:8; 55:5; 56:9). In company with his closest advisers, who were called by revelation to assist him, Joseph Smith traveled to Independence in June and July of 1831. They went by wagon to the Ohio Canal, by boat and then by stage to Cincinnati, then down the Ohio River, thence to the Mississippi River, and on to St. Louis. Joseph used the Boonslick and Santa Fe trails as he walked the rest of the way. Some of his party went by steamer up the Missouri River. At the same time a whole congregation, the Colesville Branch of the Church from Colesville, Ohio, traveled to Independence using the same combination of water and land routes. Another 30 missionaries or so traveled in pairs toward Missouri, preaching and establishing branches along the way.

As some of these Saints established various small settlements in Jackson County in 1831 and 1832, the call went out to other members of the Church to "gather to Zion." By October 1833, when original settlers drove the Mormons out of the county, approximately 1,500 Mormons had come from the East to Missouri. From May 5 to July 3, 1834, Joseph Smith led the paramilitary group, Zion's Camp, to Missouri to "redeem Zion." But when they arrived, a revelation instructed them to disband. Instead, the Saints established more permanent Mormon settlements in Liberty and in the surrounding Clay County countryside.

From mid-1834 to mid-1836, approximately 500 more Saints gathered to Missouri, all the while hoping, with their Church leaders, that Zion might still be redeemed. Instead, Clay County citizens became increasingly nervous about the burgeoning LDS presence in their midst and ordered the Mormons out. Missouri Church leaders explored new gathering spots and found relatively uninhabited territory in northern Missouri. By early 1837 most Missouri members resided in the newly created Mormon county of Caldwell.

Waves of Latter-day Saints traveled from the Kirtland area to Missouri in 1838. Joseph Smith and Sidney Rigdon fled for their lives from their Kirtland enemies in January 1838 and arrived in Far West, Caldwell County, in March. Wanting to be near their Prophet, numerous others followed. Finally, in the summer of 1838, about 550 Saints who banded together in covenant as the Kirtland Camp traversed the same general route to Missouri that Zion's Camp had used four years earlier. The Kirtland Camp arrived in Missouri just as hostilities were breaking out between Missouri militia units and the Mormons in the so-called Mormon War. This war resulted in the mass migration of virtually all Latter-day Saints to Illinois the following year.

Milton V. Backman, Jr., *The Heavens Resound: A History of the Latter-day Saints in Ohio, 1830–1838* (1983); Stanley B. Kimball, *Historic Sites and Markers along the Mormon and Other Great Western Trails* (1988).

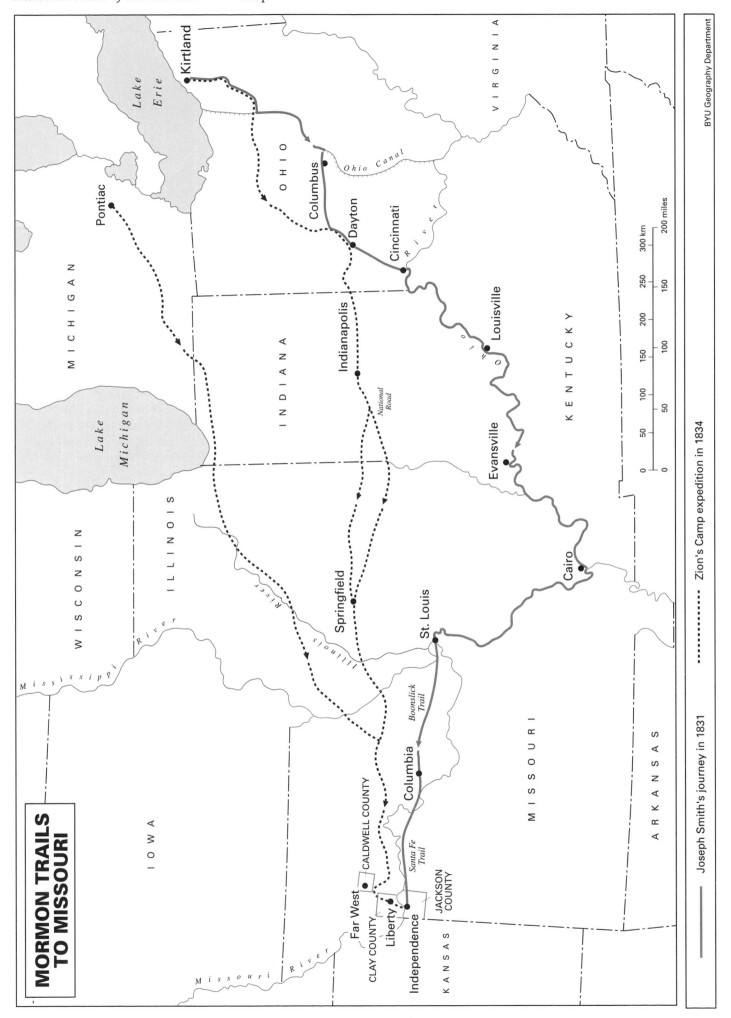

MORMON TRAILS
TO MISSOURI

Lake Erie

Kirtland

Pontiac

OHIO

Ohio Canal

Columbus

Dayton

Cincinnati

Ohio River

MICHIGAN

Lake Michigan

INDIANA

Indianapolis

National Road

Louisville

KENTUCKY

Evansville

WISCONSIN

ILLINOIS

Mississippi River

Illinois River

Springfield

St. Louis

Cairo

IOWA

Boonslick Trail

Columbia

Santa Fe Trail

CALDWELL COUNTY

Far West

CLAY COUNTY

Liberty

Independence

JACKSON COUNTY

MISSOURI

KANSAS

ARKANSAS

Missouri River

VIRGINIA

200 miles

300 km   150   200   250

0   50   100   150

0   50   100

BYU Geography Department

—————— Joseph Smith's journey in 1831

·············· Zion's Camp expedition in 1834

27

EXPEDITIONS FROM KIRTLAND

Bruce A. Van Orden

Latter-day Saints made two major expeditions from Kirtland to Missouri during the 1830s: the march of Zion's Camp in 1834, and the Kirtland Camp trek of 1838. The former included about 205 men, plus a few women and children, and the latter consisted of approximately 550 persons. They followed an almost identical route. In both cases nearly everybody walked the entire 900 miles.

Zion's Camp was a combined relief force and military body sent to escort fellow Mormons back to their homes in Jackson County, Missouri. The previous November, original Jackson County settlers, angry over the Mormons' distinctive beliefs and rapidly increasing numbers, had driven Missouri Saints north across the Missouri River into Clay County. Missouri governor Daniel Dunklin had promised to send a militia to provide necessary protection.

A revelation on February 24, 1834 (D&C 103), commanded Church leaders to recruit participants for a march. Joseph Smith was not pleased with the response, with just over a hundred men joining the march. But as the march proceeded, other recruits joined en route.

A party of 20 left Kirtland on May 1, 1834, to prepare the first camp at New Portage, Ohio, near present-day Akron. The march was officially inaugurated on May 9, near the Kirtland town square. Through Ohio, Indiana, and Illinois, Zion's Camp largely followed existing roads. In Indiana they picked up the famous National Road, later U.S. Route 40.

The marchers were well armed, carrying muskets, pistols, swords, and knives. Joseph Smith, their commander, organized them into groups of 10 and 50, with a captain over each. Lacking military training, participants conducted military exercises along the route. Days began with prayer at 5 A.M. Animals were rested every two hours. Marchers camped before dark, averaging about 25 miles per day.

Physical hardships became a major challenge. Marchers suffered from blistered feet, insufficient clothing, oppressive heat, heavy rains, humidity, hunger, and thirst. Members often had to eat limited portions of coarse bread, rancid butter, cornmeal mush, strong honey, raw pork, rotten ham, and maggot-infested bacon and cheese.

Despite these hardships and its military orientation, Zion's Camp emphasized spirituality. In addition to company prayers, leaders enjoined associates to pray privately morning and evening. The camp rested on Sundays and held worship services. One of the most prized memories was hearing Joseph Smith's teachings.

On June 6 the marchers were joined at the Salt River near Paris, Missouri, by men recruited from Pontiac, Michigan. When the expanded camp reached Richmond on June 18, they learned that armed men from Jackson and surrounding counties planned to engage them in battle. Church leaders also discovered that Governor

Dunklin had withdrawn his promise, realizing that it could lead to civil war.

A terrible thunderstorm halted the Missourians near Liberty. An ensuing revelation (D&C 105) commended participants for their sacrifice and directed them not to fight but to wait for the Lord to redeem Zion in his own way and time. Zion's Camp disbanded shortly thereafter, and supplies were distributed to refugees. Most marchers returned to Ohio. Zion's Camp proved to be a valuable training exercise for future Church leaders and an essential experience for future overland treks.

In 1837, the Church's bank, the Kirtland Safety Society, failed in Ohio. Mass apostasy followed. Faithful members in the Kirtland area suffered intense persecution. Starting in December 1837, approximately 1,600 Church members departed Ohio for Missouri, usually in groups of no more than 50 persons. Few enjoyed the luxury of water transportation. Since most were poor, they went on foot, suffering illness, fatigue, muddy conditions, biting cold, blistered feet, and thirst.

Members of the Three Quorums of Seventy—the Church's missionary cadre—made plans in the spring of 1838 for their families to travel together. As plans matured, other destitute families asked to join the company. Intending to leave in May, the group—by then known as Kirtland Camp—did not depart until July 6 due to lack of funds and provisions. The initial company consisted of 515 (249 men and 266 women).

Camp members sought employment along the way to obtain needed funds. Because of the camp's size and because of young children, the group walked only 15 miles per day. Because 10 of the group had participated in Zion's Camp, Kirtland Camp essentially followed the earlier route. Accidents and illness constantly afflicted these pioneers. Death periodically struck the camp, especially the young. The non-Mormon response to this large movement varied from curiosity to threats. In early September in Indiana, leaders directed the camp to speed up to 20 miles per day.

After the camp reached Missouri in late September, members heard of war threats against fellow Saints. Upon arrival, camp members scattered among various Mormon settlements. Some later became victims of the Haun's Mill Massacre, the attacks in Adam-ondi-Ahman, and the siege of Far West.

Milton V. Backman, Jr., *The Heavens Resound: A History of the Latter-day Saints in Ohio 1830–1838* (1983); Stanley B. Kimball, *Historic Sites and Markers along the Mormon and Other Great Western Trails* (1988); Roger D. Launius, *Zion's Camp* (1984); Bruce A. Van Orden, "Zion's Camp: A Refiner's Fire," in Larry C. Porter and Susan Easton Black, editors, *The Prophet Joseph: Essays on the Life and Mission of Joseph Smith* (1988).

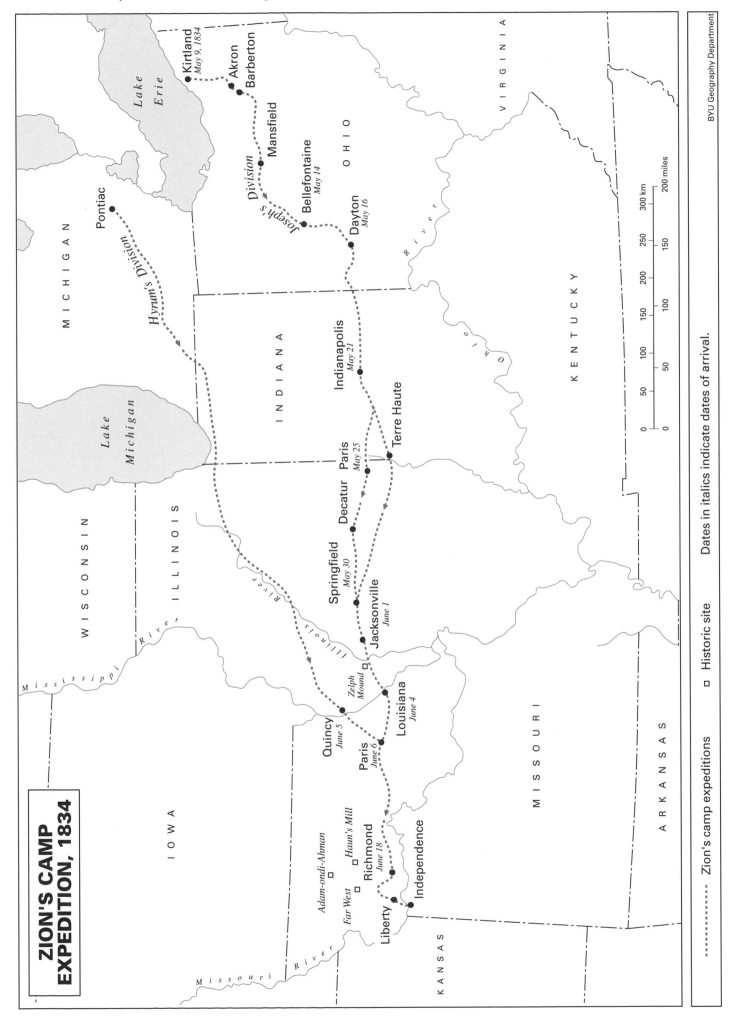

ZION'S CAMP EXPEDITION, 1834

Kirtland
May 9, 1834

Akron

Barberton

Mansfield

Bellefontaine
May 14

Dayton
May 16

O H I O

V I R G I N I A

Joseph's Division

Lake Erie

Pontiac

Hyrum's Division

M I C H I G A N

Lake Michigan

Indianapolis
May 21

Terre Haute

Paris
May 25

Decatur

Springfield
May 30

Jacksonville
June 1

I N D I A N A

River

Ohio

K E N T U C K Y

W I S C O N S I N

I L L I N O I S

Illinois River

Mississippi River

Zelph
Mound

Quincy
June 5

Paris
June 6

Louisiana
June 4

I O W A

Adam-ondi-Ahman

Haun's Mill

Far West

Richmond
June 18

Liberty

Independence

Missouri River

K A N S A S

M I S S O U R I

A R K A N S A S

0   50   100 150 200
0   50   100 150 200 250 300 km
     200 miles

BYU Geography Department

Dates in italics indicate dates of arrival.

□ Historic site

------ Zion's camp expeditions

EARLY MISSIONARY JOURNEYS IN NORTH AMERICA

Arnold K. Garr

One of the most important aspects of early Mormon missionary work was that the majority of proselyting was carried out in the United States and Canada, then known as British North America. From 1830 to 1837, the year the British Mission was established, all of the Church's missionary activity took place in North America. Even though the British Mission experienced phenomenal success in its early years, the primary emphasis on missionary work throughout Joseph Smith's entire ministry remained centered in the United States and Canada. Of all missionaries who received calls between 1830 and 1844, 96 percent labored in North America.

The center for Mormon missionary work during most of the 1830s was Kirtland, Ohio. In June 1831, during a conference in Kirtland, Smith received a revelation calling 14 pairs of elders to go on missions to Missouri. They were instructed to travel by different routes and preach the gospel along the way. Two of these elders were Reynolds Cahoon and Samuel Smith, brother of Joseph Smith. En route to Missouri they were the first Mormon missionaries to enter the states of Kentucky and Indiana. Little is known of their proselyting activities in Kentucky, but we do know that they preached in the Indiana cities of Unionville, Madison, and Vienna.

In January 1832, Joseph Smith received another revelation that led to further pioneer proselyting. Samuel Smith and Orson Hyde were called to preach in the eastern states. Obedient to their call, they became the first known missionaries in four New England states: Connecticut, Rhode Island, Maine, and Massachusetts. There is no record of them converting anyone in Connecticut, but in Rhode Island they baptized at least two persons before persecution drove them from the state. In Maine they converted enough people to start a branch in Saco, York County; and in Massachusetts they baptized enough people to organize two small branches.

In the 1832 revelation, Orson Pratt and Lyman Johnson were also called to the eastern states. These two pioneered missionary work in New Jersey and New Hampshire. Little is known of their activities in New Jersey. But during their four-week stay in New Hampshire they baptized at least 20 people in the town of Bath, including Amasa M. Lyman, a future Apostle.

At this same time, Luke Johnson and William E. McLellin were called to labor in the southern states. They began as companions, but soon thereafter, Elder McLellin found employment and ended his mission. He was replaced by Seymour Brunson. Johnson and Brunson traveled through Ohio, Virginia, and Kentucky. They baptized more than 100 people and organized branches in Lawrence County, Ohio, and Cabell County, Virginia (now West Virginia). The new branch in Virginia became the first branch of the Church in the southern states.

Another pioneer missionary was Jedediah M. Grant. In 1837, he initiated missionary work in Delaware and Maryland. Then, in 1838, he became the first elder to enter the state of North Carolina. There he preached for about six months in Rockingham, Stokes, and Surry counties, baptizing at least four people. In 1840 he was joined by other missionaries and they soon brought six or eight more converts into the Church.

Probably the first missionaries to enter British North America (Canada) after the Church was organized were Joseph Smith, Sr., and his son Don Carlos. They visited a few villages north of the St. Lawrence River in September 1830, but probably baptized no one. Two of the most successful early missionaries in Canada were John E. Page and Parley P. Pratt. Elder Page baptized more than 600 people and Elder Pratt converted John Taylor, a future president of the Church.

In 1835 a major reorganization in Church government took place in Kirtland that had a profound effect on missionary work: the Quorum of Twelve Apostles and the first Quorum of Seventy were organized. For a time, the precise responsibilities of these two quorums were not completely clear, but in March 1835, they were given the responsibility to preach the gospel "in all the world." Soon thereafter the Twelve left on a mission to the eastern states. From May to October, they conducted a series of conferences throughout the Northeast in New York, Maine, Vermont, Massachusetts, New Hampshire, and Canada.

During the 1830s and early 1840s, the Church had taken the message of the gospel into every state of the Union and parts of eastern Canada. It had thus laid the foundation for taking the message of the Restoration to "all nations, kindreds, tongues, and people."

LaMar C. Berrett, "History of the Southern States Mission, 1831–1861" (Master's thesis, Brigham Young University, 1960); Davis Bitton, "Kirtland as a Center of Missionary Activity, 1830–1838," *BYU Studies* 2 (Summer 1971):497–516; *Deseret News 1993–1994 Church Almanac* (1992); Gordon Irving, "Numeric Strength and Geographic Distribution of the LDS Missionary Force, 1830–1974," *Task Papers in LDS History* 1 (1975).

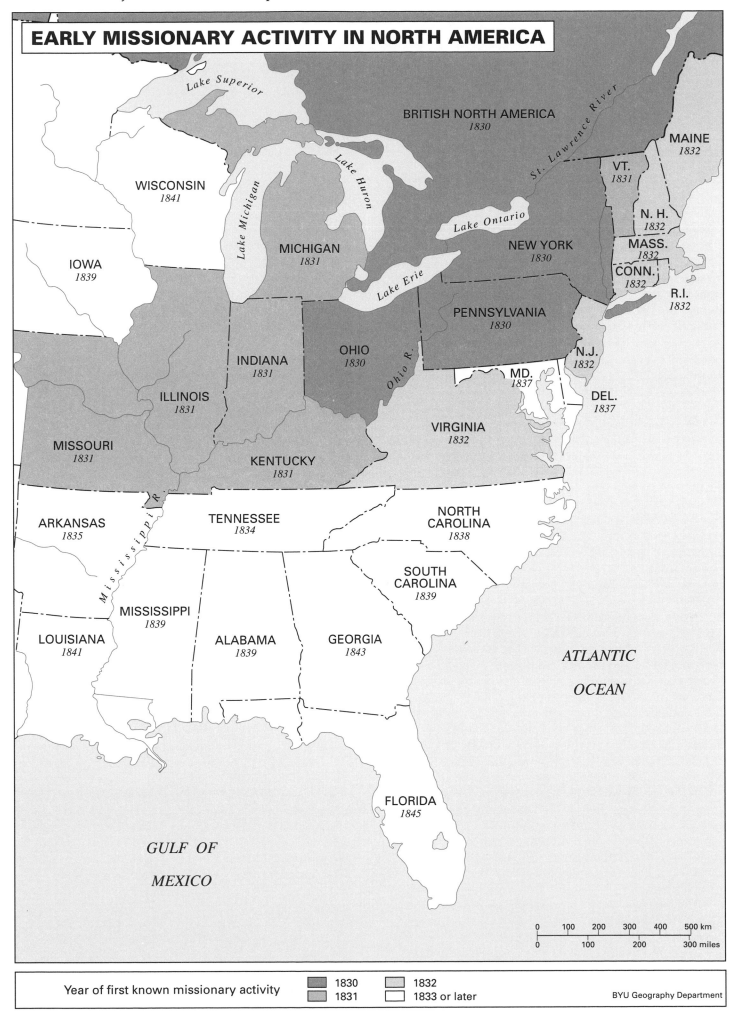

EARLY MISSIONARY ACTIVITY IN NORTH AMERICA

Lake Superior

BRITISH NORTH AMERICA
1830

MAINE
1832

St. Lawrence River

Lake Huron

VT.
1831

Lake Michigan

N. H.
1832

Lake Ontario

NEW YORK
1830

MASS.
1832

WISCONSIN
1841

MICHIGAN
1831

CONN.
1832

Lake Erie

R.I.
1832

IOWA
1839

PENNSYLVANIA
1830

INDIANA
1831

OHIO
1830

N.J.
1832

Ohio R.

MD.
1837

ILLINOIS
1831

DEL.
1837

VIRGINIA
1832

MISSOURI
1831

KENTUCKY
1831

Mississippi R.

ARKANSAS
1835

TENNESSEE
1834

NORTH
CAROLINA
1838

SOUTH
CAROLINA
1839

MISSISSIPPI
1839

ATLANTIC

OCEAN

LOUISIANA
1841

ALABAMA
1839

GEORGIA
1843

FLORIDA
1845

GULF OF

MEXICO

| 0 | 100 | 200 | 300 | 400 | 500 km |

| 0 | 100 | 200 | 300 miles |

Year of first known missionary activity

| | 1830 | | 1832 |
| | 1831 | | 1833 or later |

BYU Geography Department

MISSIONARY JOURNEYS TO FOREIGN COUNTRIES

David J. Whittaker

Missionary work has been a central concern of the Mormons since their beginnings in 1830. In their study of the Bible, particularly the New Testament, Mormon leaders identified with early Christian missionaries who were commissioned by Jesus to "go ye therefore, and teach all nations" (Matt. 28:19). Further, their own scriptures both reemphasized and reinforced this international missionary outlook. Many passages in the Book of Mormon and the Doctrine and Covenants described the world as a field, which was white and ready to harvest; and the faithful were assured that no joy would be greater than what came as a result of successful missionary work.

Historically, missionary work has served to revitalize membership at critical periods of stress and strain. New converts also brought badly needed skills and talents during the hectic pioneer period of the Church's history. The history and development of the various missions of the Church were often the testing ground for Church leaders as well as for Church programs and publications. Problems of government and administration—internal and external to the Church—that arose in the various mission fields forced Church leaders very early to deal more comprehensively with matters of organization, licensing, discipline, publishing, immigration, and management of finances.

Church membership grew from six original members in 1830 to 268,331 in 1900, by which time missionaries had preached in nearly all the countries of the world. The first foreign mission attempted was to Canada. From 1832 on, individuals or groups of missionaries hazarded trips there, and notwithstanding the few converts in these early years, those who were baptized became instrumental in opening the British Mission, the next foreign mission attempted by the Church. From its first beginnings in 1837, the British Mission became the most successful foreign mission of the Church in the 19th century.

Much of the early missionary work in England was performed by members of the Quorum of the Twelve. Apostle-missionaries such as Wilford Woodruff achieved phenomenal success in bringing new converts into the Church. From 1840 to about 1900 it is estimated that over 50,000 converts emigrated to the United States from Britain.

Very early in their history Mormons also sent missionaries into other countries besides Canada and Britain. Even before the death of Joseph Smith, elders were sent to Australia, India, South America, Germany, and Jamaica. Although he failed to go, one man was even called to go to Russia. Apostle Orson Hyde visited and dedicated Palestine in 1841.

In 1843, Noah Rogers and Addison Pratt opened missionary work in the Society Islands (Tahiti), establishing a foothold for the Church on the Tubuai Islands and Tahiti. This was the first missionary foray among the Polynesians. Thus a substantial effort had been expended in international missionary work by 1844, when Joseph Smith died.

From England early missionaries first made proselyting thrusts into Ireland, Wales, Scotland, and eventually continental Europe, and then gradually extended themselves in more organized ventures. John Taylor of the Quorum of the Twelve started missionary work in Ireland and on the Isle of Man while Alexander Wright and Samuel Mulliner carried the gospel for the first time to Scotland. In 1849, the Italian, French, and Scandinavian missions were organized. A mission to Hawaii came in 1850, another to South America in 1851. Although some missionaries had visited Germany as early as 1841, the first formal work in that European country took place in 1851, when Daniel Garn arrived from America. In 1852, missionaries were dispatched to Gibraltar, India, Hindustan (India), Siam (Thailand), China, South Africa, the West Indies (Caribbean), British Guiana, and again to Australia. Although few of these latter missions were successful during the 19th century, the very attempt suggests the international outlook and millennialism of the early Mormon Church. It is also clear that much of the early missionary work followed the paths and locations of the British Empire throughout the world.

Despite a period of anti-Mormon persecution and prosecution in the United States in the 1880s, foreign missionary efforts continued. Missionary work had begun in Mexico in 1875, but it ended about 1889. It was reopened again in 1901. In 1865, the first contacts were made in Austria and Hungary; in 1883, several missionaries preached there, but for many years little was accomplished there. In 1885, missionary work was begun in Turkey. In 1885 and 1891, respectively, missions were organized in Samoa and in Tonga.

By the end of the 19th century, Latter-day Saint missionaries had begun to preach the gospel in the four corners of the earth. For them, the gospel message had been carried to almost every nation, kindred, tongue, and people.

James B. Allen, Ronald K. Esplin, and David J. Whittaker, *Men with a Mission: The Quorum of the Twelve Apostles in the British Isles, 1837–1841* (1992); R. Lanier Britsch, *Unto the Islands of the Sea: A History of the Latter-day Saints in the Pacific* (1986); William Mulder, *Homeward to Zion: The Mormon Migration from Scandinavia* (1957); Spencer J. Palmer, *The Expanding Church* (1978); P. A. M. Taylor, *Expectations Westward: The Mormons and the Emigration of Their British Converts in the Nineteenth Century* (1965).

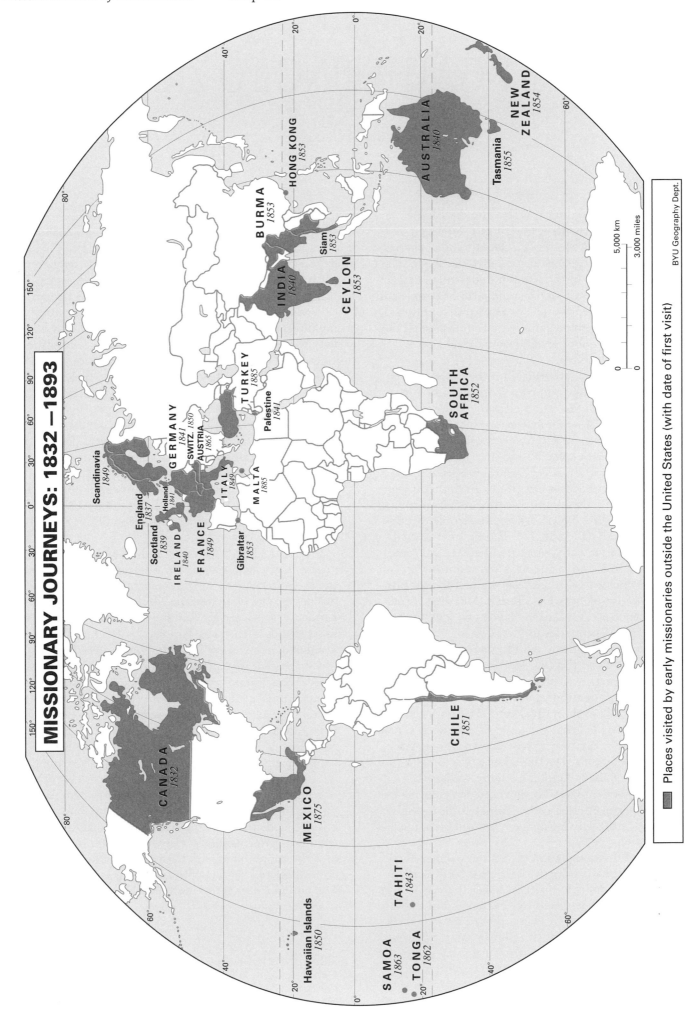

MISSIONARY JOURNEYS: 1832–1893

NEW ZEALAND
1854

AUSTRALIA
1840

Tasmania
1855

HONG KONG
1853

BURMA
1853

Siam
1853

INDIA
1840

CEYLON
1853

TURKEY
1885

Palestine
1841

GERMANY
1841

SWITZ.
1850

AUSTRIA
1865

Scandinavia
1849

England
1837

Holland
1841

Scotland
1839

IRELAND
1840

FRANCE
1849

ITALY
1849

MALTA
1885

Gibraltar
1853

SOUTH AFRICA
1852

CANADA
1832

MEXICO
1875

CHILE
1851

Hawaiian Islands
1850

TAHITI
1843

SAMOA
1863

TONGA
1862

5,000 km

3,000 miles

BYU Geography Dept.

Places visited by early missionaries outside the United States (with date of first visit)

33

FIRST GATHERING TO ZION

Richard H. Jackson

One of the oldest doctrines of The Church of Jesus Christ of Latter-day Saints is that of the Gathering. For Latter-day Saints this concept is related to biblical references to the Gathering of Israel and involves the bringing together of members of the Church in designated places where they can perform sacred ordinances in temples. In September 1830, the Prophet Joseph Smith mentioned that the Saints were to be gathered into one place (D&C 29:7–8), and subsequent revelations indicated specific destinations for gathering.

The earliest group gathering after the initial assembling of the first members in New York was to Ohio. Missionaries to the Indians first introduced the restored gospel to communities of northeastern Ohio in October of 1830. Approximately 130 people were baptized in and around Kirtland, with some 35 residing in Kirtland proper. Informed of the new branches in Kirtland, the Prophet Joseph revealed in December 1830 that it was the Lord's will that the members of the newly organized Church leave upstate New York and "assemble together at the Ohio" (D&C 37:3, 38:32). The Prophet moved his family to Kirtland in early February of 1831, and some 200 members followed in the next few months.

The movement to Kirtland was the first formal gathering of members of the LDS Church. Members came from the branches organized in New York, joining the Ohio converts. Missionaries to New England and Canada converted others who came west to join the Saints, but new revelations given through Joseph Smith soon affected the growth of Kirtland as a gathering place. These revelations identified another gathering place. In July of 1831, the Prophet traveled to the frontier in Missouri and revealed that the town of Independence and surrounding Jackson County were to be a second gathering place. He stated that Independence was to be the site of a new City of Zion, including a temple where the Saints could perform sacred ordinances. In consequence, two gathering places effectively competed for members during the first decade of the newly restored Church (D&C 57:1–7).

Because of the designation of Jackson County as the site of the City of Zion, many of the first New York migrants to Kirtland continued on to Missouri in 1831. The Prophet Joseph returned to Kirtland and lived there with his family until 1838. Thereupon Kirtland became the administrative center of the Church, and the site of the first temple constructed by the Latter-day Saints. On the other hand, the Missouri gathering became a focus of efforts to recreate the model of the early Christian church by living a communitarian life-style.

Growth in the two gathering places was uneven. In Jackson County the population of Saints grew rapidly. Between 300 and 400 arrived in the spring of 1832, and by the end of the year there were over 800 members in Missouri. By the summer of 1833 there were over 1,200 Saints in Jackson County, making it the largest concentration of Latter-day Saints in the world. Unfortunately, the rapidly growing Mormon population created hostility with the non-Mormon settlers of the area. This hostility culminated in mob violence and the expulsion of the Saints from Jackson County in November of 1833.

Between 1834 and 1837, the Saints gathering to Missouri located primarily in Clay County, and after 1837, most moved to Caldwell County, where they created several settlements, including Far West. Far West ultimately had more than 3,000 inhabitants, and the Prophet Joseph moved his family there in 1838. A temple site was dedicated, and important revelations affecting the Church were received there, but by 1839 hostility with other settlers led to the expulsion of the Saints from Missouri to Iowa and Illinois.

While the Saints gathering to Missouri experienced nearly a decade of opposition, suffering, and death as they were repeatedly forced to abandon homes, farms, businesses, and churches, the Mormon population of Kirtland was engaged in building the temple and in establishing schools (the most famous was the School of the Prophets), newspapers (including the *Latter-day Saints' Messenger and Advocate*), a bank, and a variety of businesses. The temple was completed in 1836, and many Saints from Missouri joined those at Kirtland for its dedication. The Mormon population in Ohio increased from approximately 100 in 1833 to 2,000 in 1838. Because of the influx of Mormons, the population of the Kirtland township tripled between 1830 and 1837. Mormons were elected in 1837 to all township offices except that of constable. Opposition to their presence, combined with the failure of their bank (the Kirtland Safety Society) and apostasy from within, culminated in their exodus from Kirtland and vicinity in 1838. By mid-July of 1838, more than 1,600 Latter-day Saints had left the area, ultimately joining with the Saints expelled from Missouri in a new gathering at Nauvoo, Illinois.

Milton V. Backman, Jr., *The Heavens Resound: A History of the Latter-day Saints in Ohio 1830–1838* (1983); Marvin S. Hill, *Quest for Refuge* (1989); Stephen C. LeSueur, *The 1838 Mormon War in Missouri* (1990).

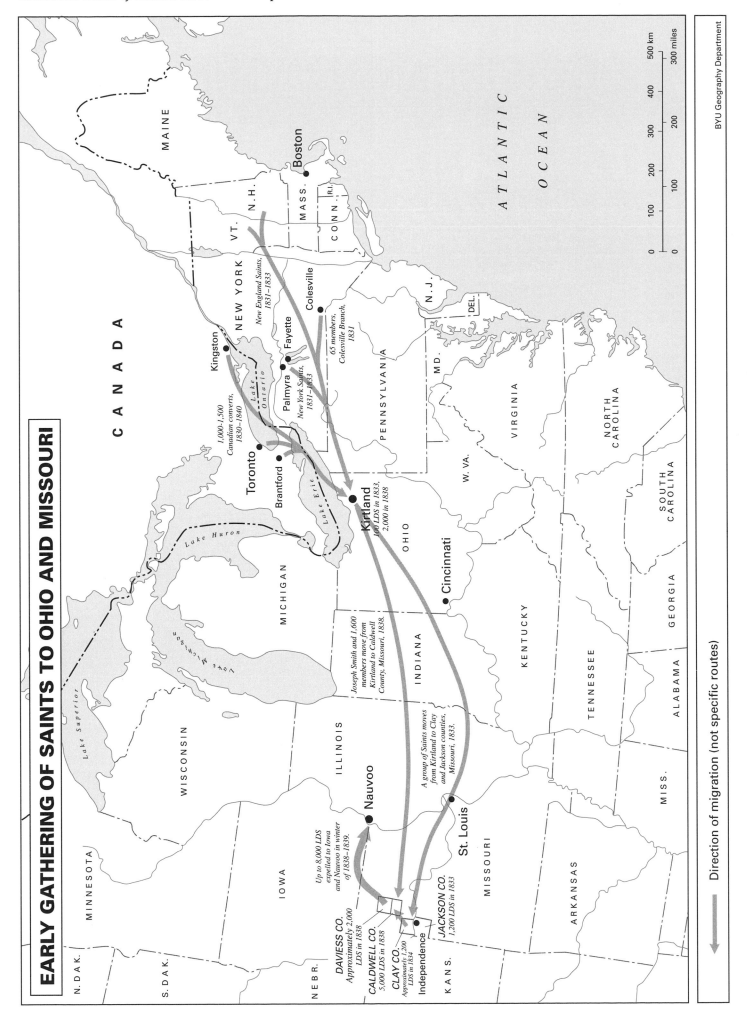

EARLY GATHERING OF SAINTS TO OHIO AND MISSOURI

N. DAK.

S. DAK.

MINNESOTA

WISCONSIN

IOWA

NEBR.

Lake Superior

Lake Michigan

Lake Huron

MICHIGAN

ILLINOIS

Nauvoo

Up to 8,000 LDS expelled to Iowa and Nauvoo in winter of 1838–1839.

*DAVIESS CO.
Approximately 2,000 LDS in 1838*

*CALDWELL CO.
5,000 LDS in 1838*

*CLAY CO.
Approximately 1,200 LDS in 1834*

Independence

*JACKSON CO.
1,200 LDS in 1833*

KANS.

MISSOURI

St. Louis

A group of Saints moves from Kirtland to Clay and Jackson counties, Missouri, 1833.

Joseph Smith and 1,600 members move from Kirtland to Caldwell County, Missouri, 1838.

INDIANA

Cincinnati

OHIO

Kirtland
100 LDS in 1833, 2,000 in 1838

Lake Erie

Brantford

Toronto

1,000–1,500 Canadian converts, 1830–1840

Kingston

Lake Ontario

CANADA

NEW YORK

Palmyra
New York Saints, 1831–1833

Fayette

Colesville

65 members, Colesville Branch, 1831

New England Saints, 1831–1833

VT.

N.H.

MAINE

MASS.

Boston

CONN.

R.I.

N.J.

PENNSYLVANIA

DEL.

MD.

W. VA.

VIRGINIA

NORTH CAROLINA

SOUTH CAROLINA

KENTUCKY

TENNESSEE

GEORGIA

ALABAMA

MISS.

ARKANSAS

ATLANTIC OCEAN

500 km

300 miles

0   100   200   300   400

0   100   200   300

BYU Geography Department

➤ Direction of migration (not specific routes)

DOCTRINE AND COVENANTS

Dale J. Stevens

The Doctrine and Covenants of The Church of Jesus Christ of Latter-day Saints is a book of scripture containing 138 sections or chapters and two Official Declarations. Most of the sections were written by Joseph Smith, the first president and prophet of the Church, as he received them as revelation or other promptings from the spirit of God. Many were in response to prayerful requests. The earliest section (Section 2) was received in Manchester, New York, on September 21, 1823, while the most recent entry is Official Declaration–2, dated September 30, 1978, in Salt Lake City, Utah.

The Doctrine and Covenants is considered by Church officials and its members to be a companion book of scripture to the Bible, the Book of Mormon, and the Pearl of Great Price. Besides containing details and instruction on church organization and practices, it contains many revelations given to Joseph Smith about issues raised as he translated the Book of Mormon and worked with the Bible. Many revelations were received for the benefit of particular individuals associated with the Church, but the information contained therein has general application as well. All revelations in the Doctrine and Covenants are considered to be *the will of the Lord, the mind of the Lord, the word of the Lord, or the voice of the Lord, and the power of God unto salvation* (see, e.g., D&C 68:4). "Its main focus is to build up the Church of Jesus Christ and to bring people into harmony with Christ's kingdom" (*Encyclopedia of Mormonism*, 1:405).

The first publication of the revelations received by Joseph Smith was attempted in Independence, Missouri, in 1833, but was destroyed by a mob before it was completed. Only a few copies were saved. The first edition of the Doctrine and Covenants, printed in 1835, contained 103 sections. A subsequent edition was printed in 1844 in Nauvoo, Illinois, and in 1845, a Liverpool, England, edition was published. Subsequent editions were published in 1876, 1879, 1921, and 1981.

A number of changes have been incorporated in each edition. The early printings contained the Lectures on Faith delivered by Joseph Smith and an article on marriage by Oliver Cowdery. Since these contributions were not considered revelations, they were eliminated in the 1921 and later editions. Other revelations, although received in the early days of the Church, were not included in the earliest editions. Neither are all of the revelations received by modern prophets of the Church recorded in the Doctrine and Covenants. Many of the revelations have been received for individuals and are not appropriate for public use. Some others are considered to be too sacred to be printed for general consumption, while others are recorded in the *History of the Church* or in other official Church publications. Currently, when

additional revelations are to be added to the Doctrine and Covenants, the First Presidency and the Council of the Twelve Apostles of the Church decide which revelations are to be included. Then the general Church membership has an opportunity to give affirmation to or vote against any proposed inclusions.

Accurate records do not exist to show how many copies have been produced since 1835. But from 1988 to 1992, for instance, approximately three million were printed. The majority of the copies are printed in what is called a "triple combination" consisting of one binding of three books: the Book of Mormon, the Doctrine and Covenants, and the Pearl of Great Price. Approximately 26 percent of the published copies have been printed separately or in combination with the Pearl of Great Price. The book is currently published in 31 different languages, with English-language editions constituting 71 percent of all copies.

Some quotations from the Doctrine and Covenants that are well known among Latter-day Saints include: "Seek not for riches but for wisdom" (D&C 11:7); "If ye are prepared ye shall not fear" (38:30); "He who doeth the works of righteousness shall receive his reward, even peace in this world, and eternal life in the world to come" (59:23); "Of you it is required to forgive all men" (64:10); "Seek ye out of the best books words of wisdom; seek learning, even by study and also by faith" (88:118); "Search diligently, pray always, and be believing, and all things shall work together for your good" (90:24).

The following table summarizes the history, geographic origin, and content of the Doctrine and Covenants.

Date	Location	Sections	General Content
1831	Ohio	1, 67–69	Preface and appendix—truthfulness of revelations
pre-1830	New York; Pennsylvania	2–19	Organizing the Church
1830	New York; Pennsylvania	20–40	Church doctrines
1831–1839	Ohio; Missouri; Massachusetts	41–66, 70–123 133, 134	Lord's laws, temples
1839–1844	Nauvoo, Illinois	124–132, 135	Salvation, eternal marriage
1847	Winter Quarters, Nebraska	136	Preparation for westward migration
1836	Kirtland, Ohio	137	Vision of the Celestial Kingdom
1918	Salt Lake City	138	Vision on redemption of the dead
1890	Salt Lake City	Declaration 1	Revoking of plural marriage
1978	Salt Lake City	Declaration 2	Priesthood deemed available to all worthy males

Bruce R. McConkie, *Mormon Doctrine* (1979); Milton V. Backman, *Joseph Smith and the Doctrine and Covenants* (1992).

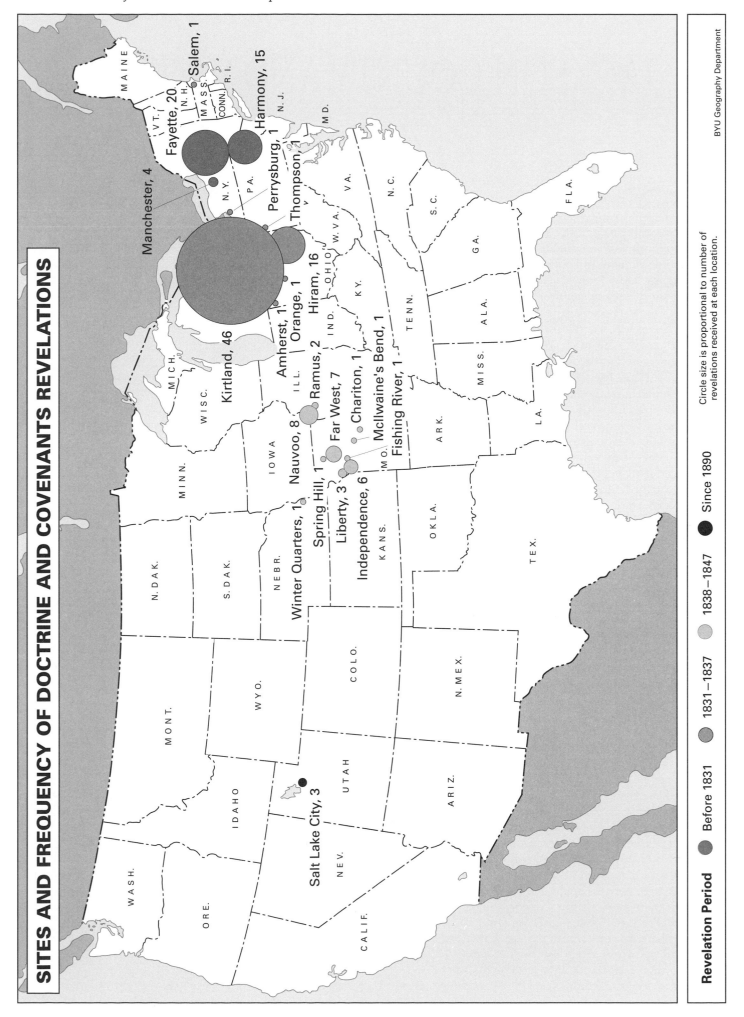

SITES AND FREQUENCY OF DOCTRINE AND COVENANTS REVELATIONS

Salem, 1
Harmony, 15
Fayette, 20
Perrysburg, 1
Thompson, 1
Manchester, 4
Amherst, 1
Orange, 1
Hiram, 16
Kirtland, 46
Ramus, 2
Far West, 7
Chariton, 1
McIlwaine's Bend, 1
Fishing River, 1
Nauvoo, 8
Spring Hill, 1
Liberty, 3
Winter Quarters, 1
Independence, 6
Salt Lake City, 3

Revelation Period Before 1831 1831–1837 1838–1847 Since 1890

Circle size is proportional to number of revelations received at each location.

BYU Geography Department

JACKSON COUNTY AND VICINITY

Max H. Parkin

Before Jackson County was opened for settlement, early promoters spoke of it as the "Garden of Missouri," and Mormons who were among its first settlers claimed it as their promised land. In February 1831, after Mormon missionaries to the Indians (Lamanites) found their mission cut short, they began proselyting settlers in Jackson County. One early convert was Joshua Lewis, a resident of Kaw Township. When Joseph Smith and other Church members arrived in the summer from Kirtland, Ohio, they congregated at the Lewis log house, where, on August 2, Sidney Rigdon dedicated Jackson County as a gathering place for the Mormons.

While Joseph Smith made Independence the center of Zion, most Mormons settled west of the village in Kaw Township, a county district west of the Blue River. At Independence, the county seat, Bishop Edward Partridge purchased land and distributed it in stewardships to Church members in the county. In this manner, four Mormon communities were established in Kaw Township and one at Independence.

Two settlements in Kaw Township were situated on the Westport road, which led from Independence to Indian lands. The closest community to Independence was the Blue River Settlement, five miles west of Independence at the point where the road crossed the Blue River. At the crossing, Orin Rockwell and his son Porter operated a ferry. Thomas B. Marsh, a future president of the Quorum of the Twelve Apostles, presided over one congregation there. By the fall of 1833, this area boasted the largest Mormon settlement in the county, with over 300 members and three Church branches.

The Timber Settlement, known also as the Whitmer Branch, was the home of David Whitmer, its presiding elder, and other Whitmer families from Fayette, New York, as well as others. Located four miles west of the Blue River on the Westport road, this settlement included the Lewis house, where Rigdon had dedicated Jackson County as the latter-day Zion, and a Mormon-built schoolhouse. The Colesville settlement was made up of the earliest group of Mormons to arrive in Jackson County; they originated in Colesville, New York. They settled two miles south of the Whitmers, near Brush Creek, where Newel Knight and his brother, Joseph, received their stewardships and constructed a gristmill. Parley P. Pratt, one of the early Lamanite missionaries, resided there; as the community grew, it added an additional presiding officer. In fact, in September 1833, the five Mormon Jackson County settlements were divided into 10 ecclesiastical branches with a presiding high priest over each.

The Prairie Settlement, near the Indian border, was led by Lyman Wight. One mile north of this settlement was Calvin McCoy's trading post, around which soon grew the important trail town of Westport. Eventually, Kansas City, Missouri, which today encompasses most of Kaw Township, grew from Westport and its landing on the Missouri River.

In the summer of 1833, mob violence against the Mormons commenced at Independence, but it was not until the last day of October that mobs attacked the Saints in Kaw Township. A mob first assaulted the Whitmer Settlement, tore off the roofs of several houses, whipped the men, and terrified the women and children; two days later a mob attacked Mormons at the Blue River Settlement and took over the Rockwell ferry. On November 4, when a mob again attacked the Whitmer Settlement, a skirmish—known as the Battle above the Blue—ensued, leaving one Mormon mortally wounded, two citizens dead, and several on both sides wounded.

On November 5, Mormons from Kaw Township rallied to assist members at Independence; state militiamen disarmed them and left them to the mercy of the armed citizens, who for several days raided all the settlements and drove the Mormons from the county. Most of the 1,200 Saints who fled withdrew north to Clay County, but some traveled south to Van Buren or east to LaFayette and other counties.

The frightful circumstances surrounding the departure of the Saints often left them without food or adequate clothing. After scattering into Clay County, they set up emergency shelters along the Missouri River bottom. Some suffering Mormons returned to Jackson County for provisions, but were beaten and sent away.

In the spring, the residents of Clay County were hospitable, and Joseph Smith's relief party, Zion's Camp, brought some help from the East in June. Joseph Smith disbanded the camp at Lyman Wight's temporary residence south of Liberty. At Wight's, the Mormon Prophet organized an ecclesiastical stake of the Church for the Missouri Saints and appointed David Whitmer its president; then he returned to Ohio, leaving the exiled people to hope for a better day.

Richard L. Anderson, "Jackson County in Early Mormon Descriptions," *Missouri Historical Review* 65 (April 1971): 270–293; Warren A. Jennings, "Zion is Fled: The Expulsion of the Mormons from Jackson County, Missouri" (Ph.D. diss., University of Florida, 1962); Max H. Parkin, "A History of the Latter-day Saints in Clay County, Missouri, from 1833 to 1837" (Ph.D. diss., Brigham Young University, 1976); Parley P. Pratt, *Autobiography of Parley Parker Pratt* (1938).

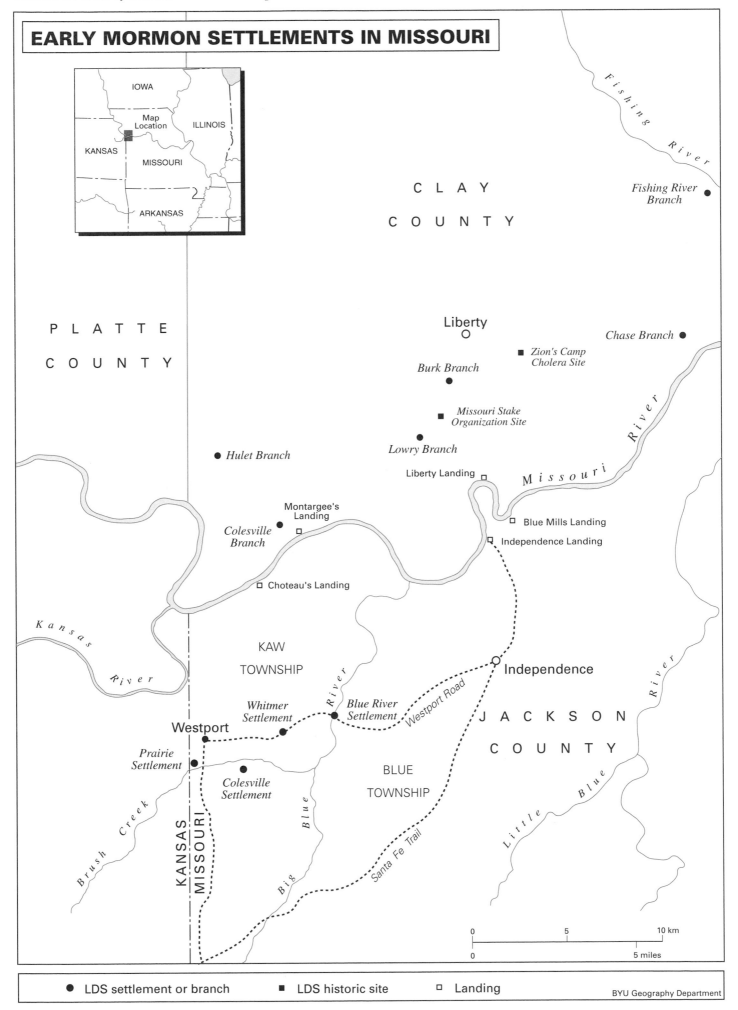

EARLY MORMON SETTLEMENTS IN MISSOURI

IOWA

Map Location

ILLINOIS

KANSAS

MISSOURI

ARKANSAS

C L A Y   C O U N T Y

Fishing River

Fishing River Branch

P L A T T E   C O U N T Y

Liberty

Chase Branch

■ *Zion's Camp Cholera Site*

Burk Branch

■ *Missouri Stake Organization Site*

Missouri River

● *Hulet Branch*

Lowry Branch

Liberty Landing

Montargee's Landing

□ Blue Mills Landing

Colesville Branch

□ Independence Landing

□ Choteau's Landing

Kansas River

KAW TOWNSHIP

River

Independence

Whitmer Settlement

Blue River Settlement

Westport Road

J A C K S O N   C O U N T Y

Westport

Prairie Settlement

BLUE TOWNSHIP

Little Blue

Colesville Settlement

KANSAS

MISSOURI

Big Blue

Santa Fe Trail

Brush Creek

| 0 | | 5 | | 10 km |
| 0 | | | 5 miles | |

● LDS settlement or branch   ■ LDS historic site   □ Landing

BYU Geography Department

INDEPENDENCE, MISSOURI

Max H. Parkin

When the first Mormon settlers arrived at Independence in the summer of 1831 from their headquarters at Kirtland, Ohio, the community was a ragged outpost on the edge of the Missouri frontier. But this seat of Jackson County was rapidly becoming the premier equipping station for merchants who plied their trade on the Santa Fe Trail and for explorers and trappers traveling elsewhere to the far West.

The village, 12 miles east of the state line that marked the border of the Indian Territory, had attracted a vanguard of Mormon missionaries to it the previous winter. Oliver Cowdery, Parley P. Pratt, and others had arrived there before crossing over to proselyte among the Indians, or Lamanites. Conflict soon arose with the Indian agent, who expelled them from the Indian reserve.

Traveling to Missouri, Joseph Smith selected Independence as the center of Zion (D&C 57:3). He dedicated a site for a temple a half mile west of the courthouse and appointed the Church bishop, Edward Partridge, both to superintend the Mormon gathering to Jackson County and to distribute Church land there to the faithful. At Independence, William W. Phelps published not only the revelations received by Joseph Smith but also a Church newspaper, the *Evening and the Morning Star*, the nation's westernmost press. Another officer managed the Church-owned store.

The gathering to Jackson County was vigorously promoted by Church leaders. When Mormons arrived, chiefly from the technically more advanced Northeast, they found that cultural differences distinguished them from the older settlers who had come principally from the south; not surprisingly, the two groups were uneasy with one another. Differences in speech, life-style, and other customs immediately set them apart. The eastern Mormons were shocked by the rugged individualism, backward ways, and occasional lawlessness of some western settlers. Both groups soon also became aware of marked religious differences.

As Mormons gathered, friction mounted. By the summer of 1833, two hundred Latter-day Saints resided at Independence and over 1,000 more had located in settlements west of the village. That summer, tensions intensified as community leaders drew up a manifesto against the Mormons, affirming their intent to drive them away. Citizens complained not only about the Mormons' gathering, but also about their published plans for the land, and the poverty of some of them. They further believed that Mormons aggravated the local slave situation. Moreover, they were uneasy with Mormon claims of certain spiritual gifts and powers. While citizens were ruefully vexed over the possibility of control of the county by the Saints, the Mormons claimed innocence of any abuses.

On July 20, 1833, about 400 aroused citizens met at the courthouse square to demonstrate violently against the Mormons. The mob tarred and feathered Bishop Partridge, tore down Phelps's printing house, and attacked the Church store. The horrified victims agreed to leave the county by the following winter and spring. But they recanted when Lieutenent Governor Lilburn W. Boggs encouraged Church leaders to protect themselves in the courts. Consequently, during fall 1833, non-Mormons reacted defiantly by brutally whipping Mormon men and terrifying Mormon villages for days. Heedless of the Mormons' unprepared condition and the inclement season, the mobs drove the Mormons northward from the county. The Saints fled Independence during a chilling downpour on November 7, 1833, and crossed the turbulent Missouri River into Clay County.

While struggling for survival that winter in a scattered and impoverished condition, the refugees turned to the courts at Independence for redress. But the state proved powerless to provide order, and efforts at promoting civil and criminal justice were ineffectual. The Mormons themselves attempted a venture in self-help from Kirtland in the form of military and humanitarian aid called Zion's Camp, but it failed to reclaim the lost Zion.

In time, the Mormons fostered another plan for return. In 1834 and 1835, Joseph Smith promoted the immigration of hundreds of Church members into Clay County from the East, hoping that the presence of a large number of Mormons would allow the exiles to return. The governor promised to help if petitioned. But the immigration agitated local citizens, some of whom turned violent. In 1836 they forced the Mormons to look for another home. Moving north, the Latter-day Saints sought peace in newly established Caldwell County.

James B. Allen and Glen M. Leonard, *The Story of the Latter-day Saints* (1976); Parley P. Pratt, *Autobiography of Parley Parker Pratt* (1938); T. Edgar Lyon, "Independence, Missouri, and the Mormons, 1827–1833," *BYU Studies* 13 (Autumn 1972): 10–19.

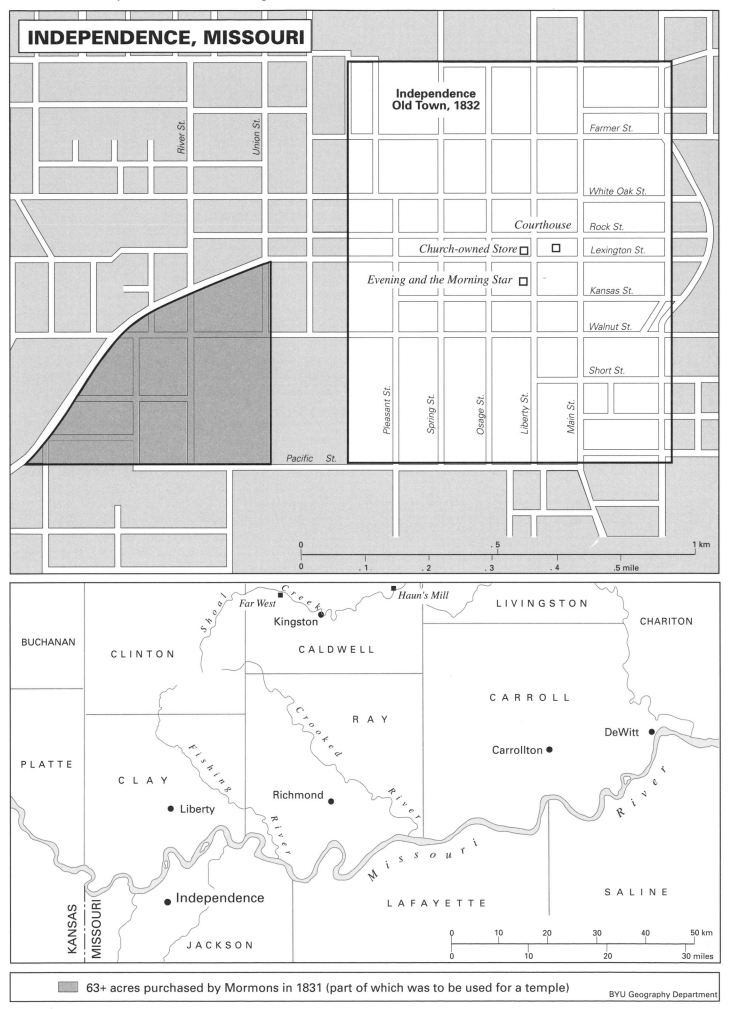

INDEPENDENCE, MISSOURI

Independence Old Town, 1832

Farmer St.

White Oak St.

Courthouse   Rock St.

Church-owned Store ☐   ☐   Lexington St.

Evening and the Morning Star ☐   Kansas St.

Walnut St.

Short St.

River St.   Union St.

Pleasant St.   Spring St.   Osage St.   Liberty St.   Main St.

Pacific St.

| 0 | | | | .5 | | | 1 km |
| 0 | .1 | .2 | .3 | .4 | | .5 mile | |

BUCHANAN

CLINTON

Shoal Creek   Far West ■   Haun's Mill ■   LIVINGSTON   CHARITON

Kingston ●   CALDWELL

Crooked River   RAY   CARROLL   DeWitt ●

Carrollton ●

PLATTE

Fishing River

CLAY

Richmond ●   *Missouri River*

● Liberty

KANSAS | MISSOURI

● Independence   LAFAYETTE   SALINE

JACKSON

| 0 | 10 | 20 | 30 | 40 | 50 km |
| 0 | 10 | | 20 | | 30 miles |

| | 63+ acres purchased by Mormons in 1831 (part of which was to be used for a temple) |

BYU Geography Department

41

NORTHERN MISSOURI

Clark V. Johnson

Mormons began to move into northern Missouri in 1834 because of persecution in Jackson County to the south. Even before Missouri became a state in 1821, Ray County had been created from Howard County (November 1820) and included the land west of the Grand River to the western boundary of the United States. Ray County is considered the mother county of Clay, Carroll, Caldwell, and Daviess counties, where persecution forced Mormons to settle.

Clay County was created January 2, 1822, from the western section of Ray County. By 1831, when Church members began to settle Jackson County, Clay County boasted more than 5,000 people. When mob pressures forced Mormons from Jackson County, the majority of the 1,200 Mormon citizens found welcome, though only temporary, relief in Clay County. By 1836, almost all of the Mormons had moved northeast to Caldwell County. While there were no Mormon settlements in Clay County, Liberty Jail remains important to Mormons because the Prophet Joseph Smith and others were confined there from December 1838 until April 1839. It was also the scene for several important revelations to Joseph Smith (D&C 121, 122, and 123).

To the east, Carroll County was created in 1833. Carrollton, the county seat, was not surveyed until 1837. About a year later, John Murdock and George M. Hinckle brought 70 Mormon families from Adam-ondi-Ahman and settled the community of DeWitt, where they quickly built about 100 homes. Situated on the confluence of the Grand and Missouri rivers, DeWitt provided a river port for the import and export of goods needed by people of northern Missouri.

Modeled after the City of Zion plat, DeWitt featured homes inside the town and farms outside. While economically and culturally this arrangement was desirable, it proved a liability. Some citizens of Carroll County rose against their Mormon neighbors and laid siege to DeWitt from mid-August to mid-October 1838, preventing DeWitt citizens from harvesting their crops located on outlying farms. Thus, little more than a year after its settlement, the starving citizens were forced to abandon DeWitt and moved to Far West for safety.

Caldwell County, created in December 1836, lies 60 miles from the state's northern boundary and 40 miles east of St. Joseph. Originally, it was about one-third timber and two-thirds prairie. Among its first settlers were John Raglin and Jesse Mann (1831), Jacob Haun (1834), and Jacob Myers (1835). When the county was organized, it included about 2,000 people, Mormons and non-Mormons. By the time Gov. Lilburn W. Boggs issued

his extermination order (1838), Caldwell County's population had increased to more than 7,000.

By 1838, two principal communities had been settled by Mormons in Caldwell County. Haun's Mill began when Jacob Haun built a gristmill on Shoal Creek in 1835. By 1838, approximately 35 Mormon families lived adjacent to the mill, with another 100 families along Shoal Creek. About 12 miles west of Haun's Mill the Saints settled Far West in 1836, which became both the commercial and ecclesiastical center for the Church, as well as the county seat. By 1838 it had 150 permanent homes, four dry goods stores, three family groceries, two hotels, several blacksmith shops, a printing shop, and a schoolhouse that also served as a courthouse and church. Hundreds of Latter-day Saints settled west of the Livingston County border along the banks of Shoal Creek. After the Missouri State Militia conquered Far West in November 1838, Kingston became the permanent county seat (1842).

Daviess County, organized to the north in 1836, was named after Col. Joseph H. Daviess, Indian fighter and lawyer. Gallatin became the county seat in 1837. When Mormons attempted to vote at an election held in Gallatin on August 6, 1838, a riot broke out. This clash was the catalyst for Governor Boggs's extermination order of October 27, 1838.

By 1836 only a few Mormons had purchased land in Colfax Township in Daviess County. But by February 1838, Lyman Wight had built a cabin on land that a few months later would become the city of Adam-ondi-Ahman. It was located on the Grand River about 50 miles from its confluence into the Missouri River. Hence the city became a port for shipping goods to and from DeWitt. Diahman, as it was called, boasted a population of 1,500 people, with more than 100 homes built by the Saints in a few months. After Far West capitulated to the Missouri State Militia on November 1, 1838, the residents in Adam-ondi-Ahman were given ten days to evacuate their homes.

By March 1839, Mormons had abandoned all settlements in Missouri, and had moved into Illinois and Iowa. Today only traces remain of the cities Adam-ondi-Ahman and Far West.

James B. Allen and Glen M. Leonard, *The Story of the Latter-day Saints* (1976); R. A. Campbell, editor, *Campbell's Gazetteer of Missouri* (1874); Clark V. Johnson, editor, *Mormon Redress Petitions: Documents of the 1833–1838 Missouri Conflict* (1992); Clark V. Johnson and Leland H. Gentry, "Missouri," in *Encyclopedia of Mormonism*, Daniel H. Ludlow, editor (1992) 2: 922–927.

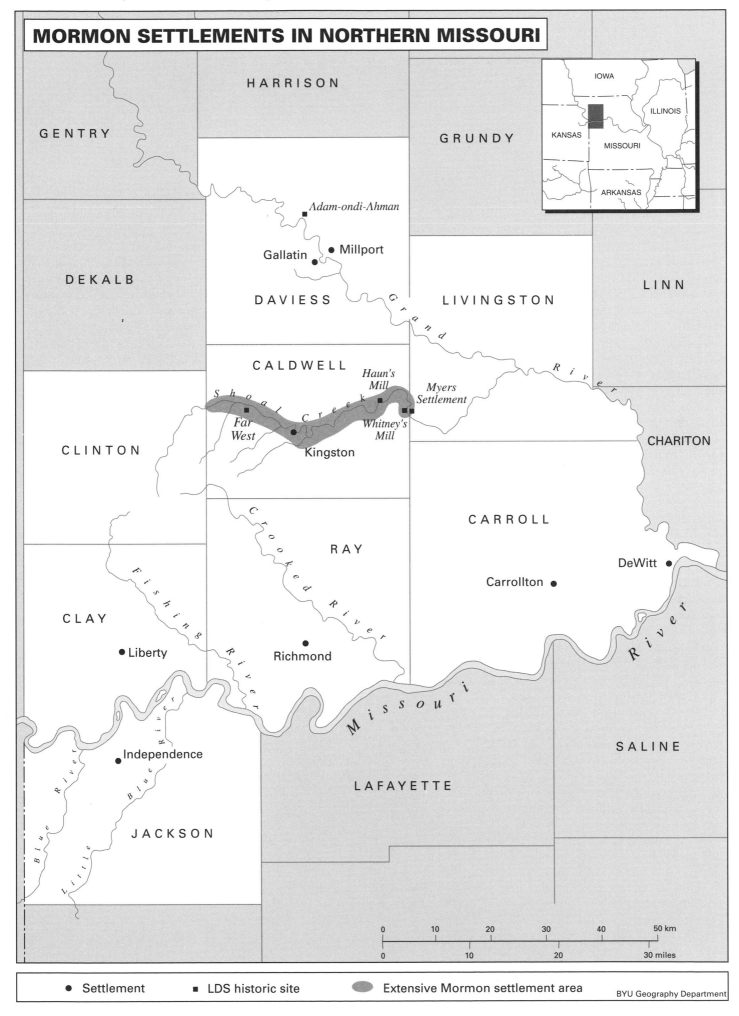

MORMON SETTLEMENTS IN NORTHERN MISSOURI

HARRISON

GENTRY

GRUNDY

IOWA

ILLINOIS

KANSAS

MISSOURI

ARKANSAS

■ Adam-ondi-Ahman

● Millport

Gallatin ●

DEKALB

DAVIESS

LIVINGSTON

LINN

CALDWELL

Haun's Mill

Myers Settlement

Shoal Creek

■

Far West

●

Whitney's Mill

■

CLINTON

Kingston

CHARITON

CARROLL

Crooked River

RAY

DeWitt ●

Carrollton ●

CLAY

Fishing River

● Liberty

Richmond ●

River

Blue River

Little Blue River

● Independence

Missouri

SALINE

LAFAYETTE

JACKSON

| 0 | 10 | 20 | 30 | 40 | 50 km |

| 0 | 10 | 20 | 30 miles |

● Settlement ■ LDS historic site ⬬ Extensive Mormon settlement area

BYU Geography Department

43

THE CITY OF ZION PLAT

Richard H. Jackson

One of the distinctive characteristics of The Church of Jesus Christ of Latter-day Saints is its emphasis on community. At a time when American farmers were creating individual farmsteads across the midwest, Joseph Smith taught that farmers needed to live in organized towns where "the farmer and his family . . . will enjoy all the advantages of schools, public lectures, and other meetings. His home will no longer be isolated, and his family denied the benefits of society" (Jackson, 230). Only three years after the Church was organized, the Prophet proposed a plan, known as the City of Zion Plat, for a community that could be replicated anywhere the Saints settled.

The City of Zion Plat, sent to Church leaders in Missouri on June 25, 1833, shows a town laid out in a regular grid pattern with north-south orientation. All of the blocks are square, with unusually wide (132-foot) streets. Such broad thoroughfares would minimize congestion, enhance safety, and allow even the largest wagons to turn easily. Blocks were divided into 20 large (one-half-acre) lots to allow for gardens in the back and shrubs and trees in front, with one house to a lot, set back 25 feet from the street. Their orientation was varied so that houses faced alternate streets on each block. Each lot was to have only one house constructed on it, and all houses were to be constructed of brick or stone. The plat required that all farms, barns, and livestock be located outside the city. The plat showed a central tier of larger blocks with 32 lots per block; the two central blocks in this tier were to be used for temples and public buildings.

The marginal notes on the City of Zion Plat indicated that it was designed to accommodate 15,000 to 20,000 people. When this size was reached, a new town was to be established far enough away to allow for enough farmland to support the residents of the new town. It is unclear whether the Prophet expected that each Mormon community would follow the City of Zion Plat. The Plat was never referred to as a revelation, which would have given it the status of a commandment to the Saints. No community founded by Mormons ever followed it precisely.

Kirtland, Ohio, was most like the City of Zion Plat. It had square blocks with 20 lots per block and lots oriented differently on alternate blocks. But Kirtland did not have a central tier of larger blocks. Later communities, developed under the direction of Joseph Smith, differed radically from his proposed City of Zion Plat. Far West,

Missouri, platted by Mormon settlers in 1836, had four large streets that were 132 feet wide bordering a central square. The balance of the streets were 82.5 feet wide, blocks were smaller than in the City of Zion Plat, and each block was divided into four equal lots. Nauvoo, the largest Mormon city in the Midwest, had streets only 49.5 feet wide, and lots were divided, as in Far West.

The most famous Mormon city is Salt Lake City. Established under the direction of Brigham Young after the martyrdom of the Prophet Joseph Smith, it resembled the city described in the City of Zion Plat in some respects. The blocks were each 10 acres in size, as proposed by the Prophet, but instead of 20 one-half acre lots, there were only eight large lots (of one and one-quarter acres) on each block. The streets were all 132 feet wide. Instead of a central tier of larger blocks, Young proposed one superblock of 40 acres (later reduced to 10 acres) to be used for a temple. Young added an additional 20 feet to the street width for sidewalks, and required that all homes be set back 20 feet from the property line. As with the City of Zion Plat, Young's instructions for Salt Lake City required building on alternate sides of the blocks to prevent homes from lining all sides of the blocks, and encouraged the planting of trees and gardens on each lot. Because of the larger lots of Salt Lake City, however, barns, livestock, and related activities were located on the town lots, creating a landscape of mini-farms in the city.

Other Mormon settlements in the Intermountain West followed the same general pattern as Salt Lake City, but the actual lot, block, and street width varies greatly from town to town. While differing in detail, the general design of regular grid survey pattern, large lots and blocks, wide streets, and use of brick and stone for construction are still distinguishing features for Mormon settlements in the Intermountain West.

Richard H. Jackson, "The Mormon Village: Genesis and Antecedents of the City of Zion Plan," *BYU Studies* 17 (Summer 1977): 223–240; Lowry Nelson, *The Mormon Village: A Pattern and Technique of Land Settlement* (1954); Joel Ricks, *Forms and Methods of Early Mormon Settlements in Utah and Surrounding Regions, 1847–1877* (1964).

ORIGINAL CITY OF ZION PLAT

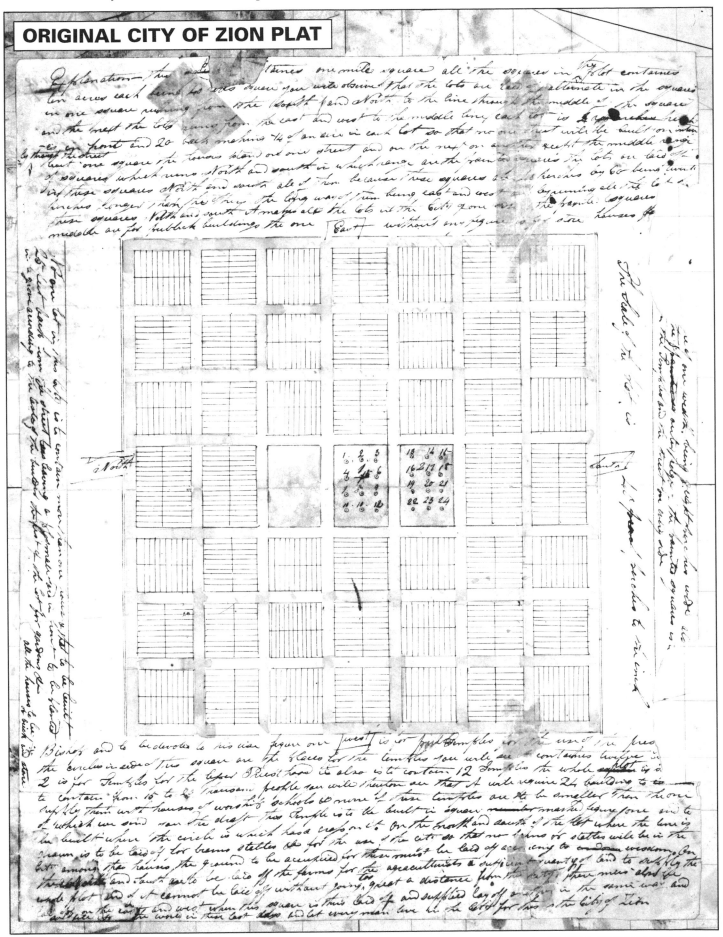

Copy of the original drawing of the City of Zion Plat by Joseph Smith
(original in LDS Church historians office, Salt Lake City).

BYU Geography Dept.

CONFLICT IN MISSOURI

Alma R. Blair

The causes of the so-called Mormon War of 1838 are complex and controversial. In December 1836 the Missouri legislature created Daviess and Caldwell counties from Ray County. Since only Caldwell was designated as Mormon, many Missourians assumed Daviess and surrounding counties were to be non-Mormon. The small groups of Saints settling in Caldwell and adjoining counties through 1837 were generally welcomed. However, in 1838, as many as 8,000 Saints migrated to Missouri. Mormons soon outnumbered Daviess County Missourians by two to one, and the 40 to 50 Missourians in DeWitt were inundated by 150 to 200 Saints. This dramatic growth led some Missouri extremists to charge that the Mormons were bent on taking over all the western counties of Missouri.

The Mormon immigrants, mostly Yankee and Canadian, were more communal, more sympathetic toward Indians, and more antislavery (though not abolitionist) than were the individualistic southern Missourians. Missourians were intrigued with the Saints' beliefs but were apprehensive of the political and economic implications of the Latter-day Saint migration, the Saints' cohesiveness, and Joseph Smith's power as prophet and leader. Moderates predominated in both groups, but their goodwill was mixed with a wary uncertainty that might be swayed by the prejudice and bigotry of radicals. Investigation and diplomacy did resolve problems between Mormons and Missourians on several occasions, but minor incidents, fed by rumor, had the potential to become major confrontations.

State leaders did not know how to—or did not care to—stop the violence once it erupted. By October 1838 conditions had so deteriorated that Missouri militiamen could not be counted on to follow orders and truth was hardly to be found. On October 27, Gov. Lilburn W. Boggs, more politician than statesman, issued his infamous extermination order to drive the Saints from Missouri in a time of crisis—a crisis sown by his earlier neglect.

Explanations of the Mormons' role have usually centered on the semisecret Danites, a group dedicated to unequivocal support of the Church leadership. Danites quickly expelled dissidents from Far West after Sidney Rigdon's "Salt Sermon" of June 17, 1838. Rigdon's July 4 speech appealed to constitutional rights but implied vigilantism as he condemned "vexatious lawsuits" and threatened "extermination" of persecutors. Few Saints seemed to notice the violation of apostates' constitutional rights or that non-Mormons could also appeal to vigilantism to protect their larger community from unwanted Latter-day Saints.

The Missourians viewed the Danites as plunderers blindly following Smith's prophecy that God had given Missouri to the Saints for their "New Jerusalem." The Saints perceived the Missourians as bigots eager to drive out Mormons and obtain their improved lands. There was some basis for such exaggerations, but a deeper problem was the shared frontier ethos, which permitted, even

encouraged, violence in certain situations. When legal appeals and diplomacy failed and conflict was joined, a war mentality melded militiaman with mobber, Saint with radical Danite. Examination of the conflicts of 1838 indicate both sides burned homes, threatened towns, and confiscated goods and animals. Each group justified such acts as military necessity, self-defense, or proper revenge.

The so-called Mormon War ended on November 1, 1838, but persecution of the Mormons actually intensified thereafter. Homeless and with few belongings, the Latter-day Saints straggled toward Quincy, Illinois, through the winter of 1838–1839. Joseph Smith escaped his captors on April 16, 1839—one of the last Saints to leave Missouri.

Major Incidents of the Conflict

August 6–7	The "Election Day Fight" erupted at Gallatin when Saints were forbidden to vote. Joseph Smith led 150 men to protect Adam-ondi-Ahman from rumored attacks. They surrounded Justice Adam Black's home, insisting he sign a statement vowing he would administer justice fairly. Black filed a complaint of intimidation.
August 13–September 24	Saints were ordered from Carroll County. Smith and Lyman Wight were arrested and freed on bail pending a grand jury trial. State militia were mustered several times.
October 1–11	DeWitt Mormons, besieged by 400 vigilantes from Carroll and five other counties, finally surrendered and fled to Far West.
October 14–24	Smith and Rigdon led 400 men to Daviess County to protect the Saints. Mormons burned Gallatin and Millport and expelled almost all non-Mormons from Daviess.
October 25–27	Three Mormons and one Missourian were killed in the Battle of Crooked River as a company of Saints tried to free two men held by the militia. Exaggerated reports of deaths and of a Mormon "rebellion" led Governor Boggs to issue his extermination order.
October 30	Two hundred militia from Livingston County massacred 18 Saints at the small settlement of Haun's Mill.
October 31	The militia surrounded Far West. Joseph Smith and about 80 leaders gave themselves up as hostages and were soon put in jail in Richmond and Liberty.

John Corrill, *A Brief History of the Church of Christ of Latter Day Saints* (1839); *The History of Caldwell and Livingston Counties, Missouri* (1886); Richard Neitzel Holzapfel and T. Jeffery Cottle, *Old Mormon Kirtland and Missouri, Historic Photographs and Guide* (1991); Stephen C. LeSueur, *The 1838 Mormon War in Missouri* (1987); Pearl Wilcox, *The Latter Day Saints on the Missouri Frontier* (1972).

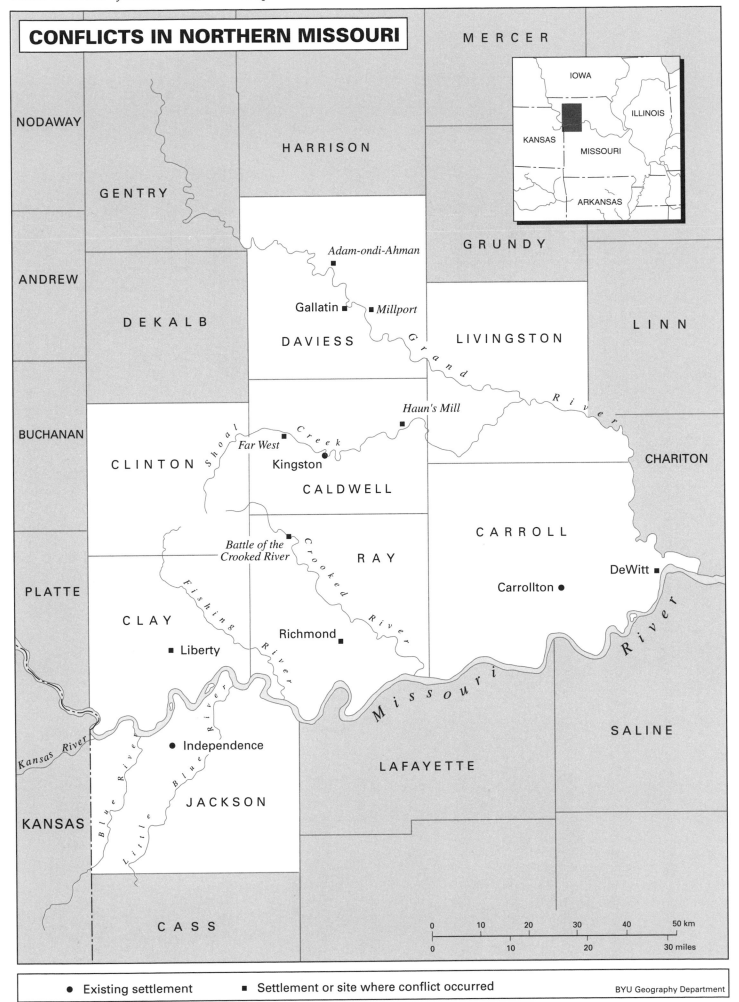

CONFLICTS IN NORTHERN MISSOURI

NODAWAY

MERCER

GENTRY

HARRISON

IOWA

ILLINOIS

KANSAS

MISSOURI

ARKANSAS

ANDREW

GRUNDY

DEKALB

■ Adam-ondi-Ahman

LIVINGSTON

LINN

Gallatin ■ ■ *Millport*

DAVIESS

Grand *River*

BUCHANAN

Creek

■ *Haun's Mill*

Shoal

Far West ■

CHARITON

CLINTON

Kingston ●

CALDWELL

CARROLL

Battle of the
Crooked River ■

Crooked

RAY

DeWitt ■

Carrollton ●

PLATTE

River

CLAY

■ Liberty

Richmond ■

Fishing

River

Missouri *River*

SALINE

Kansas River

● Independence

Blue River

Little Blue River

JACKSON

LAFAYETTE

KANSAS

0   10   20   30   40   50 km

0   10   20   30 miles

CASS

● Existing settlement   ■ Settlement or site where conflict occurred

BYU Geography Department

EXPULSION FROM MISSOURI

Sean J. Cannon

Acting on reports of Mormon violence against citizens of Daviess and Caldwell counties, Missouri governor Lilburn W. Boggs issued an order in the autumn of 1838 to the state militia to drive the Mormon populace from the state or kill them in the process. This order was responded to with enthusiasm by the military and mobs alike.

The massacre of families at Haun's Mill was followed by a hasty truce on October 31 at Far West that imposed four conditions on the Mormons. Within days of a subsequent capitulation of Mormon soldiers in Daviess County, two of the four conditions of the truce had been met: Joseph Smith and other leaders surrendered, and the citizens of Far West were disarmed. Despite continued mob violence against Mormons and their property throughout the winter of 1838, the third condition, payment of war damages, was also met. It remained only for the Saints to leave the state.

With Joseph Smith in jail, it fell to Brigham Young, Heber C. Kimball, and Edward Partridge to protect Mormon interests in Missouri. Attempts to petition the Missouri legislature to permit the Saints to remain without further reprisals were unsuccessful. The only acknowledgment of wrongdoing by the state was an appropriation of $2,000 to aid the Mormons in Daviess and Caldwell counties. After consolidating in Far West, Church members began to leave Missouri in November. As petitions to remain failed, the rest followed, fearing reprisals by mobs if they remained after February.

Some families strayed into Iowa. Most made the 200-mile journey northeast toward Quincy, Illinois, tending to follow established roads. From personal accounts of the trek, a northern route extending eastward from Far West through Chillicothe and Monroe City to Quincy, and a southern route connecting Far West with Tinney's Grove, Keytesville, Huntsville, and Quincy, appear to have been the prevalent routes. Fear of Indian attacks in the West probably kept the move directed eastward.

Soon only the poorest, mainly refugees from Daviess County, remained in Far West. Lack of food, clothing, and suitable shelter added to the misery of the harsh winter. Beginning in late January of 1839, a series of public meetings was held in Far West to call attention to the plight of indigent Church members. A committee of seven was formed to supervise the work of assisting them. Charles Bird established deposits of corn along the exodus route and contracted for a ferry at Marion City, Missouri. Theodore Turley procured teams and wagons.

As many families as possible were transported by boat from the port of Richmond down the Missouri River to St. Louis, then north to Quincy. By mid-February, a steady stream of Saints was traveling along the rugged roads from Far West to Palmyra, Missouri. A ferry near Marion City carried members across the Mississippi River to Quincy. The final work of the committee was to sell Church lands in Jackson County. Teams and wagons were then purchased in Illinois. Following a hasty transfer of Church headquarters from Far West to neighboring Tinney's Grove to avoid mobs, the final stage of the exodus was under way. By mid-April, the last Saints had left Far West.

Tremendous sacrifices of land and personal property were made as Mormons evacuated Daviess and Caldwell counties. In one instance, 40 acres of farmland were sold for a blind mare and a clock. Some families made the entire trek barefoot, while others attempted to wrap their feet in rags to protect them from the frozen earth. Despite the hospitality of some Missourians who offered their homes to refugees, many Mormons were forced to eat and sleep on the frozen ground. During February and March, 130 families found themselves stranded on the west bank of the Mississippi, opposite Quincy, unable to cross the river because of ice floes.

Upon reaching Quincy, the Saints were met with kindness and generosity by the residents of the town. The governors of Illinois and Iowa responded with similar humanity. With the purchase of lands north of Quincy, the Mormons began to settle in Iowa and Illinois, on opposite sides of the Mississippi River. The result was the establishment of the sister cities of Nauvoo, Illinois, and Montrose, Iowa. The exodus from Missouri constituted the first organized move of the Church from one central location to another. It prepared the Saints for an exodus on a much larger scale eight years later.

Leland H. Gentry, "A History of the Latter-day Saints in Northern Missouri from 1836 to 1839" (Ph.D. diss., Brigham Young University, 1965), pp. 599–657; William G. Hartley, "Almost Too Intolerable A Burden: The Winter Exodus from Missouri," *Journal of Mormon History 18* (Fall 1992): 7–40; Stephen C. LeSueur, *The 1838 Mormon War in Missouri* (1987), pp. 219–244; National Historical Company, *History of Caldwell and Livingston Counties, Missouri* (1885), pp. 139–143.

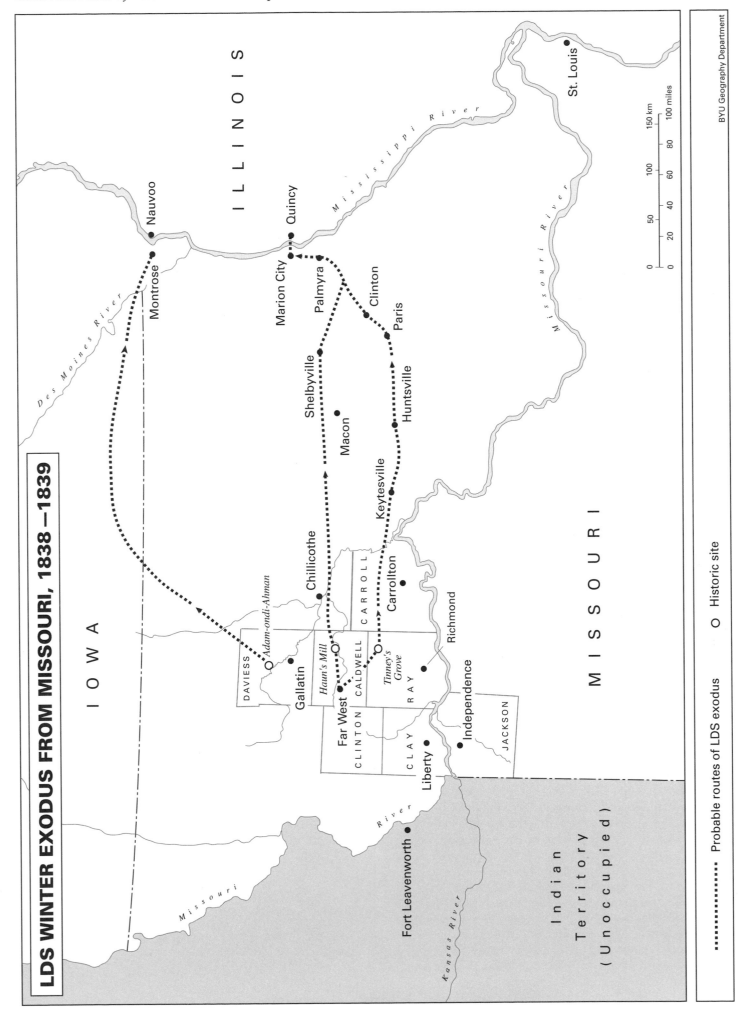

LDS WINTER EXODUS FROM MISSOURI, 1838–1839

Nauvoo

Montrose

Quincy

Marion City

Palmyra

Clinton

Paris

Shelbyville

Macon

Huntsville

Keytesville

Chillicothe

Carrollton

Adam-ondi-Ahman

Richmond

Gallatin

DAVIESS

CARROLL

Haun's Mill

CALDWELL

Tinney's Grove

Far West

CLINTON

RAY

Independence

CLAY

JACKSON

Liberty

Fort Leavenworth

I L L I N O I S

I O W A

M I S S O U R I

Indian Territory (Unoccupied)

St. Louis

Mississippi River

Missouri River

Des Moines River

Missouri River

Kansas River

150 km
100 miles
50 100
20 40 60 80 0

•••••••• Probable routes of LDS exodus   O Historic site

BYU Geography Department

NAUVOO: FRONTIER CITY

Richard H. Jackson

Nauvoo, Illinois, located on the Mississippi River, was home to the Mormons from 1839 to 1846. During seven short years the Mormons developed a bustling river port city that reached an estimated population of 15,000. The Mormon development of Nauvoo was part of the unique American frontier experience, where the tilling of virgin land created the fertile farms of rural midwestern America and land speculation gave rise to the towns and cities of urban America.

Early settlement of the midwest proceeded down the Ohio River. Settlers could take the National Road that had been completed by 1818 as far as Wheeling, West Virginia, on the Ohio. Major cities developed at favorable sites, including Pittsburgh, Cincinnati, and Louisville. The National Road passed through Indianapolis and reached the south-central Illinois community of Vandalia by the 1830s. Growing populations led to statehood in the region's territories around the time Nauvoo was founded.

During the first three decades of the 19th century, the frontier moved southwest due to the attraction of trade down the Mississippi River to New Orleans and to the Spanish settlements around Santa Fe. New towns mirrored the southwestern advance of the frontier. When Illinois became a state in 1818, the capital was in the extreme southwest at Kaskaskia. Two years later the capital was moved to Vandalia, a more central location. In 1839, while the Mormons were platting the city Nauvoo, the capital was moved again to Springfield, near the center of the state. The north and eastward movement of Illinois's capital reflected the growth of settlement in the center and north of the state, especially in Chicago.

The growth of Chicago and other cities away from the main river transport routes began as the Erie Canal and canals connecting the Great Lakes to the Ohio allowed settlement to spread to the lowlands around the Great Lakes. Completed in 1825, the Erie Canal made possible the shipping of bulk products to the markets of the northeastern United States, while the emergence of steamboats capable of traveling up the Mississippi and its tributaries after 1815 strengthened the importance of river locations for cities. Cincinnati grew from 6,000 people in 1815 to over 12,000 by 1820. In the five years from 1826 to 1831, its population soared from 16,250 to 30,000. Other river towns did not fare so well. Cairo, Illinois, seemed to have an ideal location, but it never experienced the boom growth of Cincinnati.

Nauvoo typifies the experience of both successful and unsuccessful frontier boom towns. Established in 1839 by Joseph Smith on lands purchased on contract from settlers and speculators along the east bank of the Mississippi, it was platted over the existing plats of Commerce and Commerce City, communities that existed primarily on paper with a total population of only 75 in 1837. Like Cairo, they had never been able to sustain growth.

Nauvoo grew rapidly as Mormon settlers fleeing Missouri mobs flocked to the area. At the same time, the Mormon mission system was adding new converts, especially in England, which had been opened by missionaries in 1837. Steamboats made it relatively easy for British converts to travel up the Mississippi to Nauvoo, where they found converts and members moving west from the eastern states to join those from Missouri. By 1840 there were some 7,000 people in the city, and by 1845, 11,057. Visitors compared it favorably with cities of much greater age, noting especially the use of brick to build substantial houses and businesses. Most impressive was the Nauvoo Temple that rose over the city as it neared completion in 1845.

At the same time, other cities of the urban frontier experienced even more rapid growth. Chicago increased from 4,470 residents in 1840 to 29,963 by 1850. St. Louis increased from 6,694 in 1830 to 16,469 in 1840 and 77,850 in 1850.

The assassination of Joseph Smith and his brother Hyrum in 1844, along with the increased hostility from non-Mormon settlers, forced the Mormons to abandon Nauvoo in 1846. Reduced to only 1,130 people by 1850, it never regained more than a small fraction of the population that had existed under the Mormons. The coming of the railroad made the Mississippi River less important for transport, and, in the absence of a motive such as the Mormons had in their commitment to gathering together, there has been nothing to prompt population growth in Nauvoo. Nauvoo is now just one more of the hundreds of small communities that dot the American Midwest.

Glen M. Leonard, "Nauvoo," in *Encyclopedia of Mormonism*, Daniel H. Ludlow, editor (1992) 3: 987–993; Richard Neitzel Holzapfel and T. Jeffery Cottle, *Old Mormon Nauvoo, 1839–1846* (1990); David E. Miller and Della S. Miller, *Nauvoo: The City of Joseph* (1947).

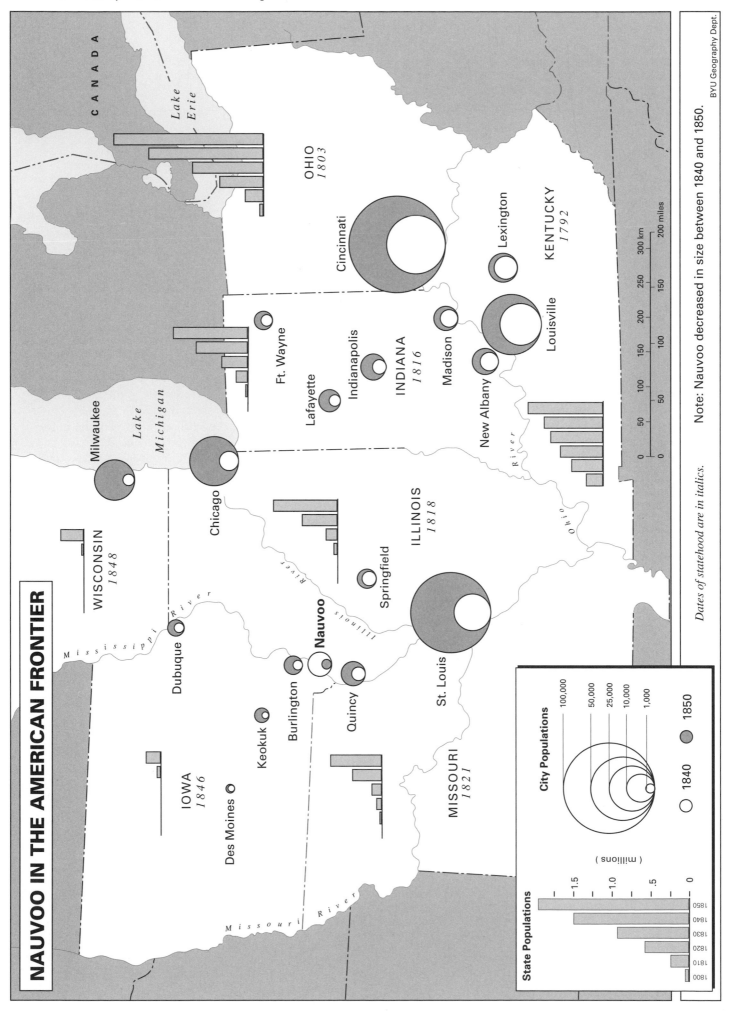

NAUVOO IN THE AMERICAN FRONTIER

CANADA

Lake Erie

OHIO *1803*

Cincinnati

Lexington

KENTUCKY *1792*

Louisville

Ft. Wayne

Indianapolis

INDIANA *1816*

Lafayette

Madison

New Albany

Ohio River

Milwaukee

Lake Michigan

Chicago

WISCONSIN *1848*

ILLINOIS *1818*

Springfield

Nauvoo

Illinois River

Mississippi River

Dubuque

Burlington

Keokuk

Quincy

St. Louis

IOWA *1846*

Des Moines

MISSOURI *1821*

Missouri River

State Populations

(millions)

1.5

1.0

.5

0

1800 1810 1820 1830 1840 1850

City Populations

100,000

50,000

25,000

10,000

1,000

○ 1840   ● 1850

300 km   200 miles

250

200   150

150

100   50

50

0   0

Dates of statehood are in italics.

Note: Nauvoo decreased in size between 1840 and 1850.

BYU Geography Dept.

51

COMMERCE, ILLINOIS

Donald Q. Cannon

About 12 miles north of the point where the Des Moines River flows into the Mississippi, the flat prairie land of western Illinois drops suddenly over a series of bluffs from which a floodplain extends toward the Mississippi River. The mud flat forms a giant horseshoe bend on the east side of the river. The area is heavily wooded with a wide variety of hardwood trees, and grass grows abundantly. The floodplain contains several springs and hence is wet and marshy. Travelers to this locale are presented a delightful view of both land and water. Such is the physical character of the place where Commerce was established in the early 19th century.

The area known as Commerce was occupied originally by Indians. The time when these first Americans settled in the area is difficult to determine. Some of the tribes that lived in the area included Pawnees, Shawnees, Ottawas, Menominees, Winnebagos, Illini, and Pottawatomies. At the time of the first white settlements, the Sac and Fox lived in a village that they called Quashquema, which was located at the head of the Des Moines Rapids. Eventually the encroachment of European and U.S. settlement on these Indian lands led to a military conflict known as the Black Hawk War (1832). The Sac and Fox Indians were driven into Wisconsin, where many of them were slaughtered.

The first whites in the area of Commerce were European explorers. Such well-known figures as Hernando de Soto, Jacques Marquette, Louis Joliet, and René-Robert La Salle explored the region in the 16th and 17th centuries as part of a major European effort to explore North America. The first Anglo-Saxon who established a residence in the Commerce area was James White, who built a stone house on the bank of the Mississippi River in 1829. White and his family established the first permanent settlement on the peninsula or horseshoe bend on the east bank of the river. Under White and his sons, Alexander, Hugh, and William, the settlement grew enough to warrant a post office, which bore the name Venus. As land speculators came into the area, the town of Venus, and indeed the entire peninsula, became known as Commerce. Eventually, by the late 1830s, two distinct entities appeared on legal papers and maps of the area, Commerce and Commerce City.

Land speculation was a popular means of making a fortune in 19th-century America, and this activity occurred in the Mississippi River Valley, too. Speculators in the Commerce area included Hugh White, William White, Isaac Galland, Horace Hotchkiss, George W. Robinson, and Hiram Kimball. As the Mormons fled from Missouri and decided to settle in the area later known as Nauvoo, they bought land through the Hotchkiss Purchase, the William White Purchase, the Hugh White Purchase, and the Galland Purchase. Isaac Galland, a speculator from Pennsylvania, sold land to the Latter-day Saints on both sides of the Mississippi, in Iowa and Illinois. During the time of these land purchases by the Mormons from Galland, he was living in the stone house that he had purchased from James White on the Illinois side of the river. Isaac Galland joined the Mormon Church in 1839 and served as a land agent for the Latter-day Saints. He remained in Iowa and did not follow the Mormons to Utah.

Finding the money to finance these real estate transactions proved very difficult for the Saints, but persistence and the influx of converts eventually brought them title to the area known as Commerce. Eventually their success, as well as their religious beliefs, made the name Commerce seem inappropriate and the name Nauvoo was assigned by their leader Joseph Smith to that fertile bend on the Mississippi.

Janath R. Cannon, *Nauvoo Panorama* (1991); Lyndon W. Cook, "Isaac Galland: Mormon Benefactor," *BYU Studies* 19 (Spring 1979): 261–284; David E. Miller and Della S. Miller, *Nauvoo: The City of Joseph* (1974).

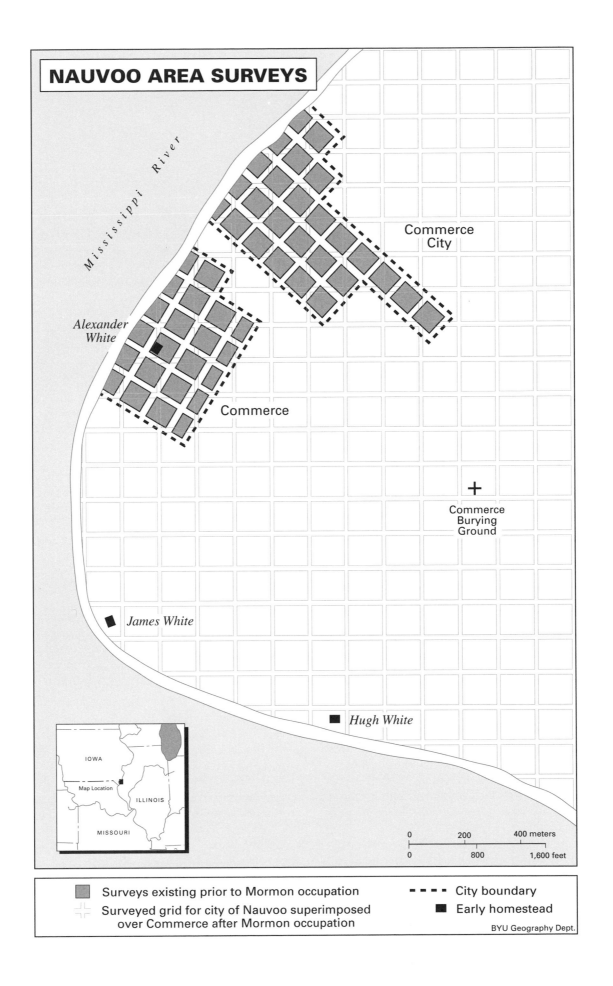

NAUVOO AREA SURVEYS

Mississippi River

Commerce City

Alexander White

Commerce

Commerce Burying Ground

James White

Hugh White

IOWA

Map Location

ILLINOIS

MISSOURI

| 0 | 200 | 400 meters |
| 0 | 800 | 1,600 feet |

Surveys existing prior to Mormon occupation

Surveyed grid for city of Nauvoo superimposed over Commerce after Mormon occupation

City boundary

Early homestead

BYU Geography Dept.

NAUVOO (1842)

Donald Q. Cannon

Less than five years after its founding in 1839, Nauvoo had become one of the largest cities in Illinois. By 1842 it had grown sufficiently to warrant the drafting of a detailed map.

Driven out of the state of Missouri, Mormons took up refuge in Quincy, Illinois. As refugees they had struggled with the decision whether to gather in one place or disperse themselves among non-Mormons. Ultimately, they decided to settle in one place. After exploration, consultation with land brokers such as Isaac Galland, and a careful consideration of their options, they chose to settle on the Illinois side of the Mississippi River at a place called Commerce, 53 miles north of Quincy.

The Mormon settlers changed the name of this settlement from Commerce to Nauvoo, a Hebrew word meaning "beautiful place." The horseshoe bend in the Mississippi and the panorama created by the heavily wooded hills certainly made Nauvoo unusually beautiful. By the end of 1839 the Mormons had established a growing community. In October of that year they organized the first stake in Illinois, the Nauvoo Stake.

While Nauvoo was the main settlement of the Mormons in Illinois, it was certainly not the only community founded by the Saints in the Prairie State. In fact, Joseph Smith and his followers established 17 communities in Hancock County besides Nauvoo. The most important Mormon settlements in Hancock County included Ramus (now Webster) and Lima. While there were other settlements, Nauvoo was by far the largest town founded by the Latter-day Saints in Illinois.

Joseph Smith envisioned a city on a grand scale and one that was well planned and orderly. The city of Nauvoo covered the entire floodplain along the Mississippi River as well as a part of the prairie land above the bluffs on the east. Surveyors platted Nauvoo in 1839 with a square grid system. Within the town itself, there were 150 square blocks of four acres each. The streets ran north-south and east-west. With the exception of Main and Water streets, the streets measured 49.5 feet in width. Main Street was 57 feet wide and Water Street 60.

As the city grew, the Saints built several important public buildings. Some of the most noteworthy include the Red Brick Store, the Seventies Hall, the Masonic Hall (Cultural Hall), and the Times and Seasons Complex.

In January 1841, Joseph Smith received a revelation commanding the Saints to build a temple in Nauvoo, effectively duplicating the divine instructions to ancient Israel for constructing first a movable tabernacle and then a temple. In this heavenly communication, now known as Section 124 of the Doctrine and Covenants, members of the Church received enlightenment on the purpose of temples as well as details of construction, including a description of building materials. The temple, a magnificent edifice for its day, was erected by a people who had very few financial resources. In place of monetary donations, the building was constructed by voluntary labor. Sacrifice was the required order of the day.

What was life like for the citizens of Nauvoo? Basically, they experienced the same kind of successes and difficulties that most 19th-century Americans did. Agriculture played a major role in the economic life of the city, with every family tending at least a household garden. Some cooperated in farming outside the city. Still others owned large farms on the prairie, where they raised wheat, oats, rye, and potatoes. Livestock included cattle, sheep, and hogs. More than one-third of the male inhabitants of Nauvoo were farmers, while another third were stonemasons, bricklayers, blacksmiths, and shoemakers. Others earned a living by gathering rags, painting portraits, selling hats, or trapping animals. A few were doctors, lawyers, dentists, or teachers.

Recreational activities corresponded to those of small-town America in the early 19th century. Often recreation had a practical character, such as joint woodcutting efforts, quilting bees, and cooperative house and barn construction. The Mississippi River provided recreational opportunities in both summer and winter. In warm weather, boating excursions were popular, and in cold weather, the surface of the river froze and the Saints engaged in sleigh riding and skating. Other diversions in Nauvoo included lectures, theater, and singing.

The map that appears opposite is a partial reproduction of the original map prepared by the Mormons in 1842. The 1842 map of Nauvoo was drawn from the plat of the original surveys by Gustavus Hills, a professor of music at the University of Nauvoo who lived on Mulholland Street. To conform to an act of Congress, the map was entered in the clerk's office of the District Court of Illinois. The lithography was done in New York City by J. Childs of 90 Nassau Street. Nauvoo Restoration, Inc., published a new edition of the map in 1971.

Donald Q. Cannon, "The Founding of Nauvoo," *The Prophet Joseph: Essays on the Life and Mission of Joseph Smith*, Larry C. Porter and Susan Easton Black, editors (1988): pp. 246–260; David E. Miller and Della S. Miller, *Nauvoo: The City of Joseph* (1974); Janath Cannon, *Nauvoo Panorama* (1991); Melinda Evans Jeffress, "Mapping Historic Nauvoo," *BYU Studies* 32 (Winter and Spring 1991): 269–275.

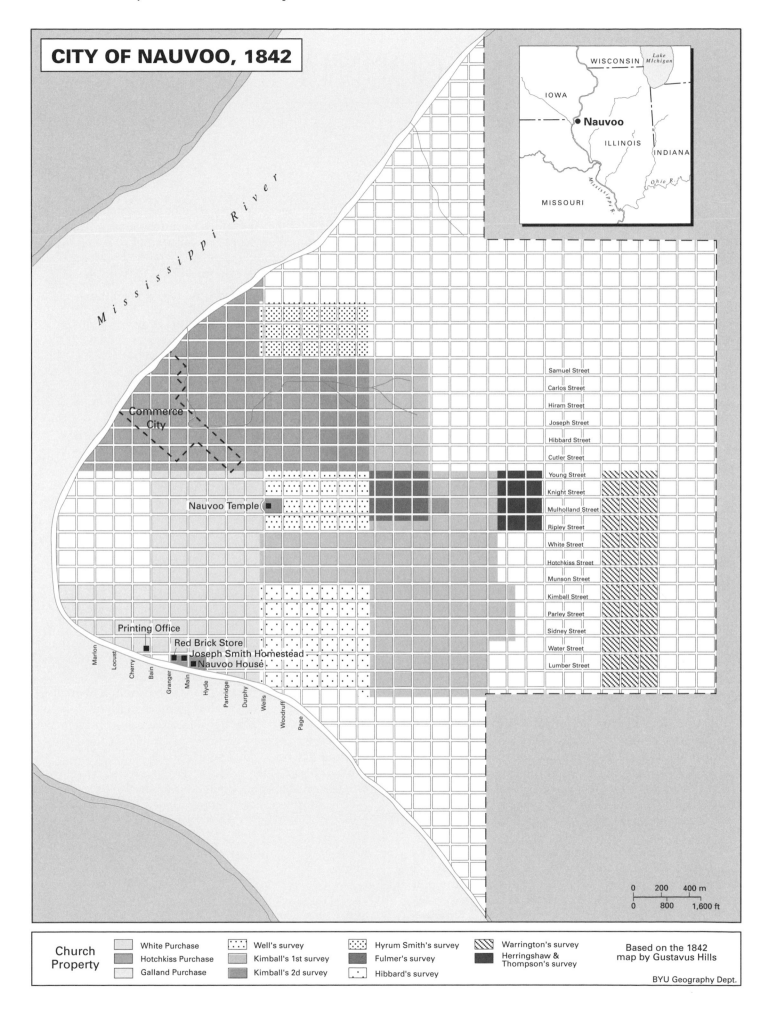

CITY OF NAUVOO, 1842

WISCONSIN
Lake MIchigan

IOWA

● Nauvoo

ILLINOIS

INDIANA

MISSOURI

Mississippi River

Ohio R.

Mississippi R.

Commerce City

Nauvoo Temple ■

Printing Office ■
Red Brick Store ■
Joseph Smith Homestead ■
■ Nauvoo House

Marion
Locust
Cherry
Bain
Granger
Main
Hyde
Partridge
Durphy
Wells
Woodruff
Page

Samuel Street
Carlos Street
Hiram Street
Joseph Street
Hibbard Street
Cutler Street
Young Street
Knight Street
Mulholland Street
Ripley Street
White Street
Hotchkiss Street
Munson Street
Kimball Street
Parley Street
Sidney Street
Water Street
Lumber Street

0	200	400 m
0	800	1,600 ft

Church Property	White Purchase	Well's survey	Hyrum Smith's survey	Warrington's survey	Based on the 1842 map by Gustavus Hills
	Hotchkiss Purchase	Kimball's 1st survey	Fulmer's survey	Herringshaw & Thompson's survey	
	Galland Purchase	Kimball's 2d survey	Hibbard's survey		BYU Geography Dept.

HANCOCK COUNTY, ILLINOIS

Donald Q. Cannon

The Latter-day Saints established several planned settlements in Hancock County, Illinois. Joseph Smith's vision of the Mormon-settlement pattern was not limited to Nauvoo, the chief city. It is important to realize that he and his followers planned settlements according to their expected function.

Hancock County was created January 13, 1825, from 797 square miles of unorganized territory attached to Pike County, and was named for John Hancock (1737–1793). Carthage became the county seat in 1833. The Mississippi River forms the western border, while Hancock County is bounded on the north by Henderson County, on the east by McDonough County, and on the south by Adams County.

The 17 communities that the Latter-day Saints either planned or established in Hancock County can be divided into at least five categories. The first are the major colonies of Ramus (Webster and Macedonia) and Lima. The second are the minor colonies of Plymouth, Green Plains, Golden Point, Yelrome (Tioga), and Camp Creek. A third were missionary towns where the Saints lived among non-Mormons, hoping to convert them to the faith. Such towns included Carthage, Bear Creek, La Harpe, and Fountain Green. Several small settlements surrounding Nauvoo might be called Nauvoo suburbs, including String Town, Mormon Springs, Rocky Run, Sonora, and Davis Mound. The Saints planned one settlement that never came into being. This town, to be called Warren, might be designated a "paper town," meaning that it never got beyond the planning stage. There were also important non-Mormon towns in the area, such as Warsaw and Pontoosuc.

The largest and most important settlement was Ramus. Also known as Macedonia and Webster (its present name), Ramus was located 20 miles southeast of Nauvoo, 12 miles south of La Harpe, and 8 miles northeast of Carthage. The town was established entirely by Latter-day Saints and was clearly regarded as an important settlement in the plans developed by Joseph Smith because of its size and location.

The establishment of Ramus was largely the work of the Joel H. Johnson family, who had settled in Carthage before the selection of Commerce (Nauvoo) as the principal settlement location. As a result of missionary work performed by Joel Johnson and others, several families along Crooked Creek joined the Church. Soon residents organized the Crooked Creek Branch and selected a site for the town. The inhabitants chose the name "Ramus" for their town. The word *ramus* is a Latin term meaning "branch," and may indicate the strong interest of the early

Saints in ancient languages. When the Mormon settlers built the city, they introduced a more extensive Church organization. What had been called the Crooked River Branch became the Ramus Stake. Hyrum Smith organized the Ramus Stake on July 15, 1840, with Joel H. Johnson as stake president.

The members of the Ramus Stake built their own meetinghouse, an unusual practice in the early days of the Church. Most Church meetings were then held in homes or out of doors. The building erected by the Saints in Ramus may have been the earliest meetinghouse built by Latter-day Saints.

Joseph Smith frequently visited Ramus. He stopped there en route to other destinations, held Church conferences, convened disciplinary courts, and visited relatives. Perhaps his most celebrated visits occurred in 1843, when he received two revelations, (now D&C 130 and 131). One other significant fact emerges from the study of Ramus. It is commonly believed that all Mormons left Hancock County in 1846, as they began their exodus to the west. In fact, some Latter-day Saints remained in Ramus until 1850.

Carthage, a missionary town comprising mostly non-Mormons, is very important in LDS history. The county seat of Hancock County, Carthage is located at its geographic center. It is best known as the place where the martyrdoms of Joseph and Hyrum Smith occurred. On June 27, 1844, a number of men in a mob of 150 to 250 persons forced their way into Carthage Jail and murdered the two brothers, who were being held on an unsubstantiated charge of treason.

Warsaw, the most significant non-Mormon town in Hancock County, was located 16 miles south of Nauvoo. This river town became notorious as an anti-Mormon community. The person most responsible for the anti-Mormon activities was Thomas Sharp, editor of the *Warsaw Signal*. The *Warsaw Signal* published dozens of vitriolic anti-Mormon articles during the 1840s.

The Mormon settlements in Hancock County constituted an important Mormon presence in western Illinois between 1839 and 1846. Along with Nauvoo they were home to the vast majority of Mormons in the state of Illinois.

Donald Q. Cannon, "Spokes on the Wheel: Early Latter-day Saint Settlements in Hancock County, Illinois," *Ensign* 16 (February 1986): 62–68; Susan Sessions Rugh, "Conflict in the Countryside: The Mormon Settlement at Macedonia, Illinois," *BYU Studies* 32 (Winter and Spring 1991): 149–174; Bruce A. Van Orden, "Items of Instruction: Sections 130 and 131," *Hearken O Ye People* (1984), pp. 231–247; Robert M. Cochran, *History of Hancock County, Illinois* (1968).

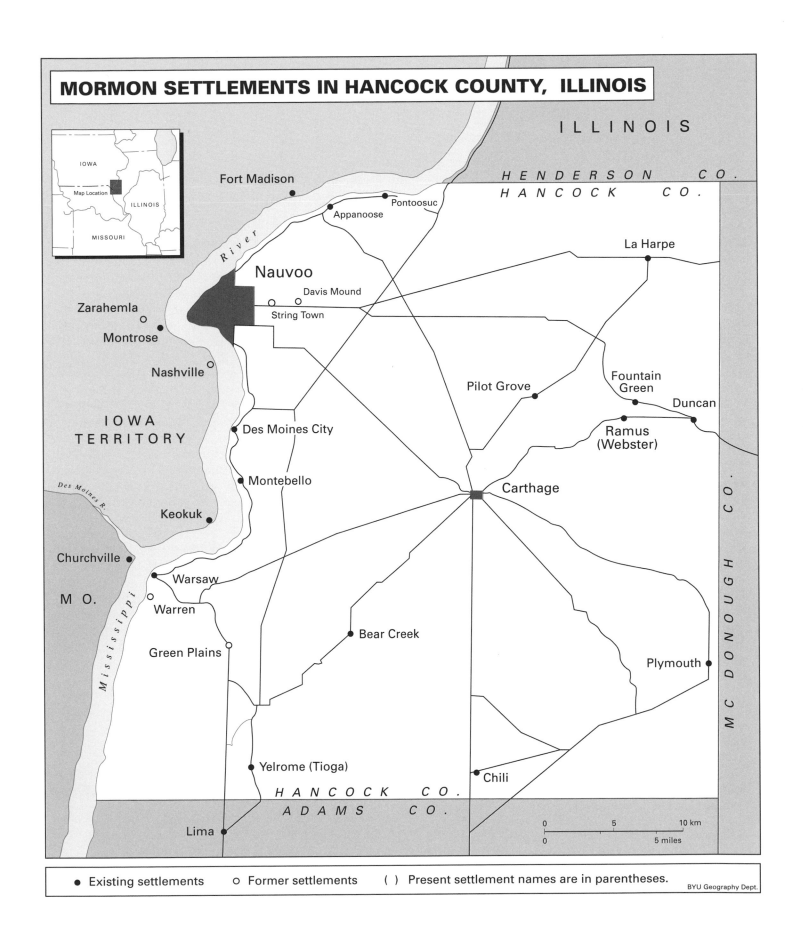

MORMON SETTLEMENTS IN HANCOCK COUNTY, ILLINOIS

ILLINOIS

IOWA

Map Location

ILLINOIS

MISSOURI

Fort Madison

HENDERSON   CO.

HANCOCK   CO.

Pontoosuc

Appanoose

La Harpe

River

Nauvoo

Davis Mound

String Town

Zarahemla

Montrose

Nashville

Pilot Grove

Fountain
Green

Duncan

Ramus
(Webster)

IOWA
TERRITORY

Des Moines City

Des Moines R.

Montebello

Carthage

MC DONOUGH CO.

Keokuk

Churchville

Mississippi

Warsaw

Warren

Bear Creek

Green Plains

Plymouth

MO.

Yelrome (Tioga)

Chili

HANCOCK   CO.

ADAMS   CO.

Lima

0   5   10 km

0   5 miles

● Existing settlements   ○ Former settlements   ( ) Present settlement names are in parentheses.

BYU Geography Dept.

EASTERN IOWA

Stanley B. Kimball

The eastern part of Iowa, especially eastern Lee County, was considered part of greater Nauvoo, Illinois. Land was purchased on both sides of the Mississippi River at the same time from the same person, stakes were established in both places, Mormons lived on both sides of the river, Masonic lodges were founded in both places, Joseph Smith preached and visited in Lee County, the Iowa settlements were connected to Nauvoo by ferry, the Sugar Creek camp and staging ground for the 1846 trek across Iowa lay seven miles west of the Mississippi River, and the September 1846 miracle of the quails took place on the Iowa shore, as did Joseph Smith's well-known healing of Brigham Young and Elijah Fordham in July 1839.

The first Mormons in Lee County were exiles from Missouri during the expulsion of 1838–1839. Most Missouri refugees headed for ferries at Quincy, Illinois, and at Louisiana, Missouri. But some did not. Israel Barlow, for example, was made welcome at Montrose in Lee County, Iowa, on the Mississippi River directly opposite what became Nauvoo, Illinois. He was attracted to Montrose because of the abandoned Fort Des Moines, which he judged could house 40 or 50 refugee families. Among those who found temporary housing there were Brigham Young, John Taylor, Wilford Woodruff, Orson Pratt, John Smith, Elijah Fordham, and Joseph B. Noble. This sudden influx of Mormon squatters, however, alarmed some of the old settlers, who grew antagonistic.

Despite this local antagonism, the Church soon purchased the undeveloped town site of Nashville (now Galland) and 20,000 surrounding acres located on the Mississippi River, three miles south of Montrose. An additional 30,000 acres were purchased in and near Montrose, and some Mormons acquired land in Keokuk, Ambrosia, and elsewhere in Lee County. Of these communities, Montrose became most prominent. Mormon settlement commenced there in May 1839. By October of that same year there were so many Mormons in Lee County that the Zarahemla Stake, one of the 11 pre-Utah stakes, was organized there (see D&C 125:3–4).

John Smith, uncle of Joseph Smith, was set apart as (that is, designated) president, with Reynolds Cahoon and Lyman Wight as counselors. Erastus Snow, Elijah Fordham, William Clayton, and Asahel Smith served on the high council, and Alanson Ripley was called as the bishop. Montrose was the center of the stake, and the high council met regularly in the home of Elijah Fordham.

This stake soon became and remained for a short time—next to Nauvoo—the second most important stake and community of Mormons in the United States. This was especially true after May 24, 1841, when Smith discontinued all other stakes except those in Nauvoo and Lee County. By August 1841, the Zarahemla Stake consisted of 683 members in eight branches—in Zarahemla, Ambrosia, Nashville, Mecham Settlement, and Keokuk (Lee County); in Augusta (Des Moines County); and in the Van Buren and Chequest townships (Van Buren County). (The communities of Zarahemla and Ambrosia no longer exist.)

Five months later, however, during January 1842, the Zarahemla Stake was discontinued and reduced to branch status. Thus the whole life of this eastern Iowa stake was but 27 months. The dissolution of the Zarahemla Stake and the subsequent decline of the Church in eastern Iowa was caused by the continuing in-gathering to Nauvoo. Thereafter little is heard of Church activities in Iowa, although a few branches struggled on for a period.

Lee County had one more important role to play in early Mormon history. During February 1846, seven miles west of Montrose on Sugar Creek, Brigham Young established the staging ground for the exodus from Nauvoo. For months thereafter many Mormons passed through Lee County on their way west. That fall, while about 640 destitute Mormons, driven from Nauvoo by mob action, camped in and near Montrose, the dramatic miracle of the quails took place. On October 9, flocks of quail, exhausted from a long flight across the Mississippi River, fell at the feet of the Saints and were gathered for food.

Stanley B. Kimball, "Nauvoo West: The Mormons of the Iowa Shore," *BYU Studies* 18 (Winter 1978): 132–142; *Manuscript History of the Church in Iowa*, Church Historical Department, Salt Lake City, Utah; Elden Jay Watson, editor, *Manuscript History of Brigham Young: 1801–1844* (1968).

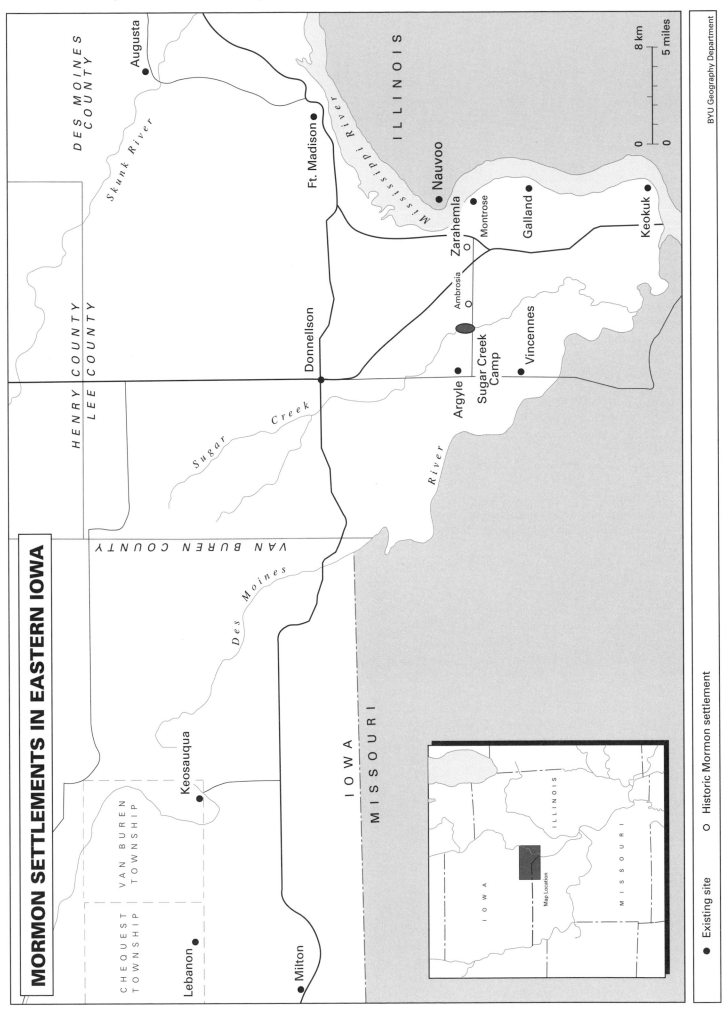

MORMON SETTLEMENTS IN EASTERN IOWA

DES MOINES COUNTY

Augusta

Skunk River

HENRY COUNTY
LEE COUNTY

Ft. Madison

ILLINOIS

Mississippi River

Nauvoo

Zarahemla
Montrose
Galland

Ambrosia

Keokuk

Donnellson

Sugar Creek

Sugar Creek Camp
Vincennes
Argyle

River

VAN BUREN COUNTY

Des Moines

Keosauqua

CHEQUEST TOWNSHIP
VAN BUREN TOWNSHIP

IOWA
MISSOURI

Lebanon

Milton

IOWA

ILLINOIS

Map Location

MISSOURI

8 km
5 miles

0
0

BYU Geography Department

● Existing site   ○ Historic Mormon settlement

59

ILLINOIS

Kenneth W. Godfrey

There are several significant Mormon historical sites in Illinois. Some of the more important of these are described here.

The Zelph Mound. On June 3, 1834, more than 200 Latter-day Saints camped near the Illinois River, one mile south of modern Valley City. While exploring what anthropologists refer to as a prehistoric middle woodland mortuary complex of the Hopewell Indian culture, these Mormons unearthed a skeleton. Joseph Smith, through a revelation, identified the bones as the remains of a Zelph, believed by Latter-day Saints to be a white Lamanite (or Indian) who may have participated in some of the last Nephite-Lamanite battles described in the Book of Mormon.

Quincy. When most Latter-day Saints resided in Kirtland, Ohio, and several northern Missouri communities (1831–1837), missionaries gleaned a few converts as they proselyted in Illinois. However, following the 1839 Mormon expulsion from Missouri, hundreds of exiles congregated at the Illinois River town of Quincy. Accepting the kind hospitality of the non-Mormon citizenry, these Latter-day Saints found shelter in Quincy for a few months and even held a general conference there to discuss their future.

Springfield. A Church branch was established in the state capital of Springfield in 1839 and a Church conference was held, a major event for Church members. Later, John C. Bennett, representing Nauvoo, was elected secretary of the meeting that organized the Illinois State Medical Society. In 1840, the Illinois State legislature met in Springfield and granted the Nauvoo Charter.

Monmouth. Joseph Smith was arrested on a Missouri writ and taken to Monmouth in Warren County, Illinois, for trial on June 1, 1841. Posting bail, the Prophet and Sheriff Thomas King of Adams County made their way to Nauvoo. King became ill and was nursed back to health by Joseph and Emma Smith. A week later, June 7, 1841, Smith went to Monmouth again and was tried before a large crowd by Judge Stephen A. Douglas. Jesse Little defended the Mormon leader, and on June 10, 1841, Joseph was acquitted.

Dixon. In June 1843, the Prophet traveled to Dixon, Illinois, to visit Emma Smith's sister, Elizabeth Wasson, and her family. While in Dixon, Sheriff Joseph Reynolds from Jackson County, Missouri, and Constable Harmon Wilson of Hancock County, Illinois, arrested the Prophet in the Wassons' yard. Illinois governor Thomas Ford had agreed to allow a warrant of extradition to Missouri to be served. The lawyer Cyrus Walker, the Whig candidate for Congress, agreed to defend the Prophet. Shortly after the arrest, Stephen Markham and William Clayton arrived and arrested Sheriff Reynolds and Constable Wilson for false imprisonment and for threatening Smith's life. Meanwhile the Nauvoo Legion, under the command of Charles C. Rich, left McQueens Mill, traveling through Ottawa and Springfield. Traveling the 200 miles in two days and 18 hours, the legion reached Dixon and their arrested leader. Escorted by the Nauvoo Legion to Nauvoo, Smith was tried and acquitted.

Norway. In May of 1843, George P. Dykes, a missionary, found a settlement of Norwegians living in LaSalle County, Illinois. Some of these Scandinavians were receptive to his message. Within three weeks, Dykes baptized many of them, including Gudmund Haugaas, a man of strong mind, skilled in the scriptures, whom he ordained an elder. Late in October 1844, two apostles visited the branch, which was located six miles northeast of Ottawa. They purchased 100 acres of ground, laid out a city, selected a site for a chapel, and appointed Dykes as the stake president. Furthermore, they set aside 10 acres for a temple. Brigham Young designated the area as a gathering place for the Scandinavian people and said that they would build the temple on the site selected and would receive their endowments in their own language.

Chicago. Mormon missionaries proselyted in the city during the years 1839 to 1846, and some Chicagoans joined the Church. Early in 1842, Joseph Smith received a letter from John Wentworth, editor of the *Chicago Democrat.* Wentworth, a New Hampshire native, had received a request from George Barstow that he contact Joseph Smith and ask him to write a sketch of his life and something about the Mormons. Smith responded to Wentworth's request and penned what has become known as the Wentworth Letter, which includes an account of the Prophet's early visions, as well as 13 succinct declarations of belief denominated "The Articles of Faith."

Amboy and Plano. Sixteen years after the murders of Joseph and Hyrum Smith, Jason Briggs, Zenas H. Gurley, H. D. Deam, and others helped convince Mormons living in Wisconsin, Iowa, and Illinois that Joseph Smith's son, Joseph Smith III, should assume leadership of what historian Alma Blair calls moderate Mormonism. On April 6, 1860, at a special conference in Amboy, Illinois, Smith expressed his willingness to lead the movement known today as the Reorganized Church of Jesus Christ of Latter Day Saints. Plano for a time served as its headquarters. Joseph Smith III moved there and the *Saints Herald,* the official organ of the RLDS church, was for a time published there.

Times and Seasons, Vols. 1–6 (Nov. 1839–Feb. 1846); *History of the Church of Jesus Christ of Latter-day Saints,* Vols. III, IV, and V (Salt Lake City: Deseret News, 1905); Paul M. Edwards, *Our Legacy of Faith* (1991).

HISTORIC LDS SITES IN ILLINOIS

WISCONSIN

Lake Michigan

M I C H.

I O W A

Elgin

Chicago

Dixon

Amboy

Walnut

Norway

La Salle

Ottawa

Toulon

Monmouth

Nauvoo   Macomb

Pekin

I L L I N O I S

Rushville

INDIANA

Quincy

Springfield

Zelph Mound

Jacksonville

Edwardsville

Fairfield

Missouri River

MISSOURI

Mississippi River

Ohio River

KENTUCKY

| 0 | 50 | 100 | 150 | kilometers |

| 0 | 25 | 50 | | 100 miles |

● Settlement   ○ Non-settlement historic site

BYU Geography Department

IMMIGRATION TO NAUVOO

Kenneth W. Godfrey

Fleeing north and east in late November 1838, Israel Barlow and other Mormons lost their way and arrived at the Des Moines River in Iowa Territory. There these religious refugees discovered some abandoned barracks and met their owner, Isaac Galland. They began negotiations to purchase land in Iowa known as the Half Breed Tract as well as land and buildings across the Mississippi River in Commerce, Illinois, that Galland seemed eager to sell.

While Barlow and others conferred with Church leaders, Galland began promoting the Mormon cause among the Illinois citizenry, including his friends Attorney Gen. Van Allen and Gov. Robert Lucas. Assured that the Mormons were welcome in Illinois, Joseph Smith, then imprisoned, sent Bishop Edward Partridge a letter instructing him to purchase Galland's lands. After escaping from Missouri officers, Smith arrived in Quincy, Illinois, in April 1839, joining his exiled family and hundreds of his followers. Within a week, he had met with Galland and acquired title to three parcels of ground in Commerce. By the summer of 1839, Smith had purchased available land on behalf of the Church and had plotted a city to be named Nauvoo, a Hebrew name connoting "beautiful place." More than 1,000 Latter-day Saints fled their temporary Quincy quarters and in the summer and autumn of 1839 emigrated to Nauvoo preparing to acquire land, build homes, and participate in establishing a new Zion. By letter, Church leaders encouraged members still scattered as far east as Kirtland, Ohio, to hasten to Nauvoo.

Even as Smith and his followers labored to establish a city from land that included a large swamp, he called the Twelve Apostles to leave on a mission to England. Leaving behind ill, impoverished families, these men, traveling largely without purse or scrip, reached Great Britain before the end of September 1839. Proselyting during the winter of 1839–1840, these missionaries baptized hundreds. They subsequently prepared these new converts for emigration to Nauvoo.

William Clayton, an English convert, set sail for America in September of 1840. His diary records that the whole company became ill. One young girl became so frightened in the midst of a gale that she lost her reason, and died three days later. The company captain, Theodore Turley, read the burial service, and the body was committed to the deep. Six days later, another child died. Turley instructed the Saints to be clean and to take care of the sick. One Mormon in Clayton's company caught a shark and another went swimming in the ocean on a calm day. At times Clayton writes of neglected meetings and of some Saints stealing water when it had to be rationed. On October 11, 1840, Clayton's feet touched American soil and his first purchase was an apple, which cost him a penny. Traveling by river, the Mormons traversed the state of New York, finally landing in Chicago before traveling by wagon to Rock Island, Illinois, 130 miles north of Nauvoo. Here they boarded a boat, finally docking in the Mormon capital on November 24, 1840, having traveled 5,000 miles in 11 weeks and 10 hours.

Before the Mormons left Nauvoo in 1846, almost 4,500 English converts would call Nauvoo home. They came on 22 different sailing vessels and usually landed in Boston, New York, or New Orleans, and then, like the Clayton company, traveled by boat or wagon or both to Nauvoo. The largest company numbered 270 and the smallest 41.

As missionaries proselyted England's citizenry, other "elders," as they were called, continued seeking converts in the United States and Canada. Small Latter-day Saint branches were organized in more than 100 American communities. These units ranged in size from only two members in the Minissink, New Jersey, branch, to more than 135 members in the New York City branch and the Brandywine, Pennsylvania, unit. Many Church members in these branches gathered to Nauvoo as commanded. These emigrants, too, came by boat, wagon, or buggy, or even walked.

In the fall of 1846, Jane Elizabeth Manning, a free black woman, left her Wilton, Connecticut, home, traveling by canal to Buffalo with her three brothers, two sisters, a brother-in-law, and a sister-in-law. From there they began walking the 800 miles to Nauvoo.

The influx of converts from England and parts of the United States and Canada swelled Nauvoo's populace until, by 1845, Nauvoo became one of the largest cities in Illinois.

M. Hamblin Cannon, "Migration of English Mormons to America," *American Historical Review* 5:2 (1946–1947), 441; Robert Bruce Flanders, *Nauvoo: Kingdom on the Mississippi* (1965); Conway B. Sonne, *Saints on the Seas* (1903).

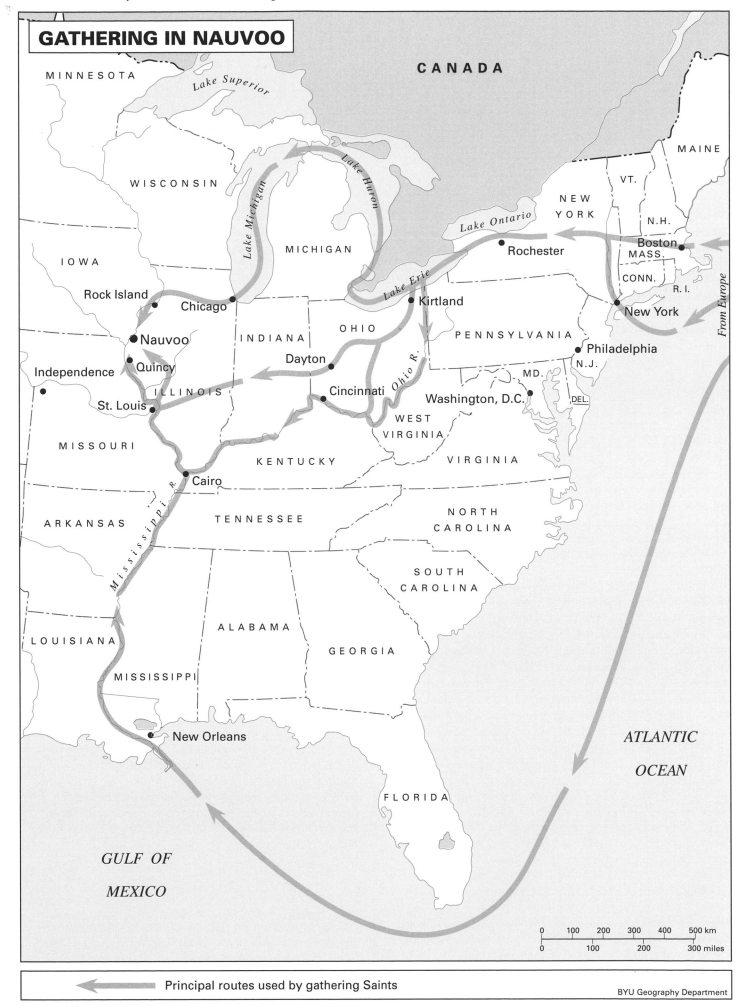

GATHERING IN NAUVOO

CANADA

MINNESOTA

Lake Superior

WISCONSIN

MICHIGAN

Lake Michigan

Lake Huron

IOWA

Lake Ontario

NEW YORK

VT.

MAINE

N.H.

MASS.

Boston

CONN.

R. I.

Rochester

Lake Erie

Kirtland

Rock Island

Chicago

INDIANA

OHIO

PENNSYLVANIA

New York

Nauvoo

Dayton

Philadelphia

Quincy

Ohio R.

N.J.

Independence

ILLINOIS

Cincinnati

MD.

DEL.

St. Louis

Washington, D.C.

From Europe

MISSOURI

KENTUCKY

WEST VIRGINIA

VIRGINIA

Mississippi R.

Cairo

ARKANSAS

TENNESSEE

NORTH CAROLINA

SOUTH CAROLINA

ALABAMA

GEORGIA

LOUISIANA

MISSISSIPPI

ATLANTIC OCEAN

New Orleans

FLORIDA

GULF OF MEXICO

| 0 | 100 | 200 | 300 | 400 | 500 km |
| 0 | | 100 | | 200 | 300 miles |

Principal routes used by gathering Saints

BYU Geography Department

63

LAND OWNERSHIP IN NAUVOO AND VICINITY

James L. Kimball, Jr.

The City of Nauvoo was incorporated by the General Assembly of Illinois in December of 1840. Its charter delineated boundaries that made Nauvoo, territorially, the largest city in the state. Roughly six square miles, the city contained 3,733 acres located on a peninsula in the northwestern corner of Hancock County, Illinois. Only a small portion of this was originally divided into lots. Encircled by the Mississippi River on three sides, the area was naturally divided into two geographic regions. From the river's edge the flat sloped gently upward some 65 feet to a bluff, which in turn stretched eastward to the prairie. The northern part of Nauvoo was interspersed with several ravines, springs, and streams, while some 15 or 20 acres on the central western edge was considered wet and swampy. Several large and small thickets of trees speckled both flat and bluff. All these elements lent to the entire area an unusually pleasing aspect. One can easily comprehend why Joseph Smith named the city Nauvoo after a Hebrew term connoting "pleasant." Not surprisingly, the entire peninsula upon which Nauvoo developed had been purchased by speculators by the mid 1830s and three town sites laid out to lure prospective buyers.

Between 1839 and 1846 some 16,000 converts gathered at the site at the behest of their prophet-leader Joseph Smith. To aid the newcomers, many of whom were sick and poverty-stricken, Joseph Smith purchased 660 acres from non-Mormons Hugh and William White, Isaac Galland, and Horace Hotchkiss. These lands were then resold in parcels of various sizes to the new arrivals. Additions to the newly plotted town extended the borders of the newly plotted community to the east upon land included in the original charter. Located on the bluffs, these additions were known by the name of their original owner or developer. The largest additions were made by the family of Phineas Kimball of Orange County, Vermont. He and his sons, Ethan and Hiram, were responsible for three additions. Hiram, who acted as a resident agent for the family, was easily the most prosperous and influential. Daniel H. Wells also held sizable tracts of land and was active in Nauvoo governmental functions. His addition to Nauvoo was adjacent to those of the Kimballs. Other additions on the bluffs of the city were Davidson Hibbard (two), Hyrum Smith (two), heirs of James Robison (two), Hugh Herringshaw and Edward Thompson (two), Benjamin Warrington (one), William Spears (one), and George W. Robinson (one).

Nauvoo citizens were natives of almost every state in the Union, Canada, and the British Isles. Nearly one-third of the emigrants spoke with a British accent, but German-speaking Saints also held regular church meetings. Native Norwegian converts came from Norway, Illinois, and at least 21 African Americans resided in Nauvoo, contributing to a diverse ethnic mix. Adults over age 20 tended to be natives of New England and those under 20 of New York and Illinois.

Generally, antebellum towns and villages did not exceed 2,500 in population. This was particularly true in Illinois, where most settlements rarely surpassed 1,000 occupants. After only a few years, however, Nauvoo jumped from a few families to roughly 3,000 people, equaling in size the capital, Springfield, and other comparable communities of the time such as Quincy, Alton, and Peoria. Moreover, given the imperfect and impressionistic nature of 19th-century census data, there remains a remote possibility that from 1843 to 1844, Nauvoo may have rivaled Chicago, the most populous city in the state.

Since Nauvoo's economy did not have much in the way of manufacturing, transportation, or marketing, its chief business item was real estate. Buying, selling, and trading land was a popular business in Nauvoo beginning in 1839.

Collecting money to pay for the land was a problem. At the first general conference held in the Nauvoo area, Lyman Wight preached a sermon encouraging the Saints to pay for the land they had received so that the Church might be in a position to pay its debts to Isaac Galland and others.

Most of the lots in Nauvoo consisted of one square acre. This large plot was designed to provide space for a home as well as a garden large enough to provide for some of the family's food supply. Individuals also owned farms outside of the city on the prairie, including the Joseph Smith farm. The cemetery was located adjacent to the city limits but outside of the territory included in the Nauvoo Charter.

James B. Allen, *Trials of Discipleship: The Story of William Clayton, a Mormon* (1987); Robert B. Flanders, *Nauvoo: Kingdom on the Mississippi* (1965); David E. Miller and Della S. Miller, *Nauvoo: The City of Joseph* (1974).

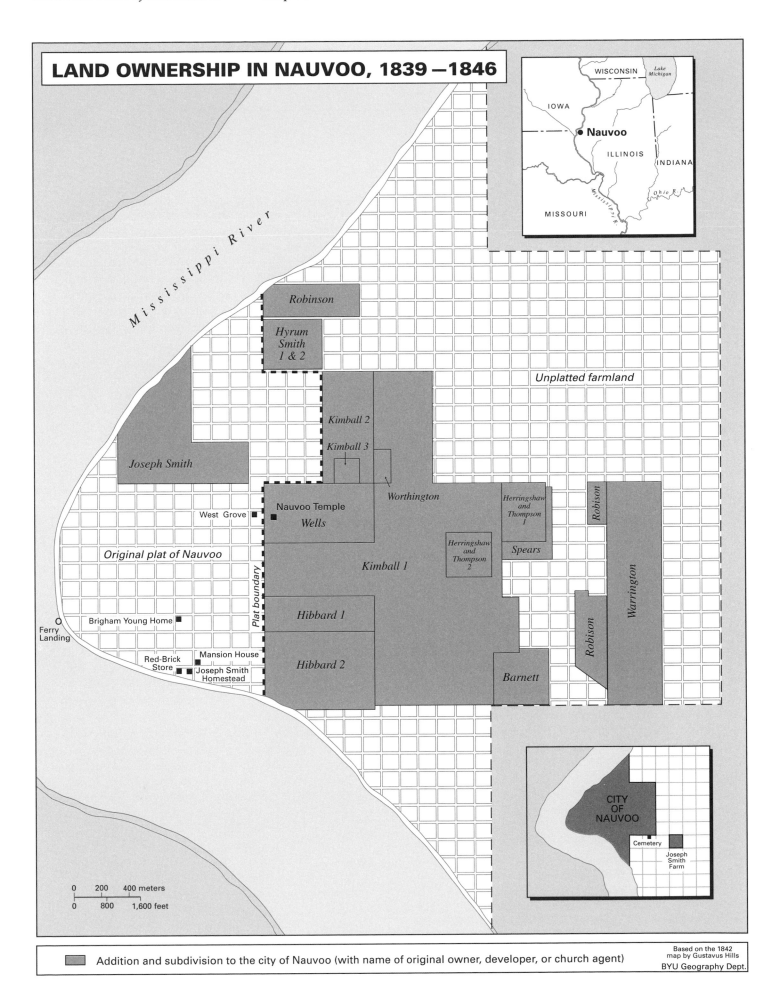

LAND OWNERSHIP IN NAUVOO, 1839–1846

WISCONSIN
Lake Michigan
IOWA
Nauvoo
ILLINOIS
INDIANA
Mississippi R.
MISSOURI
Ohio R.

Mississippi River

Robinson

Hyrum Smith 1 & 2

Unplatted farmland

Kimball 2

Kimball 3

Joseph Smith

Worthington

Herringshaw and Thompson 1

Robison

West Grove

Nauvoo Temple

Wells

Kimball 1

Herringshaw and Thompson 2

Spears

Warrington

Original plat of Nauvoo

Brigham Young Home

Hibbard 1

Ferry Landing

Plat boundary

Robison

Red-Brick Store
Mansion House
Joseph Smith Homestead

Hibbard 2

Barnett

0   200   400 meters
0   800   1,600 feet

CITY OF NAUVOO

Cemetery

Joseph Smith Farm

Addition and subdivision to the city of Nauvoo (with name of original owner, developer, or church agent)

Based on the 1842 map by Gustavus Hills
BYU Geography Dept.

DIVERGENT PATHS FROM NAUVOO

Steven L. Shields

For 20 years after Joseph Smith's death in 1844, the church that he founded was in a state of fragmentation. Nearly 30 different individuals or groups contended with Brigham Young for its leadership. By 1865, six distinct church organizations remained, continuing to the present.

Sidney Rigdon, an early contender with Brigham Young for leadership at Nauvoo, had been a member of the First Presidency. Rigdon perceived himself to be similar to a vice president. When a special conference in August 1844 refused to grant him guardianship over the Church, Rigdon worked privately to gain supporters, eventually settling in Pittsburgh, Pennsylvania, designating himself president of a reorganized church. Although Rigdon's church essentially fell apart in 1846, there was a revival in the 1860s, which continued briefly after Rigdon's death in 1876.

The heritage of Rigdon's church continues in The Church of Jesus Christ (Monongahela, Pennsylvania), first organized by William Bickerton in 1862 at Greenock (or Green Oak), Pennsylvania. Bickerton was an 1845 Rigdon convert who was left without a church when Rigdon's group fell apart. Bickerton and his associates organized branches and held conferences for several years prior to the official organization of this church, which in 1994 has some 15,000 members and is involved in missionary work overseas.

James J. Strang was Brigham Young's most serious contender in 1844. Strang claimed that, in addition to possessing a letter appointing him to be the next prophet, he was ordained by an angel when Joseph Smith died. Strang successfully persuaded a number of Nauvoo residents as well as several branches of the church to follow his leadership. Strang's several thousand followers located near Burlington, Wisconsin, but later moved to Beaver Island in Lake Michigan. Shot by two disgruntled followers, Strang died in 1856, leaving his church without a prophet. The Church of Jesus Christ of Latter Day Saints remains located mainly in the Burlington, Wisconsin, area, where there are two different buildings used by different groups of Strang's 200 or 300 followers.

Alpheus Cutler began the trek from Nauvoo to the West but remained in western Iowa with several other families. In 1853 Cutler claimed he had received a vision telling him that the church should be reorganized. Followers established a community at Manti, Iowa, where they remained until the late 1860s, when they moved to Clitherall, Minnesota. In the 1920s, a mission was sent to Independence, Missouri, where the church, called The Church of Jesus Christ and numbering about 30 members, is headquartered today.

The Reorganized Church of Jesus Christ of Latter Day Saints (RLDS) emerged out of a grass roots movement of the 1850s. Unwilling to follow Brigham Young's leadership, several local leaders looked to others for prophetic leadership, such as that offered by James J. Strang and William Smith (brother of the slain prophet), but were disappointed each time. Joseph Smith III was eventually persuaded to take the leadership of this group of Latter Day Saints after experiencing what he called "a power not my own." At a conference at Amboy, Illinois, in 1860, the church was officially reorganized.

The Reorganized Church was headquartered at Nauvoo, Illinois, until 1866, when Smith moved to Plano, Illinois. Headquarters were moved to Lamoni, Iowa, in 1881, and finally to Independence, Missouri, in 1921, where it remains today. The RLDS Church is the second largest of the Latter Day Saint churches, with about 250,000 members.

After the death of Joseph Smith, a group of unaffiliated branches located in and near Bloomington, Illinois, concluded, after years of examination, that all the other leaders were in error and looked to Granville Hedrick for leadership. Hedrick and his band returned to Independence, Missouri, in 1867 and bought land in the area where land had been purchased under Joseph Smith's direction in 1831. The Church of Christ is today headquartered in Independence, Missouri, and claims about 3,000 members.

Other would-be leaders included William McLellin, James Brewster, Hazen Aldrich, and Zadoc Brooks, who each attempted to establish their headquarters in the Kirtland (Ohio) Temple. The Lyman Wight colony in Texas was quick to join with the Reorganized Church of Jesus Christ of Latter Day Saints under the leadership of Joseph Smith III. William Smith, brother of the slain prophet, established his own church organization but eventually united with the Reorganized Church. Charles B. Thompson led a community at Preparation, Iowa, having started his work in St. Louis, Missouri. The community came apart in 1858 when Thompson was accused of misappropriating community resources.

Through the years prior to Joseph Smith's death, and continuing to the present day, the Latter Day Saint movement has been touched by schismatic tendencies. Occasionally a schism provides serious concern for leaders and believers of the organized churches; most often, though, these unique schismatic movements provide a colorful footnote in the broader history of the movement at large.

Robert Bruce Flanders, *Nauvoo: Kingdom on the Mississippi* (1965); Richard P. Howard, *The Church Through the Years*, Vol.1 (1992); Steven L. Shields, *Divergent Paths of the Restoration*, 4th ed.(1982); Steven L. Shields, *The Latter Day*

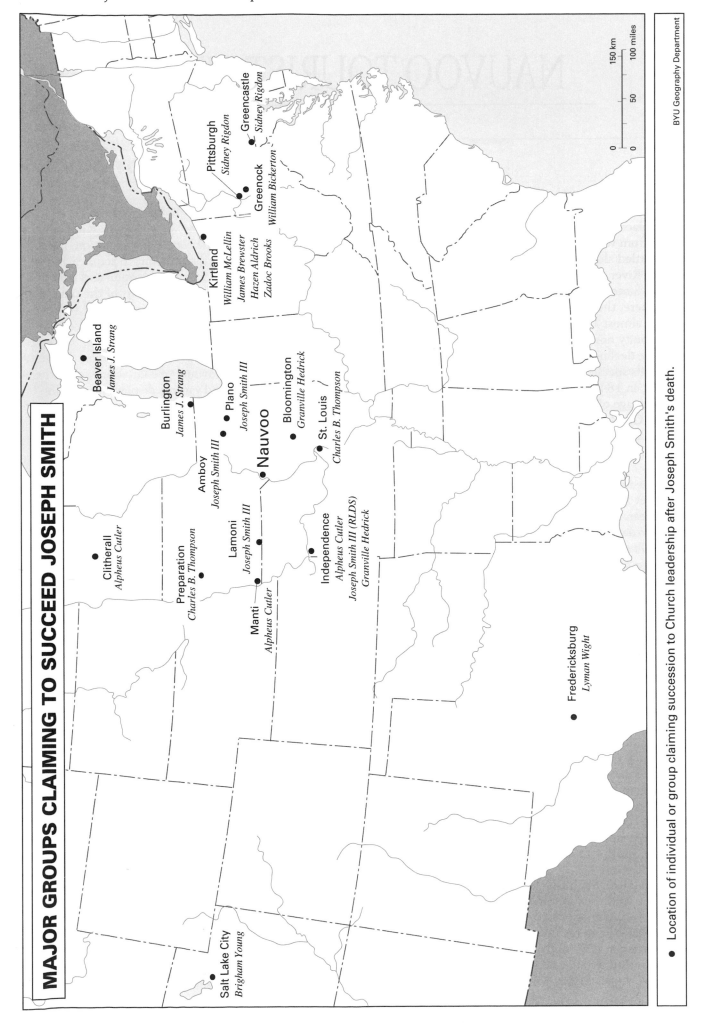

MAJOR GROUPS CLAIMING TO SUCCEED JOSEPH SMITH

Pittsburgh *Sidney Rigdon*

Greencastle *Sidney Rigdon*

Greenock *William Bickerton*

Kirtland
William McLellin
James Brewster
Hazen Aldrich
Zadoc Brooks

Beaver Island *James J. Strang*

Burlington *James J. Strang*

Plano *Joseph Smith III*

Bloomington *Granville Hedrick*

St. Louis *Charles B. Thompson*

Nauvoo

Amboy *Joseph Smith III*

Clitherall *Alpheus Cutler*

Preparation *Charles B. Thompson*

Lamoni *Joseph Smith III*

Manti *Alpheus Cutler*

Independence
Alpheus Cutler
Joseph Smith III (RLDS)
Granville Hedrick

Salt Lake City *Brigham Young*

Fredericksburg *Lyman Wight*

150 km

100 miles

50

0

0

BYU Geography Department

• Location of individual or group claiming succession to Church leadership after Joseph Smith's death.

FROM NAUVOO
TO COUNCIL BLUFFS

Stanley B. Kimball

The approximately 1,300-mile-long trek from Nauvoo to the Great Salt Lake valley occurred in two stages: the 265-mile march across Iowa in 1846, and the 1,032-mile journey across the plains of Nebraska and Wyoming into Utah in 1847. The Iowa portion of the trail was used relatively little, mainly by the Mormons fleeing Illinois in 1846, and by some other Mormons departing from Keokuk, Iowa, in 1853. The trail was again used in 1856 and 1857 by seven Mormon handcart companies that left from Iowa City, intersecting the 1846 Mormon trail at what is now Lewis in Cass County. Thousands of other Mormons crossed Iowa as late as 1863 both on variant spurs of the 1846 trail and on different trails. All trails, however, intersected the route of 1846 in western Iowa.

Iowa consists mainly of rolling lowlands and is less visually dramatic than Nebraska, Wyoming, and Utah. Distinguishing natural features in Iowa consist largely of streams and rivers. These water sources largely fix the route of the trail, and along them many important events of Mormon history took place. The most important of the streams and rivers are Sugar Creek, Des Moines River, Fox River, Chariton River, Shoal Creek, Locust Creek, Medicine Creek, Weldon River, Grand River, Nodaway River, Nishnabotna River, and, of course, the Missouri River.

In Iowa the trail generally followed primitive territorial roads as far as Bloomfield in Davis County; then it followed vague Indian and trading trails along ridges from one water source to another, ending at an Indian agent's settlement on the Missouri River at Council Bluffs. Little remains of the old trail in Iowa; time and the plow have erased almost all of it.

Because Mormons left Nauvoo in February 1846, earlier than really necessary, and because they were ill-prepared and inexperienced in moving large groups of people, the pioneers suffered more crossing Iowa in 1846 than they did traveling through Nebraska, Wyoming, and Utah. The skills acquired and lessons learned in Iowa, however, later served them well on the trail and in the Great Basin. The first companies probably totaled about 500 wagons and 3,000 people.

The trail of the pioneers of 1846 set out from Parley Street in Nauvoo. Arriving on the other side of the Mississippi River, they proceeded west some seven miles to the Sugar Creek staging ground. Thence they traveled by a variety of roads to Bonaparte, where they forded the Des Moines near the bridge on present-day Highway 79, where a marker commemorates this fact.

The wagons continued west, crossing Big Indian Creek and the Fox River, to Bloomfield. From Bloomfield they bore toward modern Cincinnati. Three miles into Wayne County is Locust Creek, along which William Clayton composed the words to the noted Mormon hymn "Come, Come, Ye Saints."

The pioneers next set up an important shelter at Garden Grove, the first permanent camp for the benefit of the Mormons who would follow. North and west the wagons reached Mt. Pisgah, which became the second permanent camp. Here an official Iowa state marker and an LDS kiosk tell the story of Mt. Pisgah.

The wagons proceeded west to present-day Bridgewater. The modern Mormon Trail Park and the best Mormon trail ruts in Iowa are found near here. From Bridgewater they traveled west to present-day Lewis. Near Lewis, the Handcart Trail of 1856 from Iowa City intersected the Iowa trail of 1846. From Lewis the pioneers pressed west to Council Bluffs. The Mormons finally reached present-day Council Bluffs in June. From there the Mormon Battalion marched to war with Mexico. By September, the remaining Mormons had crossed the Missouri River and made another permanent camp at Winter Quarters, present-day North Omaha. Many Mormons remained in Council Bluffs for years.

Stanley B. Kimball, "The Mormon Trail Network in Iowa, 1838–1868," *BYU Studies* 21 (Fall 1981): 417–430; Stanley B. Kimball, *Historic Sites and Markers along the Mormon and other Great Western Trails* (1988); Elden J. Watson, editor, *Manuscript History of Brigham Young: 1846–1847* (1971).

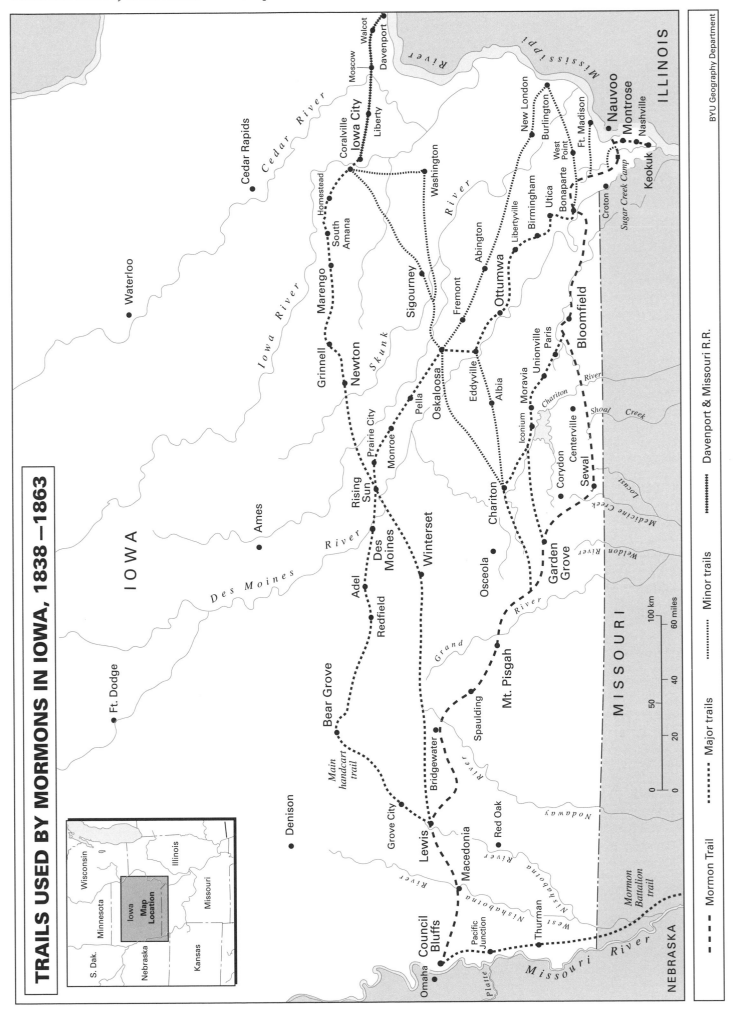

TRAILS USED BY MORMONS IN IOWA, 1838–1863

ILLINOIS

BYU Geography Department

Davenport & Missouri R.R.

Minor trails

Major trails

Mormon Trail

Walcot
Moscow
Davenport
Mississippi River
River
Cedar River
Cedar Rapids
Liberty
Coralville
Iowa City
Nauvoo
Montrose
Keokuk
Nashville
Sugar Creek Camp
New London
Burlington
Ft. Madison
West Point
Homestead
Washington
Utica
Bonaparte
Croton
South Amana
Libertyville
Birmingham
Marengo
Abington
Ottumwa
Sigourney
Fremont
Bloomfield
Iowa River
Grinnell
Newton
Skunk River
Oskaloosa
Eddyville
Albia
Moravia
Unionville
Paris
Chariton River
Centerville
Shoal Creek
Prairie City
Pella
Iconium
Corydon
Sewal
Waterloo
Monroe
Rising Sun
Chariton
Medicine Creek
Locust
Des Moines River
Des Moines
Winterset
Osceola
Garden Grove
Weldon River
Ames
Adel
Redfield
Mt. Pisgah
Grand River
Ft. Dodge
IOWA
Bear Grove
Spaulding
Main handcart trail
Bridgewater
River
100 km
60 miles
50
40
20
0
Grove City
Lewis
Macedonia
Red Oak
Nishnabotna River
Nodaway
Denison
Council Bluffs
Pacific Junction
Thurman
West Nishnabotna River
Mormon Battalion trail
MISSOURI
Omaha
Platte
Missouri River
NEBRASKA

Wisconsin
Minnesota
S. Dak.
Nebraska
Kansas
Missouri
Illinois
Iowa
Map Location

RAIL ROUTES (1831–1869)

Stanley B. Kimball

The effective beginning of railroad travel in the United States came in May 1830 with the opening of the first division of the Baltimore and Ohio line, an event that would greatly affect Mormon immigration. The story of Mormon immigrants and the railroads is little known. Generally, little attention has been paid to pioneer immigrants except as travelers in wagons. Yet very few Mormons went west solely by wagon.

Most Mormon immigrants began their wagon journey at the Missouri River by first taking various rivers and railroads from Canada and the East Coast, a distance up to 1,300 miles—the same distance between Nauvoo and Salt Lake City. At various times, Mormons traveled by a variety of rail and water routes to reach their destinations, starting as early as 1837. By 1856, rail travel extended west of Chicago and St. Louis when the Chicago and Rock Island railroad reached Iowa City, Iowa. By 1869, the Union Pacific reached Utah. Thereafter, Mormons were able to travel by rail all the way from the East Coast to Utah.

Starting in 1840, the first Mormon immigrants sailed to the United States. By February 1855, ninety-three percent of European immigrants entered the United States at New Orleans and took riverboats initially to Illinois (1839–1846), later to their wagons on the Missouri River. Thereafter, because of the developing railway network, emigration patterns changed and all European immigrants entered at Philadelphia, New York, and Boston. They then took various railroads as far as possible, at first to Chicago and St. Louis, thence by other rail lines (and Missouri River boats) to their wagons on the Missouri River at places such as Westport, Independence, Weston, and St. Joseph, Missouri; Leavenworth and Atchison, Kansas; Nebraska City and Wyoming, Nebraska; and Council Bluffs, Iowa. Train travel was cheaper, faster, and safer—safer because immigrants were not exposed to the river-borne scourge of cholera.

These observations mean that some 34,000, or 49 percent, of the approximately 70,000 LDS pioneers who crossed the plains before 1869 traveled by railroad to their waiting wagons. Mormon immigrants did not routinely travel by train, however, until 1856, when the Chicago and Rock Island railroad reached Iowa City, Iowa. The first Mormons to use this route were the handcart pioneers.

Over the years the most important midwestern railroads used by Mormons were the Chicago and Rock Island, 1856–1859 (now the Iowa Interstate), the Chicago, Burlington, and Quincy, 1859–1866 (now the Burlington Northern and part of the Amtrak system), the Hannibal and St. Joseph, 1859–1866 (now mainly the Burlington Northern), the Missouri Northern, 1859–1868 (now the Norfolk Southern), the Chicago and Northwestern, 1867–1869 (still the C&NW), the Chicago and Alton, from 1854 on (now the Illinois Central and Gulf and part of the Amtrak system), and the Pacific Railroad, from 1854 on (now the Union Pacific and part of the Amtrak system). A few also rode the Council Bluffs and St. Joseph line and the Keokuk and Fort Des Moines railroad. Some, usually missionaries, also went east by railroad.

A most important year in Mormon rail travel was 1859, when the Hannibal and St. Joseph railroad reached the Missouri River (the first railroad to do so) at St. Joseph, Missouri. Mormons could then ride all the way from the East Coast to St. Joseph by rail. In 1867 the Chicago and Northwestern reached Council Bluffs, Iowa, where Mormons crossed the Missouri and picked up the Union Pacific railroad—a fact that soon permitted Mormons to ride the rails from the East Coast to Utah, thereby becoming "Pullman pioneers."

The Union Pacific railroad started west from Omaha in 1865, but the Mormons generally did not use this route until 1867, when the tracks reached as far west as North Platte, Nebraska, and the Chicago and Northwestern reached Council Bluffs. In 1868, Mormons took the Union Pacific to Cheyenne, Laramie, and Benton, Wyoming; and thereafter, all the way to Ogden, Utah.

Because they almost always traveled in inexpensive "emigrant cars" rather than in the first-class and "Palace Cars," Latter-day Saints experienced most of the discomforts typical of mid-19th-century railroads. Among standard problems were crowding, uncomfortable cars, poor heating and ventilation, insufficient lighting, primitive sanitary facilities, inadequate eating conveniences, a lack of drinking water, noise, smells, jolting, shaking, vibration, fatigue, dirt, lice, soot, sparks, smoke, fire, gamblers, thieves, tramps, drunks, "mashers," loss of luggage, snow, ice, sickness, bad brakes, derailment, accidents, wrecks, delays, and deaths.

Kate Carter, "People Who Came on the First Trains," *Our Pioneer Heritage* (1965); Richard L. Jensen, "Steaming Through: Arrangements for Mormon Emigration From Europe, 1869–1887," *Journal of Mormon History* 9 (1982): 3–23; Stanley B. Kimball, "Rail/trail Pioneers to Zion: 1855–1869: A Preliminary Study," paper presented at Mormon History Association Conference, May 1992.

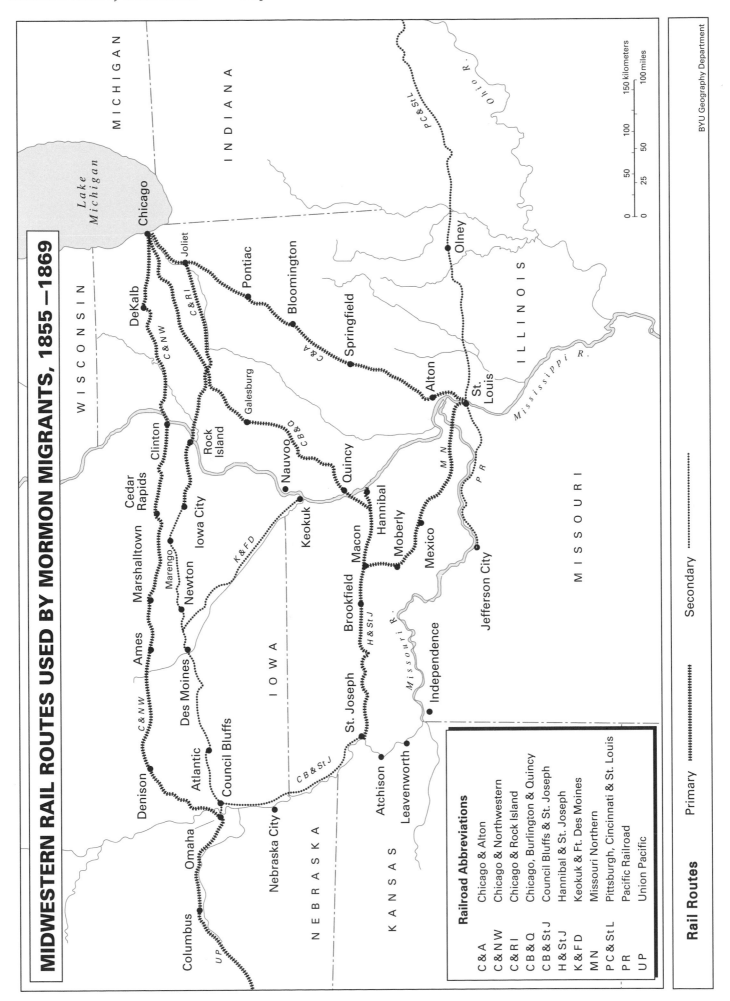

MIDWESTERN RAIL ROUTES USED BY MORMON MIGRANTS, 1855–1869

MICHIGAN

Lake Michigan

WISCONSIN

INDIANA

ILLINOIS

IOWA

MISSOURI

NEBRASKA

KANSAS

Chicago

Joliet

DeKalb

Pontiac

Bloomington

Springfield

Olney

Alton

St. Louis

Galesburg

Rock Island

Clinton

Cedar Rapids

Nauvoo

Quincy

Hannibal

Moberly

Mexico

Jefferson City

Marshalltown

Iowa City

Marengo

Newton

Keokuk

Macon

Brookfield

Ames

Des Moines

St. Joseph

Independence

Denison

Atlantic

Council Bluffs

Omaha

Nebraska City

Atchison

Leavenworth

Columbus

Mississippi R.

Ohio R.

Missouri R.

C & A

C & NW

C & RI

CB & Q

PC & StL

MN

PR

K & FD

H & StJ

CB & StJ

UP

Railroad Abbreviations

C & A	Chicago & Alton
C & NW	Chicago & Northwestern
C & RI	Chicago & Rock Island
CB & Q	Chicago, Burlington & Quincy
CB & StJ	Council Bluffs & St. Joseph
H & StJ	Hannibal & St. Joseph
K & FD	Keokuk & Ft. Des Moines
MN	Missouri Northern
PC & StL	Pittsburgh, Cincinnati & St. Louis
PR	Pacific Railroad
UP	Union Pacific

Rail Routes

Primary ++++++++++++++++++++

Secondary ....

0   25   50   100   150 kilometers
0   50   100 miles

BYU Geography Department

THE MISSOURI RIVER VALLEY

Gail Geo. Holmes

The breadth and depth of Mormon farming and community development in southwest Iowa, 1846–1853, created a watershed in the history of the Middle Missouri Valley. From the early 1700s the region had sustained little except Indian fur trade with the French, then with the Spanish, and finally with the Americans.

Delays that hampered the 1846 Mormon exodus from western Illinois and southeast Iowa to Salt Lake Valley proved a blessing to southwest Iowa. Mormons cut roads through its beautiful loess hills and built bridges and ferries over streams in Iowa and Nebraska. Thousands of acres of sod were broken. The Saints developed productive farms and established schools, churches, mills, blacksmith shops, large supply houses, hotels, newspapers, and related businesses.

Latter-day Saints organized town and county governments for the 16,000 to 18,000 original refugees. Several thousand more immigrants arrived from other parts of the United States and Canada. Additionally, more than 8,000 came from Europe. Mormons held elections, organized courts, and kept careful property records long before a federal land office was opened in Council Bluffs in 1853. In 1848 all southwest Iowa became Pottawattamie County. Soon, other counties were carved out of Pottawattamie.

In 1849, 10,000 California Gold Rushers opened a huge market for the more than 80 southwest Iowa communities. In succeeding years, steamboats brought merchandise to Emigrant Landing at Council Point to supply mercantile houses booming in Kanesville and other towns. Dozens of LDS communities traded grain, wood, and leather products besides engaging in milling, blacksmithing, tinsmithing, and wagon making.

Three Indian tribes occupied the Middle Missouri Valley when the first LDS wagon trains arrived at the Missouri River on June 14, 1846. Chiefs of about 2,250 Pottawatomie-Ottawa-Chippewas, in five scattered villages of southwest Iowa, had agreed just weeks before in Washington, D.C., to sell their lands and to move to the northeastern part of Kansas territory. About 1,300 Omaha and 930 Oto-Missouri Indians lived west of the Missouri River in five or six villages clustered near the confluence of the Platte and Missouri rivers. U.S. Indian agents at Bellevue and Point aux poules did not object to the amicable LDS presence, nor did the Indians themselves.

LDS officials, before continuing west, seem to have left city and county records in Iowa. A few of these carefully handwritten records are still available in Pottawattamie County. Significant gaps exist, however, in city and county records throughout southwest Iowa. When the Mormons left, town and even street names were changed by new owners, new squatters, claim jumpers, and, in most instances, new officials. There followed even periods of no government at all. As a result,

city and county governments today cannot find consistent records from before 1853.

A few communities such as Honey Creek, Macedonia, Magnolia, and Pisgah retain their original LDS names. Still waiting to be plotted on maps are such staging communities as Bertrand, Brownell's Grove, Davis Camp, Highland Grove, Kidd's Grove, McClellin's Camp, Nishnabotna, Perkins' Camp, Pleasant Valley, Shirts' Branch, Springville, Unionville, and West Boyer.

Communities that may have been known by two names include Allred's Camp/South Pigeon, Big Bend/Browning's Camp, North Keg Creek/Upper Crossing Keg Creek, Potter's Camp/Cutler's Camp, Dutch Hollow/Studyville, and Trading or Traders Point/Point aux poules. There may have been other LDS communities with more than one name. Occupied by Latter-day Saints but not established by them were Point aux poules, Old Agency, and probably Whipple. String Town may have been only a four-mile straggle of buildings south along the road from Kanesville to Council Point.

Some LDS settlements must have been very small, such as Plum Hollow, Green Hollow, Dutch Hollow/Studyville, and Dawsonburg, a cluster of communities within a radius of about six miles, 35 miles south of Kanesville. Unlike most LDS towns, Big Grove was not renamed (Oakland) until 1881 and Plum Hollow (Thurman) until 1890.

It is unlikely that the 98 presently known names of LDS communities constitute a complete list. Pioneer letters and journals indicate substantial movement away from wagon train organization, beginning in 1846. Families and individuals easily moved from community to community while pursuing free enterprise.

Of the several hundred Mormons who remained in or returned to Iowa, some objected to the collection of taxes or to punishments for immorality. Others disagreed over who should direct missionary work among Indians. Some left their LDS communities in order to live in Point aux poules or Old Agency. Others broke with the Church and built their own settlements, such as Manti and Preparation Canyon. Others waited for Mormon Battalion husbands or sweethearts. A few induced returning veterans to remain rather than move to Utah. Some went west to Utah and then returned. Migrating east or west, these pioneers wrote new pages of trans-Mississippi history.

Ruth Daugherty, *Unpublished Notes, Papers, and Maps of Harrison and Shelby, Iowa, Counties* (1960–1992); *Frontier Guardian* (Kanesville, Iowa), Orson Hyde, editor (1849–1852); David C. Mott, *Abandoned Towns, Villages & Post Offices of Iowa* (1973); George M. Hilton, Maps and Survey Notes of Original (1851–1852) Government Survey of Pottawattamie County, Iowa, Pottawattamie County Engineer's Office, Council Bluffs, Iowa [1950s].

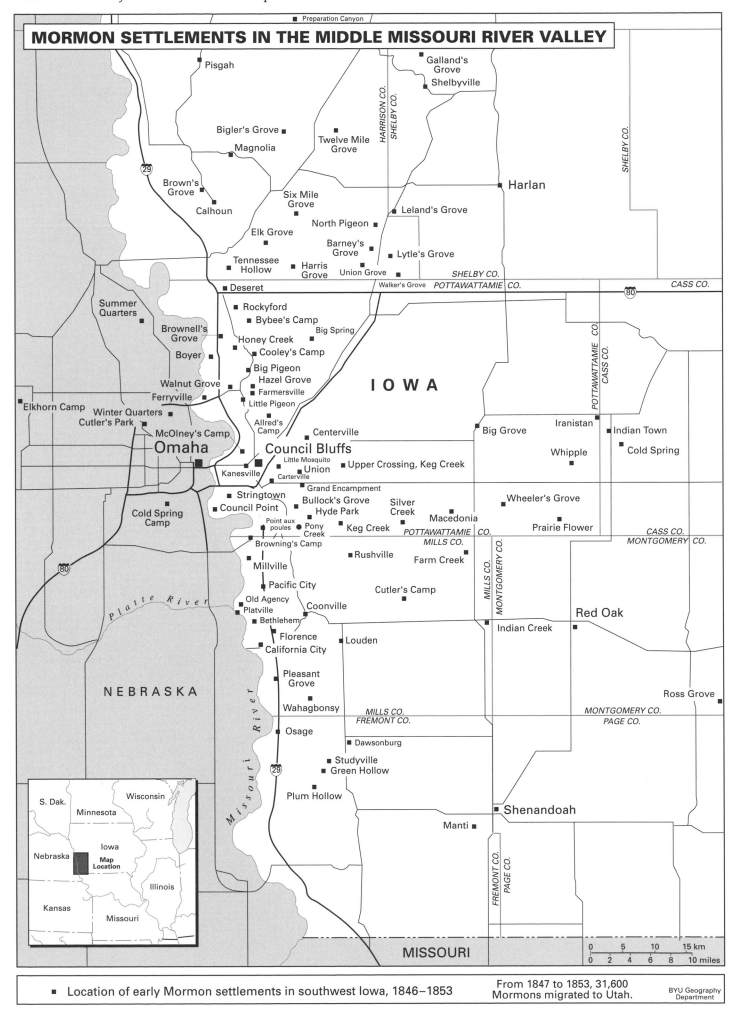

MORMON SETTLEMENTS IN THE MIDDLE MISSOURI RIVER VALLEY

Preparation Canyon

Pisgah

Galland's Grove

Shelbyville

HARRISON CO.

SHELBY CO.

SHELBY CO.

Bigler's Grove

Magnolia

Twelve Mile Grove

Harlan

Brown's Grove

Calhoun

Six Mile Grove

Leland's Grove

Elk Grove

North Pigeon

Barney's Grove

Lytle's Grove

Tennessee Hollow

Harris Grove

Union Grove

SHELBY CO.

Deseret

Walker's Grove

POTTAWATTAMIE CO.

CASS CO.

Summer Quarters

Rockyford

Bybee's Camp

Big Spring

IOWA

POTTAWATTAMIE CO.

CASS CO.

Brownell's Grove

Honey Creek

Cooley's Camp

Boyer

Big Pigeon

Hazel Grove

Walnut Grove

Farmersville

Ferryville

Little Pigeon

Elkhorn Camp

Winter Quarters

Cutler's Park

Allred's Camp

Centerville

Big Grove

Iranistan

Indian Town

McOlney's Camp

Whipple

Cold Spring

Omaha

Council Bluffs

Little Mosquito

Union

Upper Crossing, Keg Creek

Kanesville

Carterville

Grand Encampment

Wheeler's Grove

Stringtown

Bullock's Grove

Silver Creek

CASS CO.

Council Point

Hyde Park

Macedonia

MONTGOMERY CO.

Cold Spring Camp

Point aux poules

Pony Creek

Keg Creek

Prairie Flower

POTTAWATTAMIE CO.

Browning's Camp

MILLS CO.

Rushville

Farm Creek

MILLS CO.

Millville

MONTGOMERY CO.

Pacific City

Cutler's Camp

Old Agency

Coonville

Red Oak

Platville

Bethlehem

Indian Creek

Florence

Louden

California City

NEBRASKA

Pleasant Grove

Ross Grove

Wahagbonsy

MILLS CO.

MONTGOMERY CO.

FREMONT CO.

PAGE CO.

Osage

Missouri River

Dawsonburg

Studyville

Green Hollow

Plum Hollow

Shenandoah

Manti

S. Dak.

Wisconsin

Minnesota

Iowa

Nebraska

Map Location

Illinois

Kansas

Missouri

FREMONT CO.

PAGE CO.

Platte River

MISSOURI

| 0 | 5 | 10 | 15 km |
| 0 | 2 | 4 | 6 | 8 | 10 miles |

■ Location of early Mormon settlements in southwest Iowa, 1846–1853

From 1847 to 1853, 31,600 Mormons migrated to Utah.

BYU Geography Department

MIGRATION ROUTES TO THE WEST

A. Gary Anderson

Migration routes to the west developed in the early 1800s with the acquisition of the Oregon Territory on one hand and the autonomy of Mexico on the other. The interest developed further with the Mormon migration west in 1847, followed by the California gold rush in 1849.

Santa Fe Trail. When Mexico achieved independence from Spain in 1821, William Becknell, "Father of the Santa Fe Trail," forged westward from Franklin, Missouri, to Santa Fe to sell his goods, guided by a group of Mexican soldiers, thereby establishing a 900-mile trail. From 1827 until 1876, Independence, Missouri, served as the main outfitting point for the Santa Fe Trail. Westport, established 11 miles west of Independence in 1833, broke Independence's monopoly in the mid-1840s and remained the eastern terminus of the trail longer than any other. The outbreak of the Civil War in 1861 caused the trailhead to move upriver to Fort Leavenworth for security reasons. Westport and Fort Leavenworth also served travelers going to California and Oregon.

Responding to the Mexican War in 1846, Col. Stephen Kearny led U.S. troops along the Santa Fe Trail, including 541 volunteers recruited from Mormons at Council Bluffs, Iowa. Now referred to as the Mormon Battalion, the soldiers marched from Fort Leavenworth to Santa Fe, and then to San Diego.

By the time of the Civil War, Indian resistance had forced most trail traffic to use the longer but safer Mountain Route. Thereafter, the railroad moved westward, providing cheaper and faster transportation. In February 1880, as the first steam locomotive arrived at the New Mexico capital, the Santa Fe Trail's era passed silently into memory.

Oregon Trail. When Thomas Jefferson secured the Louisiana Purchase in 1803, the first to respond to a new interest in the West were fur trappers. A party led by Robert Stuart returned to St. Louis from the Columbia River to become the first group to travel the Oregon Trail in 1813, although in reverse. These mountain men became the guides to future emigrants.

Independence, Missouri, marked the beginning of the Oregon Trail in 1827, but by 1848 other cities upstream along the Missouri River took precedence. Westport and Fort Leavenworth gained prominence during the gold rush era of 1849–1852. By steaming two more days upstream from Independence to St. Joseph, emigrants saved almost two weeks of travel. The Pony Express also began here in 1860. The Council Bluffs area became the chief jumping-off point for all westward migration during the 1859–1886 period. The initial Mormon migration left from nearby Winter Quarters in 1847.

At least two government expeditions along the Oregon Trail ignited interest in westward expansion. Capt. Benjamin Bonneville headed west in 1832 with wagons along the Platte River through South Pass to the Green River area and later into Idaho. Lt. John C. Fremont's exploration expedition, guided by Kit Carson, traveled along the trail in 1842 to the Rocky Mountains and South Pass and then in 1843 and 1844 continued to Oregon. Fremont's maps plotted the route, and many emigrants used them, including Mormons.

After a group of Nez Perce and Flathead Indians traveled to St. Louis in 1831 seeking the "white man's book" (the Bible), Christian missionaries also turned their efforts to the West. A small slate marker on the Oregon Trail shows where Narcissa Prentiss Whitman and Eliza Hart Spalding, as part of the Whitman Mission to the Indians in 1836, became the "first white women to cross South Pass."

Mormon Trail. The Mormon Pioneer Trail stretches approximately 1,300 miles from Nauvoo, Illinois, to Salt Lake City. The first segment of the trail from Nauvoo to Council Bluffs, Iowa, approximately 265 miles in length, followed territorial roads and Indian trails across Iowa. Kanesville (now Council Bluffs) became the nucleus of the Mormon emigration.

The second and major segment of the trail stretched from present North Omaha (earlier Winter Quarters) and Florence, Nebraska, across Nebraska and Wyoming into Utah (1,032 miles). This part of the trail was used extensively from 1847 until completion of the transcontinental railroad in 1869.

The Latter-day Saints followed the Great Platte River Road, traveling the north branch of the Oregon Trail. Beginning in 1849, substantial numbers of Latter-day Saints traveled the southern bank of the Platte River. Of the 500,000 emigrants who followed the Great Platte River Road from 1841 to 1866, approximately 185,000 followed the northern route, known today as the Mormon Trail, although Mormons neither blazed the trail nor used it exclusively.

The Oregon, California, and Mormon trails are one trail from Fort Laramie to Fort Bridger. In the early development of these trails, there were many variants and cutoffs. About 1849, the nature of the Oregon Trail changed with the coming of the California gold rush and the forty-niners, the military presence, increased disease, physical improvements such as ferries and bridges, the appearance of steamboats on the Columbia River during the 1850s, and the beginnings of Indian troubles. With the 1860s came more changes—increased settlements, the Pony Express, telegraph, stagecoaches, and then the railroads. These newer modes of communication and transportation used the general route of the trail. While the railroads did not kill the use of the trail immediately, they altered the need for it.

Gregory M. Franzwa, *The Oregon Trail Revisited* (1988); Stanley B. Kimball, *Historic Sites and Markers along the Mormon and Other Great Western Trails* (1988); Merrill J. Mattes, *The Great Platte River Road* (1987); John D. Unruh, Jr., *The Plains Across* (1979).

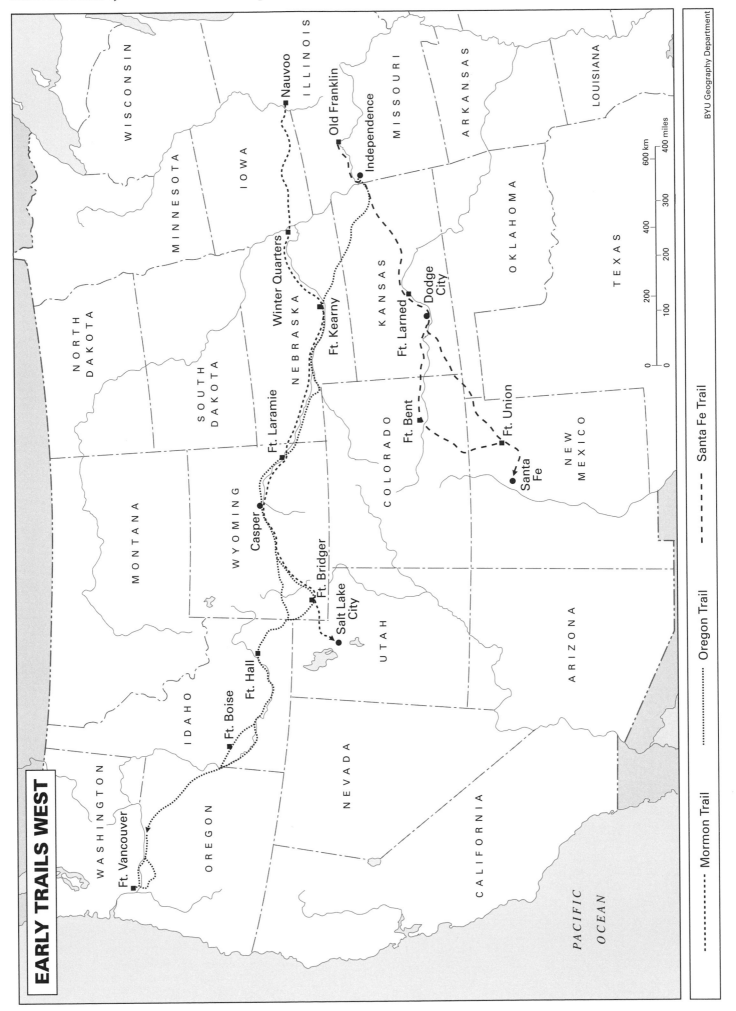

EARLY TRAILS WEST

BYU Geography Department

Mormon Trail ....

Oregon Trail ··········

Santa Fe Trail – – – –

77

SAM BRANNAN AND THE *BROOKLYN SAINTS*

Paul H. Peterson

The *Brooklyn* Saints were a group of some 220 Mormons residing in the eastern United States who traveled by sea to California. Following Brigham Young's advice to go west, they united under the leadership of Samuel Brannan and made a 17,000-mile voyage from New York City to California. Of the Latter-day Saints going westward in 1846—the Camp of Israel that went to the Great Salt Lake Valley, the Mormon Battalion, and the Mississippi Saints—the *Brooklyn* Saints alone traveled by sea.

Apostle Orson Pratt first issued the call to eastern Saints to join the general exodus westward. Angered at 16 years of persecution and convinced that Latter-day Saints would not find contentment in the United States, Pratt urged congregations everywhere to "be determined to flee out of Babylon, either by land or by sea" (*History of the Church* 7:520–522). In accord with Brigham Young's instruction, Samuel Brannan, publisher of the Church newspaper in New York City, was appointed to head the expedition. The ambitious Brannan, anticipating the eventual establishment of a Mormon headquarters on the Pacific coast, viewed the journey as an opportunity to gain influence and wealth. Conversely, Brigham Young envisioned Mormon settlers establishing not a permanent settlement but a way station in California where arriving Saints could rest and resupply themselves before making the final journey to Salt Lake City.

Of the 230 who sailed, all but 12 were Latter-day Saints. There were 70 men, 60 women, and 100 children. Adults paid $75 and children $37.50. They brought books, a printing press, guns, 800 pounds of paying freight bound for the Sandwich Islands, and enough agricultural and mechanical tools to equip 800 laborers. All of the people and cargo were crammed onto the ship *Brooklyn*, which Brannan had leased at the inexpensive rate of $1200 per month plus expenses. An average-size ship for its day, *Brooklyn* was 125 feet long and 28 feet across the beam and weighed about 445 tons.

Brooklyn sailed from New York harbor on February 4, 1846. Four days out, the ship encountered a severe gale that its experienced captain, Abel Richardson, pronounced the worst he had ever seen. Surviving the storm with the loss of only two cows, they proceeded south through the Atlantic toward Cape Horn. After three weeks, the ship passed near the Cape Verde Islands, off the African coast. Given the winds and currents, this was the most efficient route to California. When passing the equator, they were becalmed for three days. Boredom soon gave way to apprehension as they approached the dreaded Cape Horn. Captain Richardson avoided difficulty by bearing directly south several miles in order to

gain longitude west. The ship was soon sailing north along the coast of Chile.

The *Brooklyn* Saints had now been three months at sea and provisions had become scarce. A severe storm prevented a landing at Valparaiso, but on May 4 they landed at Juan Fernández Island. After five days of rest and replenishing, they set sail for the Sandwich Islands (Hawaiian Islands), arriving at Honolulu harbor on June 20, 1846. Here they learned that the United States was warring with Mexico and would likely seize California. *Brooklyn* left Hawaii on June 30 and sailed into Yerba Buena (now San Francisco) on July 31, where the U.S. flag flew over California. Their valorous voyage now complete, most of the Saints found work. Many helped build up the frontier village of Yerba Buena, while about 12 families founded the short-lived agricultural community of New Hope (1846–1848). Most, including Brannan, stayed in California, but some eventually moved to Utah.

The voyage of *Brooklyn* was both typical and eventful. The voyagers endured two severe storms, one in each ocean. Regular religious services were held, and, in general, the behavior of the Saints was laudable. There were two births; the infants were named, respectively, Atlantic and Pacific, after the oceans where they first saw life. Sadly, there were also twelve deaths: ten passengers and one crewman died at sea, and one small infant died of sickness at the Sandwich Islands.

The voyage of *Brooklyn* had significance for both western U.S. and Mormon history. On the one hand, the *Brooklyn* Saints served a largely symbolic role. They were too late to be included in that group of hardy pioneers who helped prepare California for eventual U.S. settlement. Further, despite the hopes of Brannan and others, they were never meant to serve as a vanguard for a permanent Mormon headquarters in California. On the other hand, like other contingents of Saints, whether encamped on the Great Plains or plodding through the desert with the Mormon Battalion, they were part of a courageous people who in 1846 opted to flee persecution and worldly allurement in order to establish a kingdom retreat in the Rocky Mountains.

Lewis Clark Christian, "A Study of the Mormon Westward Migration between February 1846 and July 1847 with Emphasis on the Evaluation of the Factors that Led to the Mormons' Choice of Salt Lake Valley as the Site of Their Initial Colony" (Ph.D. Diss., Brigham Young University, 1976), pp. 38–62; Lorin K. Hansen, "Voyage of the *Brooklyn*," *Dialogue: A Journal of Mormon Thought* 21 (Autumn 1988): 47–72.

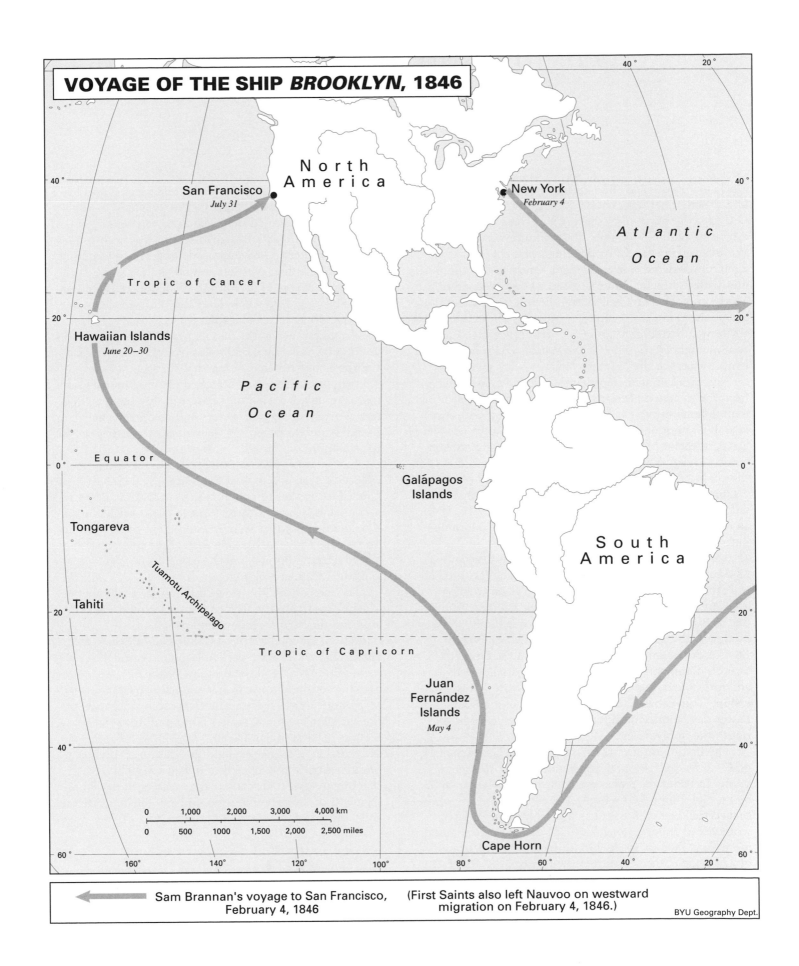

VOYAGE OF THE SHIP *BROOKLYN*, 1846

40°   20°

North America

San Francisco
July 31

New York
February 4

Atlantic Ocean

Tropic of Cancer

Hawaiian Islands
June 20–30

Pacific Ocean

Equator

Galápagos Islands

Tongareva

South America

Tuamotu Archipelago

Tahiti

Tropic of Capricorn

Juan Fernández Islands
May 4

Cape Horn

| 0 | 1,000 | 2,000 | 3,000 | 4,000 km |
| 0 | 500 | 1000 | 1,500 | 2,000 | 2,500 miles |

Sam Brannan's voyage to San Francisco, February 4, 1846

(First Saints also left Nauvoo on westward migration on February 4, 1846.)

BYU Geography Dept.

THE MORMON BATTALION

Susan Easton Black

On January 26, 1846, Brigham Young authorized Jesse C. Little to meet with national leaders in Washington, D.C., for the purpose of seeking government aid for migrating Latter-day Saints. Little journeyed to Washington in May 1846, arriving just eight days after Congress declared war on Mexico. On June 5, 1846, he met with President James K. Polk, who offered aid to the Mormon pioneers by permitting them to raise a battalion of 500 men. Little's acceptance of Polk's offer committed a Mormon battalion to join Col. Stephen Watts Kearny, commander of the Army of the West, to fight for the United States in the Mexican War.

Kearny appointed Capt. James Allen to enlist soldiers from the encamped Mormons in Iowa Territory. Allen met with disappointment as Mormons viewed him with suspicion. It was not until Brigham Young vigorously endorsed his recruitment of volunteers that the Mormon Battalion began to form. Young enthusiastically exclaimed, "Let the Mormons be the first to set their feet on the soil of California. . . . Hundreds would eternally regret that they did not go, when they had the chance." On July 16, 1846, an estimated 543 men were mustered into the Mormon Battalion at Council Bluffs, Iowa Territory.

They left Council Bluffs on July 20, 1846, accompanied by 33 women and 51 children. The soldiers trekked to Fort Leavenworth, where they were given weapons, accoutrements, and a clothing allowance of $42. The march from Leavenworth to Santa Fe was briefly delayed by the death of Allen, but under the new leadership of Lt. Col. A. J. Smith, the march to Santa Fe resumed. Smith's command was laced with dictatorial directives and forced marches. Sgt. Daniel Tyler wrote of his leadership, "I am satisfied that any other set of men but Latter-day Saints would have mutinied rather than submit to the oppressions."

The first division of the battalion approached Santa Fe on October 9, 1846, and was heralded by a 100-gun salute. In Santa Fe, Smith was relieved of his command by Lt. Col. Philip St. George Cooke. Cooke, aware of the rugged trail between Santa Fe and California, ordered women and children to accompany the sick of the battalion to Fort Pueblo. In Pueblo, three detachments, a total of 273 people, resided during the winter of 1846–1847.

The remaining soldiers, with five officers' wives, left Santa Fe for California on October 19, 1846. During this phase of the march, Sergeant Tyler wrote of Cooke's leadership, "We found the judgment of Colonel Cooke in traveling much better than that of Smith, in fact, it was first-class. He never crowded the men unnecessarily." The soldiers journeyed down the Rio Grande del Norte and crossed the Continental Divide. While moving up the San Pedro River, they were attacked by a herd of wild cattle. They continued their march toward Tucson, where they anticipated a fight with the garrisoned Mexican soldiers. The Mexican defenders had temporarily abandoned their position and no conflict ensued.

On December 21, 1846, the battalion encamped on the Gila River. Two weeks later they crossed the Colorado River into California. By January 29, 1847, they were camped at the San Diego Mission. Their military march of nearly 2,000 miles from Council Bluffs to California had ended. On January 30, 1847, Cooke penned, "History may be searched in vain for an equal march of infantry. Half of it has been through a wilderness where nothing but savages and wild beasts are found, or deserts where, for lack of water, there is no living creature."

To complete their enlistment, some soldiers were assigned to garrison duty at San Diego, San Luis Rey, and Ciudad de los Angeles, while others were designated to accompany General Kearny back to Fort Leavenworth. The battalion soldiers were mustered out of the military on July 16, 1847. Eighty-one men chose to reenlist and served eight additional months in California in Company A of the Mormon Volunteers.

The men of the Mormon Battalion are remembered for their loyalty to the United States during the Mexican War and their unprecedented march of nearly 2,000 miles from Council Bluffs to California. They are also acknowledged for their participation in the early development of the West and the building of the first wagon road over the southern route from California to Utah in 1848.

Historical sites recognizing the accomplishments of the battalion are the Mormon Battalion Memorial Visitors' Center in San Diego, Fort Moore Pioneer Memorial in Los Angeles, and the Mormon Battalion Monument at the state capitol in Salt Lake City. Monuments and trail markers have also been placed on segments of the battalion route in New Mexico, Arizona, and Colorado.

Frank Alfred Golder, *The March of the Mormon Battalion from Council Bluffs to California: Taken from the Journal of Henry Standage* (1928); Carl V. Larson, comp., *A Data Base of the Mormon Battalion: An Identification of the Original Members of the Mormon Battalion* (1987); Daniel Tyler, *A Concise History of the Mormon Battalion in the Mexican War, 1846–1847* (1969); John F. Yurtinus, "A Ram in the Thicket: The Mormon Battalion in the Mexican War" (Ph.D. diss., Brigham Young University, 1975).

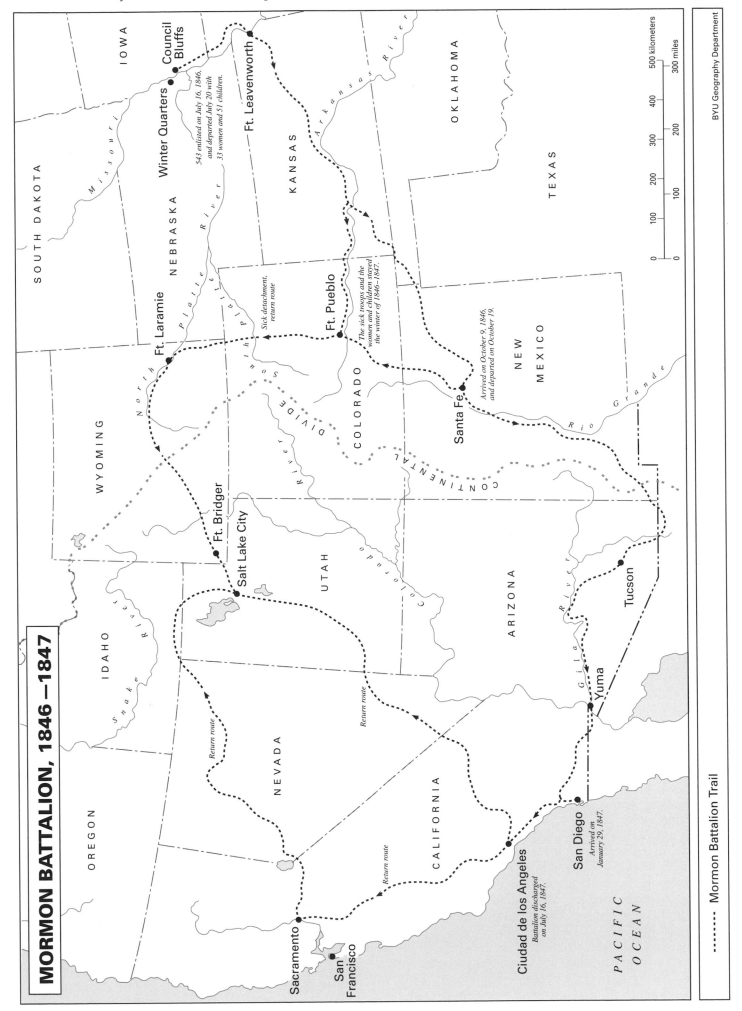

MORMON BATTALION, 1846–1847

IOWA

Council Bluffs

Winter Quarters

543 enlisted on July 16, 1846, and departed July 20 with 33 women and 51 children.

SOUTH DAKOTA

NEBRASKA

Missouri River

Ft. Leavenworth

KANSAS

Platte River

Arkansas River

OKLAHOMA

Ft. Laramie

North Platte River

South Platte River

Sick detachment, return route

Ft. Pueblo

The sick troops and the women and children stayed the winter of 1846–1847.

COLORADO

CONTINENTAL DIVIDE

Santa Fe

Arrived on October 9, 1846, and departed on October 19.

NEW MEXICO

TEXAS

WYOMING

Green River

Colorado River

Ft. Bridger

Salt Lake City

UTAH

Rio Grande

IDAHO

Snake River

OREGON

NEVADA

Return route

Return route

ARIZONA

Gila River

Tucson

Yuma

CALIFORNIA

Return route

Sacramento

San Francisco

Ciudad de los Angeles

Battalion discharged on July 16, 1847.

San Diego

Arrived on January 29, 1847.

PACIFIC OCEAN

500 kilometers

300 miles

0 100 200 300 400 500

0 100 200 300

BYU Geography Department

------ Mormon Battalion Trail

SALT LAKE CITY (1847)

Brian Q. Cannon

On Wednesday, July 21, 1847, Orson Pratt and Erastus Snow ascended Donner Hill and caught their first good view of the Salt Lake Valley. They "could not refrain from a shout of joy," Pratt recorded. Later that day, they briefly explored the valley before rejoining their company's wagon train in Emigration Canyon. On the following day, the first Mormon wagons lumbered into the valley. From the mouth of Emigration Canyon the pioneer company moved in a southwesterly direction, passing near the site of present-day Westminster College, and then turned almost due west. Oxen and wagons beat a path through thick stands of grass over six feet high. Thomas Bullock compared walking through the grass to "wading." When the wagons arrived at the north bank of Parley's Creek, near today's Fifth East between Sixteenth and Seventeenth South, they decided to stop: the site was, in Bullock's words, "bare enough for a camping ground, the grass being only knee deep, but very thick." Nine horsemen led by Orson Pratt devoted the remainder of the day to exploring the northern portion of the valley, and at length determined that the most promising site for farming lay along City Creek, two miles directly north of their temporary encampment.

Accordingly, on the following day the travelers relocated along the south bank of City Creek, between today's Third and Fourth South streets and Main and State streets. That evening Pratt designated the valley as sacred ground in a dedicatory prayer. Brigham Young and his fellow travelers entered the valley on July 24 and proceeded to the pioneer encampment.

Although they had decided to plant crops along City Creek, the pioneers continued to investigate other possible sites for a final encampment. On July 27 they met to discuss the subject. William Vance moved that the group send an expedition to the western shores of the Great Salt Lake before selecting the site for a settlement, but his suggestion inspired little enthusiasm among the other settlers. After some deliberation they opted to remain along City Creek.

Having selected the site for their settlement, the leaders began to make plans for distributing land to each household. Brigham Young indicated that "every man should have his land measured off to him for city and farming purposes, what he could till." Toward that end, Orson Pratt began a survey of the valley. Pratt's original rectangular plat, designated in subsequent years as Plat A, consisted of 135 blocks, although 22 of the blocks in the vicinity of Capitol Hill and City Creek Canyon were not divided into city lots as part of the survey. Plat A extended from Ninth South to Fifth North streets and from Fifth West to Third East streets. The survey provided for three public squares of ten acres each—the sites of Washington Square, Pioneer Park, and West High School today. The temple block, originally envisioned as a 40-acre tract, was reduced to a single ten-acre block. Aside from these public squares, city blocks consisted of eight lots of one and one-quarter acres each and were bounded by streets eight rods wide. Homes were to be built in the center of each lot and were to be set back 20 feet from the sidewalks.

While Pratt was laying out the new community, other residents labored to enclose a ten-acre public square known as the Old Fort—the site of present-day Pioneer Park—with a nine-foot-high adobe wall. Many families spent the winter there in log cabins that measured approximately 16 by 14 feet and leaked "like sieves" when it rained. To ease the crowding in the Old Fort, workers also enclosed additional tracts to the north and south of it in 1847. Approximately 1,700 settlers spent the winter of 1847–1848 in the valley.

Although some lots were tentatively assigned to residents in August of 1847, the lots were formally allotted by Brigham Young and Heber C. Kimball in the fall of 1848 following a land lottery. Men or women with families to support were entitled to a city lot along with as much farmland as they could productively utilize. Residents excavated ditches alongside the city streets to convey water from City Creek to every city lot.

Each lot was large enough to contain a small orchard and a garden. However, planners intended that large-scale farming would be conducted in the "big field," a vast area extending southward from the city. Lands from Ninth South to today's Twenty-first South were divided into five-acre parcels, with ten-acre lots extending southward from there to approximately Forty-fifth South. Although original plans called for additional plots of 20, 40, and 80 acres in the southern half of the valley, only the smaller plots of five and ten acres were allotted in 1848. The balance of the valley was initially designated as community pasture. At that early date, there was ample land in the valley for every inhabitant.

Thomas G. Alexander and James B. Allen, *Mormons & Gentiles: A History of Salt Lake City* (1984); Leland Hargrave Creer, *The Founding of an Empire: The Exploration and Colonization of Utah, 1776–1856* (1947); Richard H. Jackson, "Righteousness and Environmental Change: The Mormons and the Environment," in *Essays on the American West, 1973–74*, Thomas G. Alexander, editor (1974), pp. 321–342; John S. McCormick, *Salt Lake City: The Gathering Place* (1980).

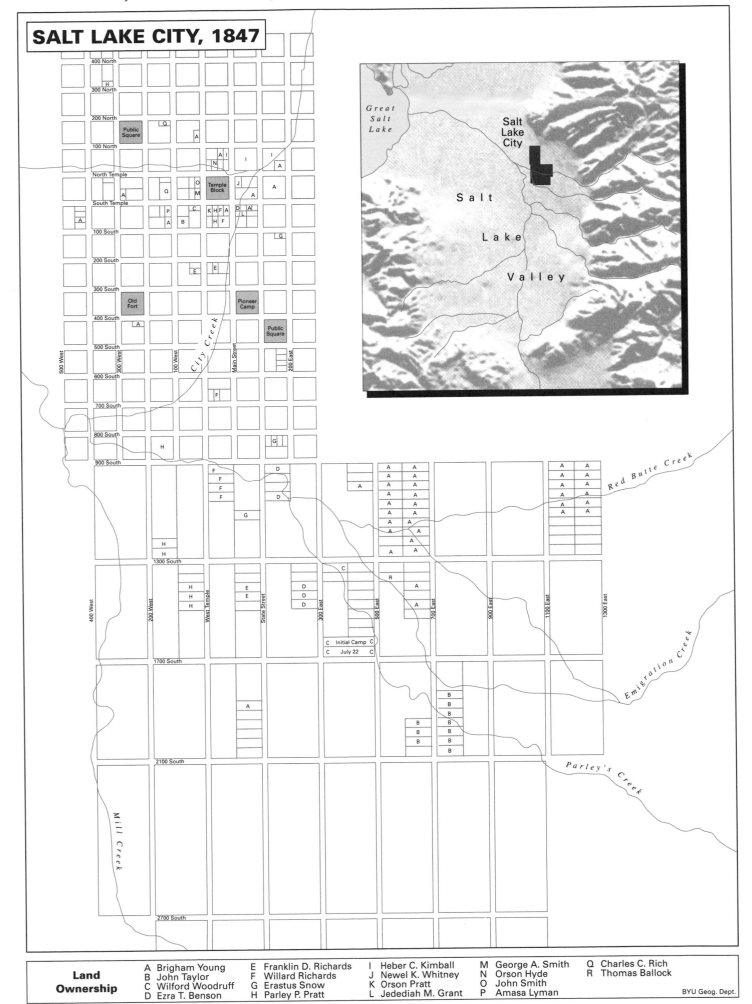

SALT LAKE CITY, 1847

Great Salt Lake

Salt Lake City

Salt Lake Valley

400 North
300 North
200 North
100 North
North Temple
South Temple
100 South
200 South
300 South
400 South
500 South
600 South
700 South
800 South
900 South
1300 South
1700 South
2100 South
2700 South

Public Square
Temple Block
Old Fort
Pioneer Camp
Public Square

City Creek
500 West
300 West
100 West
Main Street
200 East

400 West
200 West
West Temple
State Street
300 East
500 East
700 East
900 East
1100 East
1300 East

Red Butte Creek
Emigration Creek
Parley's Creek
Mill Creek

Initial Camp
July 22

Land Ownership						
A Brigham Young	E Franklin D. Richards	I Heber C. Kimball	M George A. Smith	Q Charles C. Rich
B John Taylor	F Willard Richards	J Newel K. Whitney	N Orson Hyde	R Thomas Ballock
C Wilford Woodruff	G Erastus Snow	K Orson Pratt	O John Smith	
D Ezra T. Benson	H Parley P. Pratt	L Jedediah M. Grant	P Amasa Lyman	

BYU Geog. Dept.

SALT LAKE VALLEY (1848–1870)

Brian Q. Cannon

By 1870, twenty-three years after the first Mormon settlers had arrived, Salt Lake County's population had soared to more than 18,000. Of that number nearly 13,000 resided in Salt Lake City, while 700 lived in nearby mining camps and over 4,000 inhabited farming districts in the valley.

The city itself had spread far beyond the original plat surveyed in 1847. Plat B, consisting of 63 blocks to the east of the original city, and Plat C, comprising 84 blocks to the west, had been added in 1848 and 1849, respectively. In the latter part of the 1850s, additional two-and-one-half-acre blocks had been surveyed north of South Temple Street between Third and Tenth East in the area that is today known as the Avenues. In the 1860s, additional blocks were added between Tenth and Fourteenth East. Fifty blocks were also surveyed north of Plats C and A.

By 1870, homes, farms, and villages dotted the valley beyond the city limits. Settlement of outlying farms had commenced in earnest as early as 1848, when groups of farmers had established the communities of Sugarhouse, four miles southeast of the city; East Millcreek, seven miles southeast of Salt Lake City; and Spring Creek (Holladay), nine miles southeast of the city, along Big Cottonwood Creek. In that same year, members of Amasa Lyman's pioneer company had taken up land between Big and Little Cottonwood creeks and named their settlement South Cottonwood. Other Mormons had located southwest of the city along the Jordan River at West Jordan and North Jordan (Taylorsville). In 1849, farmers established the nuclei for five other farm villages: Brighton and English Fort (Granger) along the Jordan River, Fort Union (also called Union; originally part of South Cottonwood), Butterfield (Herriman) along Butterfield Creek, 22 miles southwest of Salt Lake City, and Willow Creek (Draper), in the extreme southeastern corner of the valley. Throughout the 1850s, settlers filled in additional lands along the Jordan River, taking up farms in East Jordan (Midvale) as early as 1851 and at South Jordan in 1859.

Not only residential districts and farms but a variety of industrial enterprises and businesses were established in the valley between 1847 and 1870. Within ten years of the first settlers' arrival in the valley, over two dozen mills were operating in the valley and surrounding canyons. In 1870, businesses were concentrated in the district between West Temple and 200 East and between South Temple and 300 South. Main Street was particularly crowded with businesses, including a bakery, a furniture store, blacksmith shops, a millinery, a telegraph office, a barbershop, and dry goods and grocery stores.

The fall of 1861 brought the Overland Telegraph's utility poles and telegraph wires to the city's streets. In 1862, American soldiers under the command of Col. Patrick Edward Connor established a military reservation, Fort Douglas, on the bench east of Salt Lake City. In 1870 the Utah Central Railroad Depot opened south of North Temple Street in the block between Third and Fourth West.

Although Salt Lake County's tremendous boom in commercial mining did not occur until the 1870s, mines and mining camps were located in Bingham and Little Cottonwood canyons as early as 1863 and 1864. In 1870, Woodhull Brothers established the valley's first smelter along Big Cottonwood Creek in present day Murray.

By 1870, impressive brick and stone buildings graced Salt Lake City. The oldest of these was a two-story building of sandstone and adobe known as the Council House that was located on the southwest corner of Main and South Temple streets. Completed in 1850, the Council House served first as an office building for Mormon Church leaders and subsequently housed the legislature, the territorial public library, a fledgling university, and the *Deseret News*. In 1852, workers had constructed a tithing store and storehouse on the northeast corner of South Temple and Main streets and the Social Hall, situated on the east side of State Street between South Temple and First South streets. Also in 1852, settlers had completed an adobe tabernacle seating 2,500 on the southwest corner of the temple block. Not until 1867 was the present Mormon Tabernacle completed. Mormons also constructed the Endowment House in the northwestern portion of the temple block in the 1850s and in 1853 began work on the Salt Lake Temple. In 1862, an imposing theater with a seating capacity of 3,000 was completed on the northwest corner of First South and State streets.

Residents of the Salt Lake Valley in 1870 could take pride in many facets of the city and farms that they had created. Mormon apostle Orson Hyde, however, noted one disquieting consequence of settlement. In 1865 he reflected, "When our brethren, the Pioneers, first landed here in '47 there was an abundance of grass. . . . There is now nothing but the desert weed, the sage, the rabbit-bush and such like plants that make very poor feed for stock" (*Journal of Discourses* 11:149).

Thomas G. Alexander and James B. Allen, *Mormons & Gentiles: A History of Salt Lake City* (1984); Leland Hargrave Creer, *The Founding of an Empire: The Exploration and Colonization of Utah, 1776–1856* (1947); John S. McCormick, *Salt Lake City: The Gathering Place* (1980); Utah State Historical Society, *The Valley of the Great Salt Lake*, 3d edition (1967).

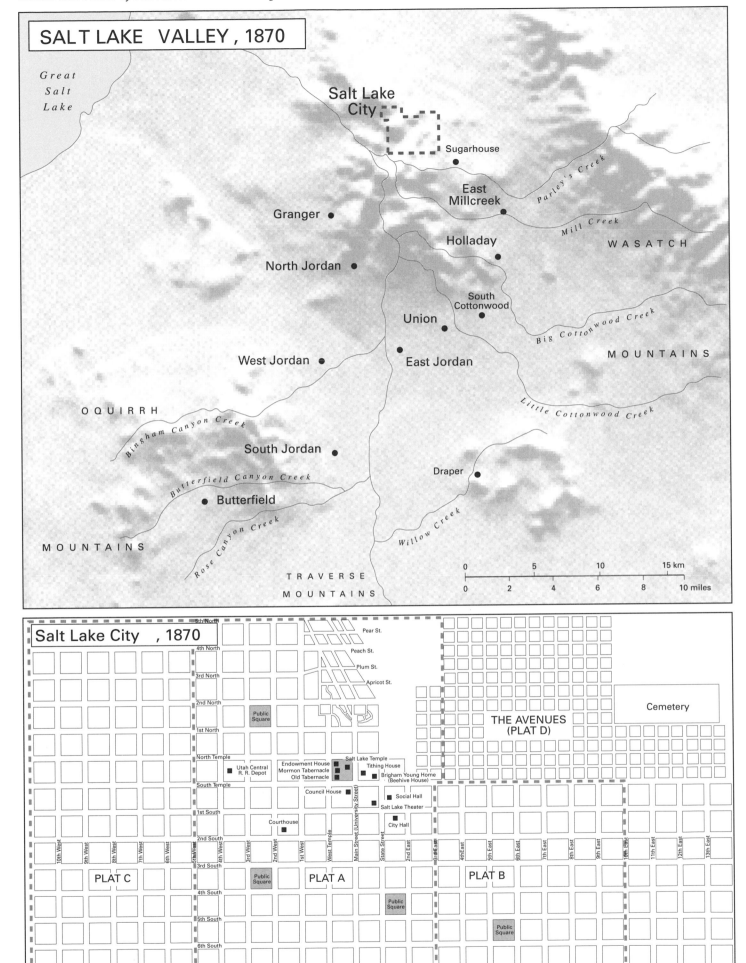

SALT LAKE VALLEY, 1870

Great Salt Lake

Salt Lake City

Sugarhouse

East Millcreek

Parley's Creek

Granger

Holladay

Mill Creek

WASATCH

North Jordan

South Cottonwood

Union

Big Cottonwood Creek

MOUNTAINS

West Jordan

East Jordan

Little Cottonwood Creek

OQUIRRH

Bingham Canyon Creek

South Jordan

Draper

Butterfield Canyon Creek

Butterfield

Rose Canyon Creek

Willow Creek

MOUNTAINS

TRAVERSE
MOUNTAINS

| 0 | | 5 | | 10 | | 15 km |
| 0 | 2 | 4 | 6 | 8 | | 10 miles |

Salt Lake City, 1870

5th North
Pear St.
4th North
Peach St.
3rd North
Plum St.
Apricot St.
2nd North
Public Square
1st North

THE AVENUES
(PLAT D)

Cemetery

North Temple

Utah Central R. R. Depot

Endowment House
Mormon Tabernacle
Old Tabernacle

Salt Lake Temple
Tithing House
Brigham Young Home (Beehive House)

South Temple

Council House

Social Hall
Salt Lake Theater

1st South

Courthouse

City Hall

2nd South

10th West
9th West
8th West
7th West
6th West
5th West
4th West
3rd West
2nd West
1st West
West Temple
Main Street (University Street)
State Street
2nd East
3rd East
4th East
5th East
6th East
7th East
8th East
9th East
10th East
11th East
12th East
13th East

3rd South

PLAT C

Public Square

PLAT A

PLAT B

4th South

Public Square

5th South

Public Square

6th South

- - - - - - — Original land surveys

BYU Geography Department

MORMON TRAIL

Wayne L. Wahlquist

The Mormon migration to the Mountain West began with the expulsion of Mormons from Nauvoo, Illinois, in 1846. The first refugees left the state in early February, and the last were driven out in September. An estimated 12,000 to 16,000 people evacuated Nauvoo and its hinterland and found themselves scattered across Iowa during 1846 and 1847. Upon reaching the Missouri River, they began congregating at the present site of Council Bluffs, which they named Kanesville in honor of Col. Thomas L. Kane, who had befriended them earlier and who then visited them on the Missouri. A larger number moved to the west side of the river. After examining several locales, a town site—Winter Quarters—was surveyed on the bluff above the west bank of the Missouri in what is now Florence in North Omaha. Here the majority built what shelters they could to enable them to survive the coming winter. Nearly 4,000 spent the winter in cabins, caves, or sod hovels. Approximately 400 did not survive because of inadequate shelter, winter cold, and an outbreak of cholera. An even larger number, approximately 10,000, were scattered in camps across Iowa. Winter Quarters served not only as a temporary hearth, where Mormon leaders could collect their flock and prepare for the long trek to the Salt Lake Valley, but also as the primary launching site for Mormon immigrants for the next several years.

Under Brigham Young, a pioneer company of 144 persons left Winter Quarters on April 14, 1847, to establish a route to the Salt Lake Valley, later to be followed by thousands of others. En route, 19 men left the company on other assignments and 35 persons were added. The company moved west to the Platte River and then continued along its north bank. A well-traveled route, the Oregon Trail, followed the river on its south side. At one point the pioneer company debated crossing the Platte and following the Oregon Trail, but determined that for the thousands to follow, it would be better to keep the Mormon Trail on the north side to minimize contact with Oregon-bound immigrants.

At first, distances were estimated; later they were measured by tying a piece of cloth to a wagon wheel and counting the revolutions. That task proved to be too laborious, and an odometer was rigged that would measure distances automatically. Not only did the pioneer company measure distances (1,031 miles between Winter Quarters and Salt Lake City); they also calculated longitude and latitude coordinates of significant points along the trail and used a barometer to determine elevations.

They also recorded vegetation and rock strata through which they passed.

The Mormon Trail followed the North Platte as far as Fort Laramie, Wyoming. Here the pioneer company crossed the river and followed the Oregon Trail to Fort Bridger. At difficult river crossings the company constructed ferries and left small contingents to operate the ferries for immigrant trains that would follow. At Fort Bridger the trails split, the Oregon Trail turning northwestward and the Mormon Trail following the Hastings cutoff southwestward to the Salt Lake Valley, the route pioneered by the ill-fated Donner-Reed company the year before.

Although the staging areas for beginning the trek west varied, the route established by the initial pioneer company became the highway for approximately 62,000 Mormons who migrated to Salt Lake Valley before the completion of the railroad in 1869. In 1849, a revolving trust—the Perpetual Emigration Fund—was established to assist refugees scattered through Iowa and Missouri to emigrate to Utah. It soon became the means of assisting thousands of European converts to immigrate whose continual influx meant that the Mormon Trail remained in use until the completion of the railroad.

An innovative transportation system was introduced in 1856 when several companies traversed the entire distance with handcarts. At first this seemed to be the fastest and cheapest method of travel. But when two companies that left too late in the season were caught by winter snows in Wyoming, 222 people perished from exposure. By 1860, handcarts had been abandoned.

The Mormon Trail has become something of an icon in Mormon culture. The shared experience of the Great Trek to the Salt Lake Valley helped to bond and solidify several generations of Mormons, who still feel a strong kinship with their pioneer ancestors. Mormon hymns, folk songs, stage productions, and pioneer day celebrations help to engrave the Mormon Trail experience deep into the Mormon psyche.

LeRoy Hafen and Ann W. Hafen, *Handcarts to Zion: 1856–1860* (1960); Stanley B. Kimball, *Historic Resource Study: Mormon Pioneer National Historic Trail* (1991); Brigham H. Roberts, *A Comprehensive History of The Church of Jesus Christ of Latter-day Saints*, Vol. 3 (1930); Wayne L. Wahlquist, "Settlement Processes in the Mormon Core Area 1847–1890" (Ph.D. diss., University of Nebraska, 1974).

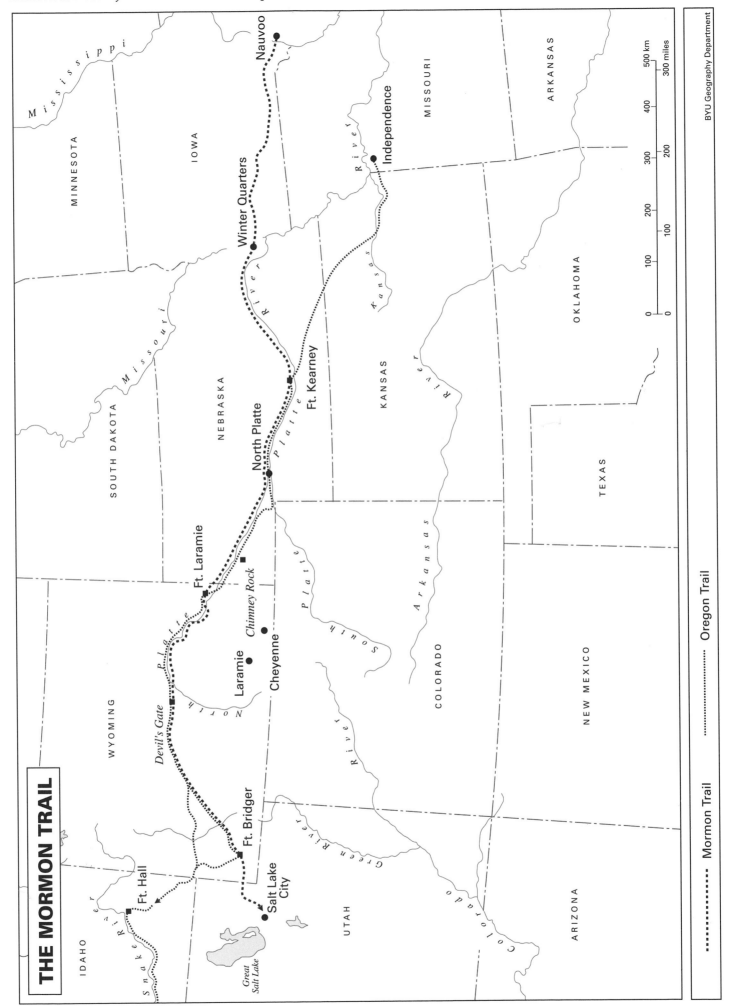

THE MORMON TRAIL

BYU Geography Department

- - - - - Mormon Trail
·········· Oregon Trail

EXPANSION ALONG THE WASATCH FRONT

Dean L. May

On July 22, 1847, the pioneer company of Latter-day Saints colonizing the Rocky Mountain West began settlement of what geographers now call the Wasatch Oasis, a series of narrow crescents of arable land rimming the western flanks of the Wasatch Mountains from present-day Brigham City southward to Nephi. The first site occupied was the northeastern part of the Salt Lake Valley. On July 22, 1847, before Brigham Young himself had entered "The Valley" (as they then and forever after called it), the pioneer company began plowing and planting. Within a few weeks they had explored the valley and its surrounding canyons, participated in a ritual rebaptism to sanctify their new beginning in the West, constructed a fort with adobe walls on three sides to enclose the rustic log cabins they were building, surveyed a city of 135 ten-acre blocks, harvested salt from the lake, put a whipsaw into operation, built a boat, hewn out a canyon road, set up a blacksmith shop, and established an adobe yard. By December 7, they had planted 2,000 acres of fall wheat, looking to the need to feed the nearly 2,000 people who already had arrived, as well as those who would be coming the next season. Great Salt Lake City, as it was then called, had been founded—the first Mormon settlement in the Great Basin, the future capital of Utah, and still a mecca for Mormons throughout the world.

The new arrivals immediately began seeking sites to settle both north and south of the city along the Wasatch Front. On September 29, 1847, Peregrine Sessions claimed land in the area that became Bountiful, directly north of Salt Lake City, making it the second oldest Mormon settlement in the region. The next year others moved farther south in the Salt Lake Valley to settle Sugarhouse, Mill Creek, and South Cottonwood; and north, occupying favorable sites at Centerville, Farmington, and Ogden, the latter including lands along the Weber River recently purchased from mountain man Miles Goodyear.

The most dramatic aspect of 1850 settlement was the further spread into the Utah valley, the site of six of nine new colonies founded that year—Alpine, American Fork, Lehi City, Payson, Pleasant Grove, and Springville. The other three were near already established towns between Salt Lake City and Ogden.

The year 1851 represented the apogee and the culmination of the Wasatch Front period of settlement. In that year, 15 new settlements were established, far more than in any year until 1859. They included Brigham City and Nephi, framing Wasatch Front expansion on the north and on the south. Also in that year the southern Utah outposts of Parowan and Cedar City were founded.

It was common, when a particular need required movement far beyond the advancing line of settlement, for Church leaders to resort to the central planning of a new colony and then call or assign leaders and settlers to launch the enterprise. Salt Lake City (1847), Provo and Manti (1849), and Parowan (1851) were founded through such means. But as soon as the new colony was established, satellite towns grew up spontaneously in each vicinity until all available sites were filled.

This technique of settlement, often noted and described as typical of Mormon colonization, was employed along the Wasatch Front only in founding Salt Lake City and the first of the Utah valley settlements, Provo. Salt Lake City, was, of course, the mother colony for the whole Great Basin region. In the Utah valley, Church leaders fostered a concerted effort because they feared (with good reason) Native American resistance. Elsewhere along the Wasatch Front, the stream of immigrants filled arable spaces spontaneously, without resort to planned and called colonization.

The rate of new foundings was strong and sustained until 1852, when the number of new colonies each year declined dramatically for a seven-year period, to surge again in 1859. Two Mormon colonies had been founded in Utah in 1847, six in 1848, nine each in 1849 and 1850, 15 in 1851, and between one and four each year until 1859, when 26 new colonies were established, a consequence of increasing population pressures pushing them beyond the safe haven of the well-established Wasatch Front to the Cache, Heber, and Pahvant valleys and to southeastern Utah.

Eugene E. Campbell, *Establishing Zion: The Mormon Church in the American West, 1847–1869* (1988); Milton R. Hunter, *Brigham Young the Colonizer* (1973); Richard H. Jackson, editor, *The Mormon Role in the Settlement of the West* (1978); Wayne L. Wahlquist, "Settlement Processes in the Mormon Core Area, 1847–1890" (Ph.D. diss., University of Nebraska, 1974).

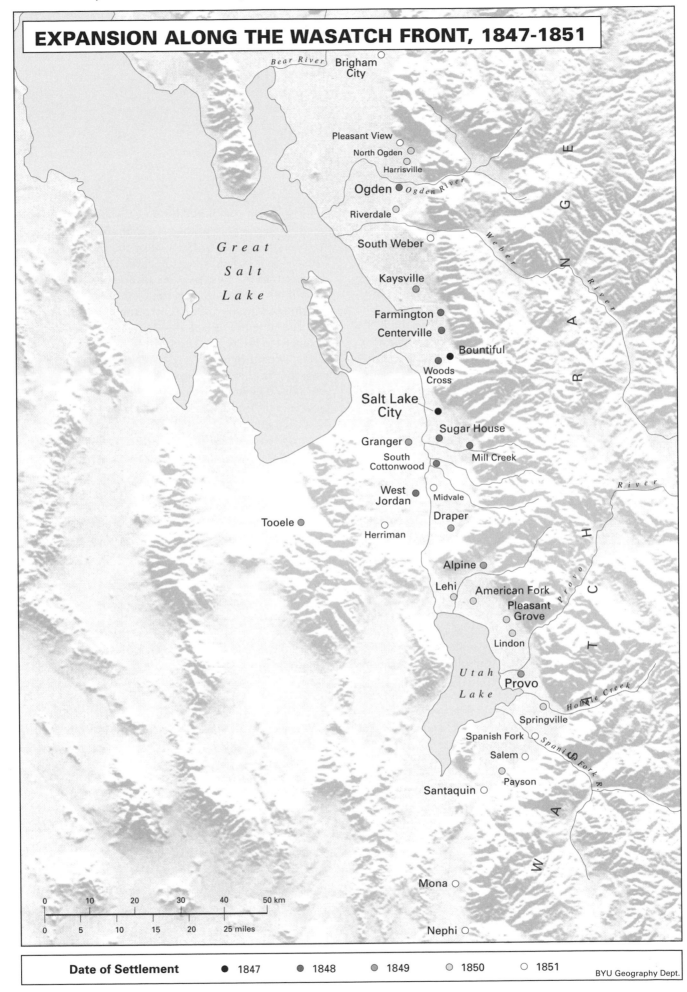

EXPANSION ALONG THE WASATCH FRONT, 1847-1851

Bear River

Brigham City

Pleasant View

North Ogden

Harrisville

Ogden — *Ogden River*

Riverdale

Great Salt Lake

South Weber

Weber River

Kaysville

Farmington

Centerville

Bountiful

Woods Cross

Salt Lake City

Sugar House

Granger

Mill Creek

South Cottonwood

River

West Jordan

Midvale

Tooele

Draper

Herriman

Alpine

Lehi

American Fork

Provo

Pleasant Grove

Lindon

Utah Lake

Provo

Hobble Creek

Springville

Spanish Fork

Spanish Fork R.

Salem

Payson

Santaquin

W A S A T C H   R A N G E

Mona

| 0 | 10 | 20 | 30 | 40 | 50 km |

| 0 | 5 | 10 | 15 | 20 | 25 miles |

Nephi

Date of Settlement   ● 1847   ● 1848   ● 1849   ○ 1850   ○ 1851

BYU Geography Dept.

THE STATE OF DESERET

Dean L. May

The earliest Anglo-American settlers of the Great Basin, like those of Oregon and California, took action to establish a provisional government while waiting for the U.S. Congress to act. The region became U.S. territory on February 2, 1848, under terms of the treaty of Guadalupe Hidalgo, which ended the war between Mexico and the United States. In December, a body of Mormon leaders called the Council of Fifty prepared a petition to the U.S. Congress for the establishment of a territorial government. They then proceeded to organize a civil government, the populace voting on March 12 to form the state of Deseret, and approving as principal officers Brigham Young, governor; Willard Richards, secretary; Heber C. Kimball, chief justice of the Supreme Court; Newel K. Whitney and John Taylor, associate justices; and local judges that included bishops of each of the 19 wards of Salt Lake City. The legislature, or General Assembly, met on July 2, chose Almon W. Babbitt to be delegate to the U.S. Congress, and then decided to petition Congress for statehood rather than territorial status.

The proposed state was to be called Deseret, a Book of Mormon word meaning "honeybee," symbolizing both industry and the cooperative, communal organization of their society. The constitution provided for a bicameral legislature and for executive and judicial branches of government. It affirmed religious freedom and separation of church and state. However, with the great majority of the population Mormon, Church leaders—especially members of the Council of Fifty—were the sole candidates for office. Mormons at the time believed that the state of Deseret was to be the beginning of the Kingdom of God on earth, would supersede all other civil authority, and should appropriately be under ecclesiastical control.

The petition proposed vast boundaries, some 490,000 square miles, extending from the Colorado Rockies to the Sierras and from the Oregon Country to the Gila River, with a southern salient stretching west to include the Pacific coast from Los Angeles to San Diego. Such extensive claims were justified by the service of Mormons in the Mexican War, the leaders maintaining in a petition to Congress that "we have done more by our arms and influence than any other equal number of citizens to obtain and secure this country to the government of the United States."

Thomas L. Kane, a friend and political adviser to the Mormons, had urged them to press for statehood rather than territorial status, but the petition became bogged down in high-level political dealing to determine the status of slavery in the territory conquered from Mexico. The wrangling was resolved in the Compromise of 1850, which denied statehood, but on September 9, 1850, created a considerably pruned-back, though still enormous, territory to be named Utah, after the most powerful of the resident Indian tribes, the Utes. A central provision of the compromise was popular sovereignty—that Congress would take no position on the status of slavery in Utah, leaving the matter ultimately to the local citizenry.

The state of Deseret was the sole functioning civil government in the region from July 2, 1849, until February 5, 1851, when Brigham Young took the oath of office as governor of the newly created Utah Territory. During this period the General Assembly of Deseret launched civil government in the Great Basin. It established a judiciary at local, county, and state levels; it passed acts incorporating major towns, cities, and institutions, including the Latter-day Saint Church. It created counties and county governments. It sought to maintain public control over canyons and canyon resources by granting rights to trusted high Church officials. The validity of these acts was affirmed by officers of the territorial government (most of them the same persons) after the General Assembly of Deseret dissolved on April 5, 1851.

The granting of territorial status to the region did not end the Mormon leaders' hopes to one day see the state of Deseret realized. Congress denied the petition, but anticipating a collapse of federal authority because of the Civil War, a ghost government, with a full slate of elected officers, was formed in 1862 and continued throughout the decade to meet each year and enact the same laws passed by the territorial legislature.

By that time the very name Deseret had come to symbolize for Mormons independence from outside control and influence, and thus carried within it political, social, and economic agendas. Attempts to gain statehood under the name of Deseret were made in 1849, 1862, 1867, and 1872. However, the constitution that was submitted to Congress in 1882, like the later ones of 1887 and 1895, contained the name Utah, suggesting a strategic retreat from earlier social values in favor of those of the American mainstream. The dream of founding a state of Deseret was realized in part when Utah became a state in 1896, but the territory it covered, like the concept itself, was shorn and altered by the realities of American political life.

Eugene E. Campbell, *Establishing Zion: The Mormon Church in the American West, 1847–1869* (1988); Gustive O. Larson, *The "Americanization" of Utah for Statehood* (1971); Edward Leo Lyman, *Political Deliverance: The Mormon Quest for Utah Statehood* (1986); Dale L. Morgan, *The State of Deseret* (1987).

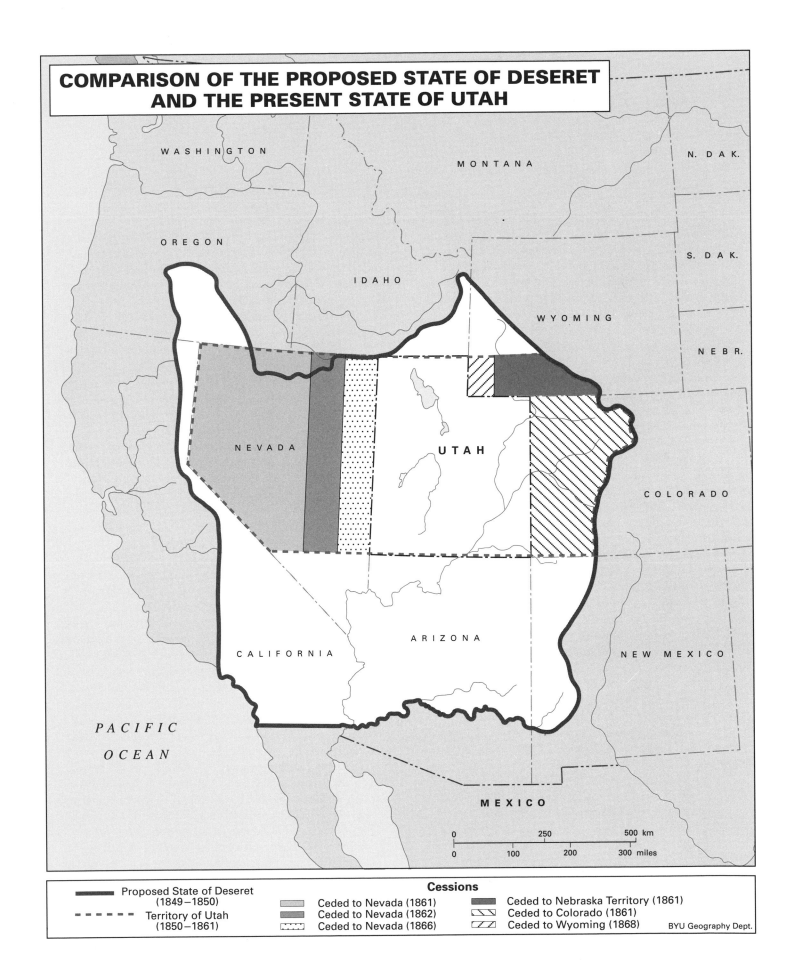

COMPARISON OF THE PROPOSED STATE OF DESERET AND THE PRESENT STATE OF UTAH

WASHINGTON

OREGON

MONTANA

N. DAK.

S. DAK.

IDAHO

WYOMING

NEBR.

NEVADA

UTAH

COLORADO

CALIFORNIA

ARIZONA

NEW MEXICO

PACIFIC OCEAN

MEXICO

| 0 | 250 | 500 km |
| 0 | 100 | 200 | 300 miles |

—— Proposed State of Deseret (1849–1850)

– – – Territory of Utah (1850–1861)

Cessions

Ceded to Nevada (1861)
Ceded to Nevada (1862)
Ceded to Nevada (1866)

Ceded to Nebraska Territory (1861)
Ceded to Colorado (1861)
Ceded to Wyoming (1868)

BYU Geography Dept.

EXPLORING THE WEST BEFORE 1847

Fred R. Gowans

By 1847, when the Mormon pioneers arrived in the valley of the Great Salt Lake, Spanish, French, and American fur traders, trappers, immigrants, and government explorers had accumulated and made available to the public a significant amount of data about the region. The discovery in the 1970s of the journal of Juan Maria Antonio Rivera in Madrid, Spain, has convinced most scholars that Rivera's journey of 1765 into the Moab area of east-central Utah represents the first documented exploration of the region.

In 1776, Spain launched the now celebrated Dominguez-Escalante Expedition. One expedition member was Don Bernardo Miera y Pacheco, whose map is the first cartographic representation of Utah's geography. Fray Francisco Atanasio Dominguez and Fray Silvestre Velez de Escalante journeyed almost 2,000 miles, traveling through large portions of New Mexico, Colorado, Utah, and Arizona. The padres' daily journal furnishes extensive information concerning present-day Utah.

Jules Remy, who visited Salt Lake City, Utah Territory, in 1855, reported that he was shown a cave located on the shore of the Great Salt Lake; the cave contained the following inscription: "Lecarne 17—." It appears that even French traders, possibly from St. Louis or Canada, had pushed their trading frontier to the Great Basin. Certainly, records in both Spanish and French archives suggest that there were other documented accounts of 18th-century activities in the Utah area that have remained elusive but that may someday be found.

In 1808, George Drouillard presented William Clark a map of the upper Missouri country that reveals there was trade between the Crow Indians and the Spanish settlements of the Southwest. This map presents the possibility of Spanish traders traversing the Great Basin and central Rockies while conducting trade with various tribes.

The Overland Astorians, under the command of Wilson Price Hunt and representing John Jacob Astor's Pacific Fur Company, left St. Louis en route to the Oregon country with aspirations of securing control of the fur trade in that region. Hunt left five men near present-day Rexburg, Idaho, with orders to explore and trap the area. The account of their wanderings during the years 1811 and 1812 discloses their presence in the Bear River country of northern Utah and southwestern Wyoming.

The failure of Andrew Henry and William Ashley (Henry-Ashley Company) to open trade relations with the Indians on the upper Missouri River in 1822 and 1823 forced the partners to send their engages to the Rocky Mountains in search of furs. Jedediah Smith, in command of a portion of the men, crossed South Pass in March 1824 and established a unique commercial system that enabled the fur companies to prosper in those remote regions and allowed their men to provide the most extensive exploration of Utah prior to the arrival of the Mormons. During the next 16 years mountaineers would add the physical geography of present-day Utah to their knowledge of the landscape of the American West and would record in journals, letters, and maps their impressions of this new land. In 1825, Étienne Provost, representing prominent Santa Fe merchants, and Peter Skene Ogden's Hudson's Bay Company Snake River Brigade were also trading and trapping along the Wasatch Front of Utah.

Exploring and trading expeditions under the leadership of Étienne Provost (1824–1825), Jedediah Smith (1824–1827), William H. Ashley (1824–1826), Daniel T. Potts (1825–1828), Peter Skene Ogden (1825 and 1829), Warren A. Ferris (1830–1835), John Work (1831), Antoine Robidoux (1832), Joseph Walker (1833–1834), and Osborne Russell (1834–1842) represent some of the documented accounts of Utah exploration.

The fashion change from beaver to silk hats destroyed the beaver trade in the central Rockies. However, as one era of western history passed away, a new one was born: the Immigrant Era. As immigrants crossed Utah's future boundaries, additional information found its way to the East. In 1841, the Bartleson-Bidwell party departed from a westbound wagon train traveling over the old fur highway en route to the Oregon country near present-day Soda Springs, Idaho. The small group, continuing to California, crossed the northwestern corner of present-day Utah, giving birth to what would become the California Trail, one of the major overland routes in the westward movement.

John C. Fremont, the most popularized government explorer, traversed present-day Utah in both 1843 and 1845, making available not only detailed reports and maps of the newly named Oregon Trail, but also significant information on the American West, including large portions of Utah. Fremont's contributions had a profound impact on the Mormons and their colonization of the Valley of the Great Salt Lake.

The year 1846 represents the close of pre-Mormon exploration, but with it came calamity. In that year four emigrant parties left the Oregon Trail at Fort Bridger to follow the highly publicized Hastings cutoff. History has recorded the tragedy of the fourth group, the Donner-Reed Party. Ironically, it was the efforts of this ill-fated party that opened the route from Fort Bridger to the valley of the Great Salt Lake for the Mormon pioneers the following year.

Angelico Chavez, translator, and Ted J. Warner, editor, *The Dominguez-Escalante Journal: Their Expedition through Colorado, Utah, Arizona, and New Mexico in 1776* (1976); William H. Goetzmann, *Exploration and Empire* (1966); Fred R. Gowans, *Rocky Mountain Rendezvous* (1976); Dale L. Morgan, *The Great Salt Lake* (1947).

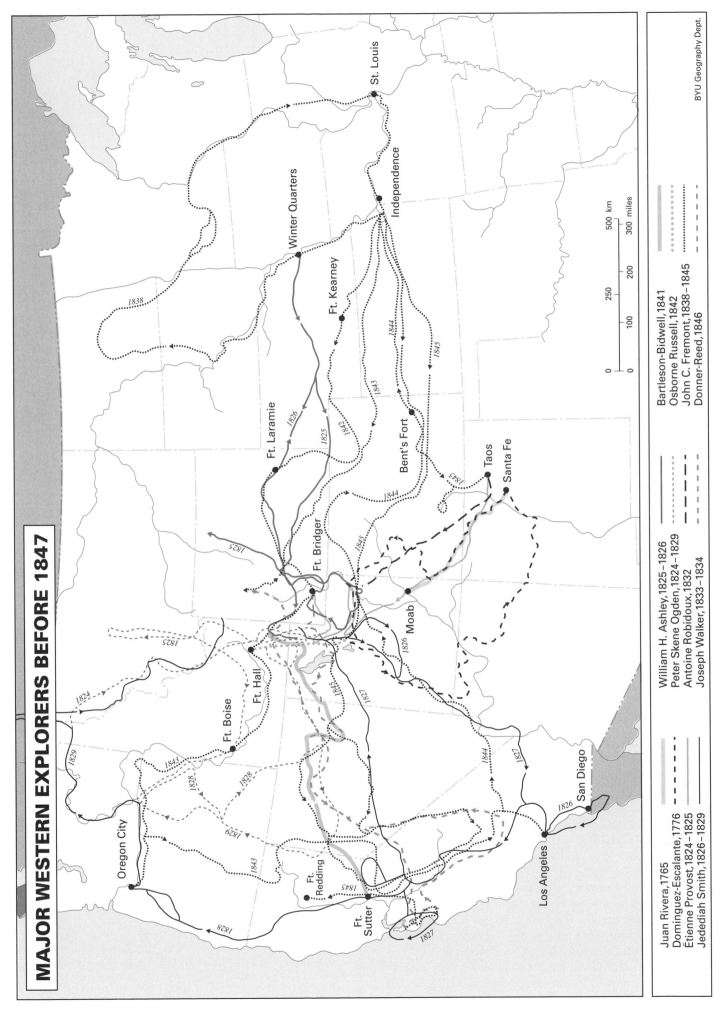

MAJOR WESTERN EXPLORERS BEFORE 1847

Juan Rivera, 1765
Dominguez-Escalante, 1776
Étienne Provost, 1824–1825
Jedediah Smith, 1826–1829

William H. Ashley, 1825–1826
Peter Skene Ogden, 1824–1829
Antoine Robidoux, 1832
Joseph Walker, 1833–1834

Bartleson-Bidwell, 1841
Osborne Russell, 1842
John C. Fremont, 1838–1845
Donner-Reed, 1846

BYU Geography Dept.

St. Louis
Independence
Winter Quarters
Ft. Kearney
Ft. Laramie
Bent's Fort
Taos
Santa Fe
Moab
Ft. Bridger
Ft. Hall
Ft. Boise
Oregon City
Ft. Redding
Ft. Sutter
San Diego
Los Angeles

500 km
300 miles
0   100   200   250

EXPLORING THE WEST AFTER 1847

Vivian Linford Talbot and Fred R. Gowans

After 1847, most of the exploration of the Great Basin was carried out by U.S. military personnel, especially members of the Army Corps of Topographical Engineers. They located and surveyed geographical features, studied the native flora and fauna, and made ethnological observations. The resulting maps, road locations, and other data were invaluable to local Latter-day Saints who could not have afforded such studies. Moreover, reports generated by the surveyors were of interest to an eastern public eager to learn more about the American West. These explorers became a link between earlier exploration by Indians and fur trappers on the one hand, and later civilian scientists on the other.

Army Corps member Howard Stansbury received orders in early spring of 1849 to make a reconnaissance of the Platte River Trail, proceeding west across the Wasatch Mountains to Salt Lake City. Stansbury's assignments included a survey of the Great Salt Lake Valley, a study of the resident Indian tribes and the Mormons, the location of a supply route from the valley north to the Oregon-California emigrant trail, and the study of the natural resources in the area. Stansbury was the first explorer known to circumnavigate the Great Salt Lake by land; his expedition completed surveys of the Jordan River and Utah Lake. On his return East in the fall of 1850, Stansbury located a new route crossing present-day Wyoming, which would later be utilized by the Overland Stage, the Pony Express, and the Union Pacific Railroad.

John Gunnison was second in command of the Stansbury expedition and supervised much of the surveying in Salt Lake Valley. He assisted Stansbury in preparing an excellent report with accompanying maps. He also wrote a well-circulated book that presented an objective view of the Mormons based on his year's stay in the valley. Commissioned to lead the survey of a possible transcontinental railroad route along the 38th parallel, Gunnison and seven of his men were killed by Pahvant Indians on the Sevier River in central Utah in 1853.

Edward Beckwith completed Gunnison's railroad survey in 1853 and 1854 and then took his party north to winter in the Salt Lake Valley. He then explored the Stansbury trails between Salt Lake Valley and Fort Bridger and proceeded west across Nevada into California along the 41st parallel. The first transcontinental railroad followed much of this route. Lt. Col. Edward J. Steptoe, after completing a government investigation of Gunnison's death in 1854 and 1855, supervised some of the improvements of the Mormon Corridor road between Cedar City and the headwaters of the Santa Clara River.

Corpsman James H. Simpson, as chief topographical engineer for Gen. Albert Sidney Johnston's Army of Utah, established a wagon road connecting Camp Floyd in Cedar Valley, Utah, with the supply depot at Fort Bridger in 1858. Two years later he began locating a similar route to Denver. During the interim period he plotted two wagon roads to California leading west from Camp Floyd but south of the existing Humboldt River route. These routes were later used by the Pony Express and Overland Stage.

In connection with the Utah War in 1857, Joseph Christmas Ives investigated the feasibility of bringing military supplies into Utah by way of the Colorado and Virgin rivers. John Newberry, a famous geologist, later joined the Ives expedition and studied the eroded plateaus of northern Arizona and southern Utah. This expedition is credited as the first by Anglo-Americans to explore the floor of the Grand Canyon.

A civilian, Clarence King, obtained federal funds to study the geological structure and mineral deposits within a 100-mile-wide strip along the Central Pacific–Union Pacific railroads from the California-Nevada border to eastern Wyoming. Work began in May 1867, and during 1869, his parties' investigations in Utah took them along the Provo, Duchesne, and Bear rivers, through Echo Canyon, and along the crest of the Uintas, and included a remapping of the Great Salt Lake, which had risen nine feet since Stansbury's survey.

In 1869, former military man John Wesley Powell and his party floated the Green and Colorado rivers to the mouth of the Virgin River—the first known to complete this expedition. Two years later Powell repeated this voyage with a sizable appropriation from Congress to map and study the Colorado Plateau region. Headquartered in Kanab, Utah, the group completed the study in 1879.

Among the last of the military surveyors, George Wheeler used surveying instruments to survey accurately the area south of Clarence King's 40th parallel surveys in 1869. This included a reconnaissance through southeastern Nevada and western Utah, the first since the mountain men to make this north-south crossing of the Great Basin. His later 100th meridian study included a detailed survey of Utah's canyonlands.

Richard A. Bartlett, *Great Surveys of the American West* (1962); William H. Goetzman, *Army Exploration in the American West, 1803–1863* (1959); William H. Goetzman, *Exploration and Empire* (1966); Frank N. Schubert, *Vanguard of Expansion, Army Engineers in the Trans-Mississippi West, 1819–1879* (1980).

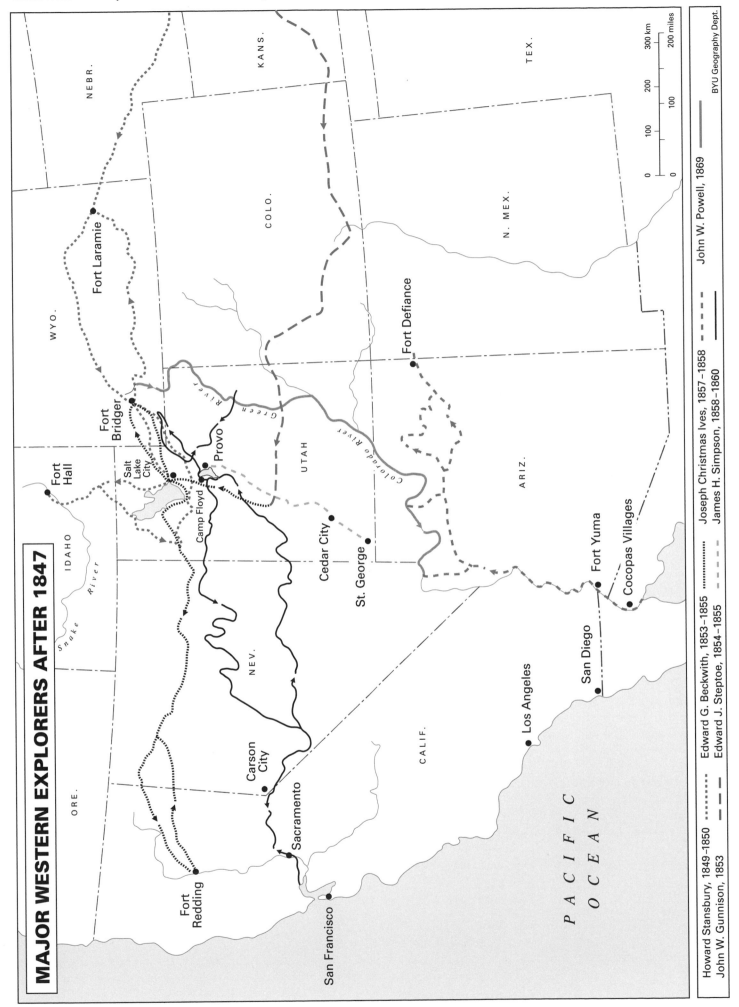

MAJOR WESTERN EXPLORERS AFTER 1847

Howard Stansbury, 1849–1850 ··········
John W. Gunnison, 1853 ── ──

Edward G. Beckwith, 1853–1855 ·········
Edward J. Steptoe, 1854–1855 ── ──

Joseph Christmas Ives, 1857–1858 ── ── ──
James H. Simpson, 1858–1860 ── ──

John W. Powell, 1869 ────
BYU Geography Dept.

EXPANSION OUTSIDE THE WASATCH FRONT

Lynn A. Rosenvall

Mormon exploration teams reconnoitered the Great Basin seeking potential farmland, water, timber, grazing lands, and other resources. Brigham Young "intended to have every hole and corner from the Bay of San Francisco to the Hudson Bay known to us [the Mormons]." Settlement sites were required for those fleeing from Missouri and Illinois and also for the thousands of anticipated converts from Europe and elsewhere. Total numbers of migrants to the Salt Lake Valley eventually exceeded 100,000. The new settlements were generally nucleated farm villages where each family lived within the village and traveled daily to and from their farmland in the surrounding area. Mormon settlement history can be divided into three periods. (1) From 1847 to 1857, contiguous growth centered on Salt Lake City, with a few outlying settlements at strategic points on the periphery. The coming of a federal army to Utah in 1857 ended this era. (2) From 1858 to 1869, colonization was wholly within the borders of the territory of Utah. This period ended with the completion of the railroad. (3) From 1870 to 1900, there was expansion into territory outside of Utah.

1847 to 1857

All of the settlements founded in the first two years, except Ogden, were located within the Great Salt Lake valley. In 1849, major settlements, such as Provo, Manti, and Tooele, became hub communities around which were located secondary villages. In this first decade the Mormons established some 100 settlements located mainly along the Wasatch Mountain Range in a discontinuous strip starting at Bear River valley in southeastern Idaho, then stretching south through Salt Lake, Utah, Juab, Pavant, and Beaver valleys and finally terminating in the Virgin River valley some 300 miles south of Salt Lake City. At strategic points on the periphery, settlements were built as way stations for moving goods and personnel into the region. Genoa (1849) and Frankton (1856) in the Carson valley were established on the west, and Fort Supply (1853) and Fort Bridger (1855), previously built as a trading post, were founded at the eastern entrance into Utah. In 1851, a Mexican ranch in Southern California was acquired as the settlement site for San Bernardino. Key settlements such as Parowan (1851) and Las Vegas (1855) were located along the Mormon Corridor route from San Bernardino to Salt Lake City. The desire to proselyte the Indians prompted the founding of Fort Limhi (1855) in the Salmon River country of Idaho and the Elk Mountain settlement (1855) on the upper Colorado River. In 1857, Mormon leaders, as a defensive response to the approaching army of Albert Sidney Johnston, recalled all of the settlers in these outlying communities.

1858 to 1869

The next decade was one of contiguous colonization, both north and south of Salt Lake City, and also into the higher valleys of the Wasatch Range. Some 149 new settlements were founded during this second period, almost all in close proximity to the hub settlements that were settled during the previous decade in the major valleys along the Wasatch Range. After the more accessible and desirable land was preempted, the valleys to the east were settled: Cache and upper Weber valleys to the north, and Heber, Sanpete, Sevier, and Panguitch valleys to the south. New settlements were located in the Virgin River valley in the southwest corner of Utah to produce cotton, grapes, figs, and other subtropical products. After the completion of the railroad in 1869, most immigrants came as individuals or families rather than groups, and the involvement of the Church in the total settlement process abruptly decreased.

1870 to 1900

From 1870 to the end of the century, almost one-half of the new settlements were interspersed among existing communities in Utah, in isolated and desolate spots such as the San Juan country or the more remote, arable valleys of eastern Utah, or in Canada and Mexico. In the two years following Brigham Young's death in 1877, more settlements were founded than in any similar period of Mormon colonization. With the diminishing prospect of arable land available within Utah in the 1870s, many sought new homes in Idaho and Arizona. Settlers soon occupied the Snake River valley, centering on Idaho Falls. In 1876, colonists were sent to establish colonies on the Little Colorado River in eastern Arizona, and other communities were founded east of Phoenix. Colonization continued southward to the San Pedro River north of the Mexican border, and beginning in 1879 settlers from the Little Colorado River moved farther south into the valley of the upper Gila River, ultimately founding settlements on the upper San Juan and the upper Gila rivers in western New Mexico. Eight settlements in Nevada, however, were established in the 1860s, when much of that area was part of the territory of Utah. With the exception of Fort Bridger and Fort Supply, the first Mormon settlements in Wyoming were founded in Star Valley commencing in 1876. In 1893, Mormons began to settle in the Big Horn country of northern Wyoming. Around the turn of the century Mormon colonization almost came to an abrupt halt, but over 500 settlements had been established in an area stretching from the Midwest to California and from Canada to Mexico.

Milton R. Hunter, *Brigham Young the Colonizer* (1945); D. W. Meinig, "The Mormon Culture Region: Strategies and Patterns in the Geography of the American West, 1847–1964," *Annals of the Association of American Geographers* 55 (1965):191–220); Joel E. Ricks, *Forms and Methods of Early Mormon Settlement in Utah and the Surrounding Region, 1847–1877* (1964); Lynn A. Rosenvall, "Mormon Settlement Patterns: 1830–1900" (Ph.D. diss., University of California, Berkeley, 1972).

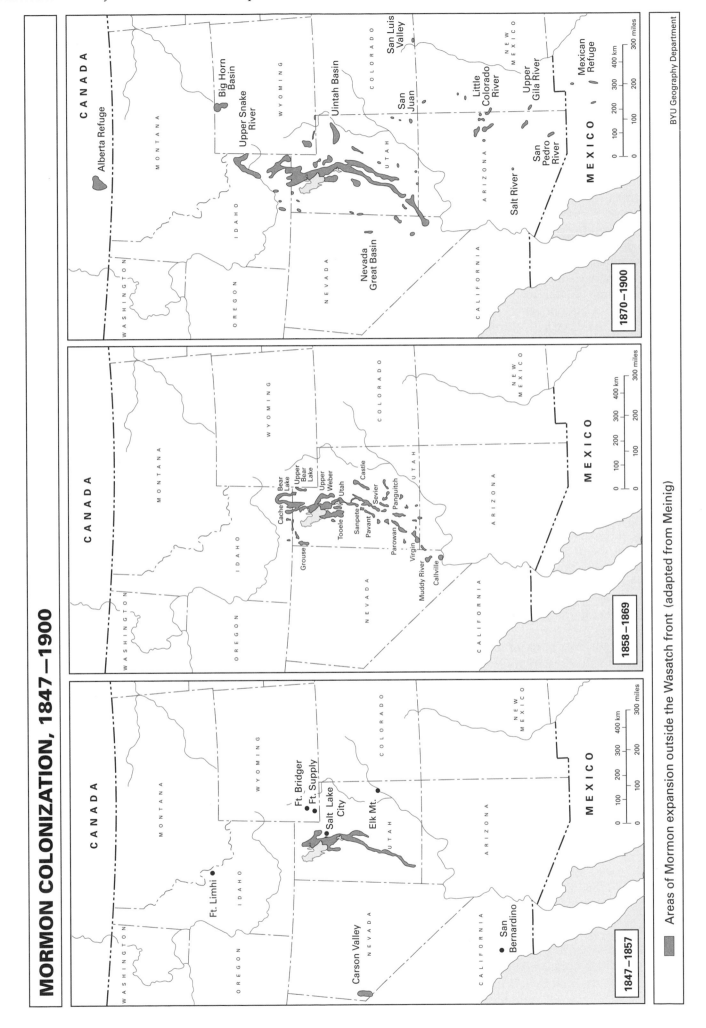

MORMON COLONIZATION, 1847–1900

BYU Geography Department

1870–1900

CANADA

MONTANA

IDAHO

WYOMING

OREGON

NEVADA
Nevada
Great Basin

WASHINGTON

CALIFORNIA

ARIZONA

UTAH

COLORADO

NEW MEXICO

MEXICO

Alberta Refuge

Big Horn Basin

Upper Snake River

Uintah Basin

San Luis Valley

San Juan

Little Colorado River

Upper Gila River

Salt River

San Pedro River

Mexican Refuge

0   100 200 300 400 km
0   100   200   300 miles

1858–1869

CANADA

MONTANA

IDAHO

WYOMING

OREGON

NEVADA

WASHINGTON

CALIFORNIA

ARIZONA

UTAH

COLORADO

NEW MEXICO

MEXICO

Bear Lake
Cache
Upper Bear Lake
Upper Weber
Utah
Castle
Sevier
Sanpete
Pavant
Tooele
Grouse
Parowan
Panguitch
Virgin
Muddy River
Callville

0   100 200 300 400 km
0   100   200   300 miles

1847–1857

CANADA

MONTANA

IDAHO

WYOMING

OREGON

NEVADA

WASHINGTON

CALIFORNIA

ARIZONA

UTAH

COLORADO

NEW MEXICO

MEXICO

Ft. Limhi

Ft. Bridger
Ft. Supply
Salt Lake City
Elk Mt.

Carson Valley

San Bernardino

0   100 200 300 400 km
0   100   200   300 miles

Areas of Mormon expansion outside the Wasatch front (adapted from Meinig)

RELATIONS WITH THE U.S. MILITARY

Audrey M. Godfrey

Unlike many frontier settlers who asked for military protection, Mormon settlers resisted the establishment of army forts in their territory, seeing such efforts as an encroachment upon their lands, government, and freedom. Through the years, Mormon-military relations have evolved from antagonism to accommodation.

Church leaders welcomed U.S. Army topographical engineers who came to Utah to chart roads for emigrants in 1849 and 1853. Capt. Howard Stansbury and Lt. John W. Gunnison received cordial treatment but carried back warnings from Mormon ecclesiastical authorities that further efforts involving military interference in the territory would be met with force.

The first large contingent of federal soldiers arrived in 1854, under Lt. Col. Edward J. Steptoe, to investigate the possibility of constructing a road from Salt Lake City to California. Liaisons between soldiers and local women resulted in a charge by the Mormons that the men brought depravity into their Victorian communities, a charge revived three years later when U.S. troops returned.

With each attempt to extend federal influence into the territory, Mormons' stubborn adherence to sovereignty sent government appointees back to the East carrying tales about the debauchery of polygamists and about the unpatriotic climate. Finally, President James Buchanan, determined to seat a non-Mormon governor by force if necessary, ordered an army to accompany his appointee, Alfred Cumming, precipitating the Utah War in 1857 and 1858.

A severe, early winter and Mormon resistance forced the army, under the leadership of Gen. Albert Sidney Johnston, into a winter bivouac, Camp Scott, near Fort Bridger. Before spring weather allowed movement, a peace commission had negotiated a pardon of the Mormons. The army then established Camp Floyd in Cedar Valley, 40 miles southwest of Salt Lake City. No battles ensued, but neither did agreement.

For three years the army remained in Utah, virtually confined to its barren valley except for forays to prevent Indian attacks, guard the immigrant road, make a show of force when a U.S. court was convened in Provo, or, most important, survey and build existing and new roads for travelers. As the Civil War threatened, regiments were withdrawn to service in other areas, and the fort was disbanded in 1861. When the military left, $4 million in stores and livestock was sold to local buyers for less than $100,000. Some businesses that had serviced Camp Floyd continued to operate, further boosting the local economy.

A year later, Col. Patrick Connor led his California Volunteers into Utah and located them in full view of the Mormon capital on its eastern bench, founding Fort Douglas. Immediately, conflict developed. The colonel believed the army's role to be more than a directive given him to protect the mail route. He believed that continued surveillance of the Mormons was necessary. He also promoted local mining, which put him at odds with Brigham Young, who championed agriculture and said that mining would bring an unsavory population and a love of wealth into Mormon communities. Young and Connor also disagreed on relations with native peoples. Young thought that the military was too quick to exterminate natives before discerning guilt. Connor maintained that Mormons instigated Indian assaults on emigrant parties and supplied the attackers with weapons.

After 1900, Fort Douglas gradually became an accepted part of the community. In 1916, the federal government used the post to train civilians in national preparedness. During both world wars, the fort was a stopping place for troops and a center for processing local draftees. Its closing in 1991 ended a long era of federal influence in Utah.

Between 1872 and 1912, three federal army posts were established to deal with Indian problems. Fort Cameron, near Beaver, was built at the time of the Black Hawk War in 1872. An outbreak on the Uintah Indian Reservation and continued conflict there prompted Maj. Thomas T. Thornburgh and 200 cavalry troops to set up Fort Thornburgh near Vernal in 1881. Intertribal warfare on the Ute Reservation led to the establishment of Fort Duchesne in 1886.

Relations between Mormons and the U.S. military at these three posts were mostly cordial. The army fed considerable funds into the areas serviced by the forts to pay for labor in their construction, to feed and clothe the men, and to provide forage for livestock. Indians also benefited through trade with the soldiers and paid labor. Many laborers freighted supplies, under contract, from the railroads to the forts. Soldiers worked at improving roads, and constructed a telegraph line from Price to Fort Duchesne. By 1912, the non-Indian population had increased, and the cessation of conflicts with Indians brought an end to the need for military intervention.

Since the 19th century, Utah has been the site for training military troops; for testing and storing weapons, equipment, and matériel; and for arms research. Utah now depends on these installations for much of its economic well-being. Since World War I, Mormon youth have been encouraged to serve in the military as a patriotic duty. With the dangers of the frontier reduced and a more diverse population in the state, there has been little friction and more cooperation between Mormons and the military.

Thomas G. Alexander and Leonard J. Arrington, "The Utah Military Frontier, 1872–1912—Forts Cameron, Thornburgh, and Duchesne," *Utah Historical Quarterly* 32 (1964):330–354; Norman F. Furniss, *The Mormon Conflict, 1850–1859* (1960); Donald R. Moorman with Gene A. Sessions, *Camp Floyd and the Mormons: The Utah War* (1992).

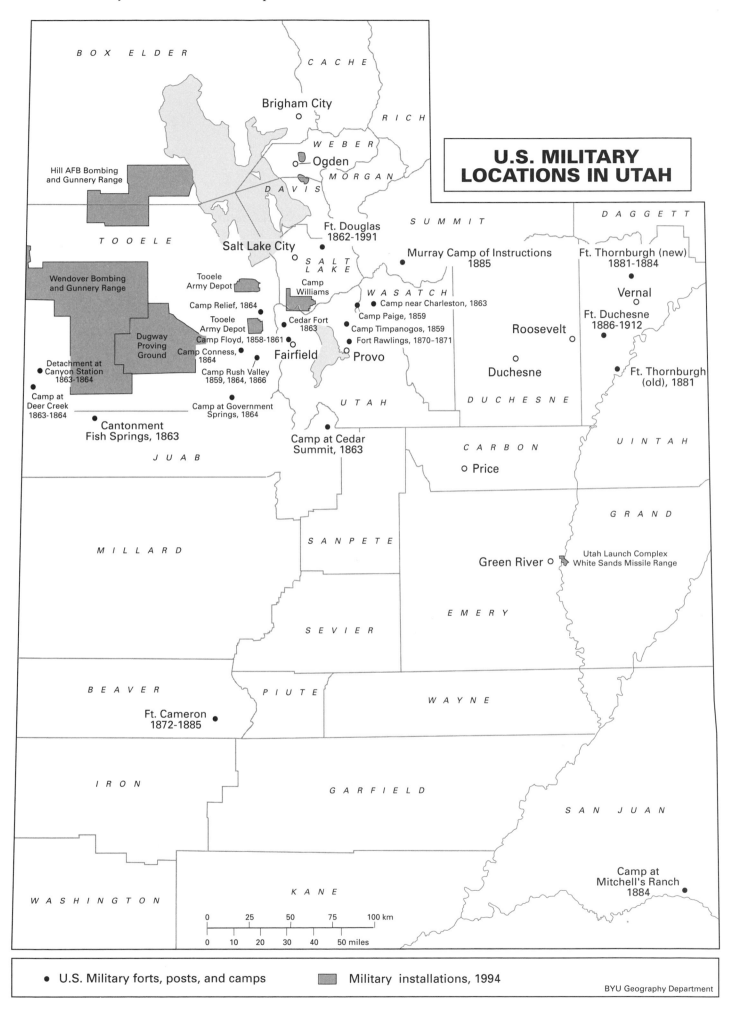

U.S. MILITARY
LOCATIONS IN UTAH

BOX ELDER

CACHE

Brigham City

RICH

WEBER

Ogden

MORGAN

DAVIS

Hill AFB Bombing
and Gunnery Range

TOOELE

SUMMIT

DAGGETT

Ft. Douglas
1862-1991

Murray Camp of Instructions
1885

Ft. Thornburgh (new)
1881-1884

Salt Lake City

SALT
LAKE

Wendover Bombing
and Gunnery Range

Tooele
Army Depot

Camp
Williams

WASATCH

Vernal

Camp near Charleston, 1863

Camp Relief, 1864

Tooele
Army Depot

Cedar Fort
1863

Camp Paige, 1859

Ft. Duchesne
1886-1912

Dugway
Proving
Ground

Camp Floyd, 1858-1861

Camp Timpanogos, 1859

Roosevelt

Camp Conness,
1864

Fairfield

Fort Rawlings, 1870-1871

Provo

Ft. Thornburgh
(old), 1881

Detachment at
Canyon Station
1863-1864

Camp Rush Valley
1859, 1864, 1866

UTAH

Duchesne

Camp at
Deer Creek
1863-1864

Camp at Government
Springs, 1864

DUCHESNE

UINTAH

Cantonment
Fish Springs, 1863

Camp at Cedar
Summit, 1863

CARBON

JUAB

Price

GRAND

MILLARD

SANPETE

Green River

Utah Launch Complex
White Sands Missile Range

EMERY

SEVIER

BEAVER

PIUTE

WAYNE

SAN JUAN

Ft. Cameron
1872-1885

IRON

GARFIELD

WASHINGTON

KANE

Camp at
Mitchell's Ranch
1884

| 0 | 25 | 50 | 75 | 100 km |
| 0 | 10 | 20 | 30 | 40 | 50 miles |

• U.S. Military forts, posts, and camps   Military installations, 1994

BYU Geography Department

ECONOMIC DEVELOPMENT IN EARLY UTAH

Leonard J. Arrington

The remoteness of early Deseret from the remainder of the nation, the difficulty of transportation, and the separatist inclinations of the settlers forced Utah in the years before the coming of the railroad to go through an almost miraculously successful stage of self-sufficiency that was more complete and long lasting than that of any other section of the United States. Any scientific investigation at the time would have concluded that the settlement of substantial numbers of people at even marginal levels was impossible. The land was too barren and the resources were too sparse to support more than a few scattered groups of people.

And yet growth and development did occur through hard work and severe sacrifice. The settlers' formula for success was a puritanical attitude toward consumption and saving and an ecclesiastically organized cooperation. With religion as an essential tool of survival, development was based on cooperative, rather than individualistic, principles. Under Church direction, there developed group colonization; cooperatively built forts; the construction of cooperative canals, roads, fences, and mills; cooperative livestock herds; and even some cooperative farming of fields. However arid and barren the territory seemed to be, the settlers had faith that God had endowed their promised land with all the resources necessary for their use. Unlike other American states and territories that started by developing extractive export industries, Utah's growth began with a local self-sufficient subsistence agricultural economy mobilized to support an ever-increasing number of people.

A closed economy of this type inevitably faces shortages of certain resources that inhibit development even though other resources lie unused. At that point further growth usually relies on export of abundant resources to exchange for resources in which the region is deficient.

In 1869, at a time when the Great Basin kingdom was beginning to run into critical bottlenecks in its resource structure, the transcontinental railroad was completed, converting the closed Mormon economy into an open one. Industry based on export of abundant minerals developed, providing the territory the wherewithal to import the machinery and equipment necessary for further development.

Instead of encouraging and supporting outside interests in the new mining and trading enterprises that were initiated, Brigham Young sought instead to preserve the political, social, and economic autonomy of the local cooperative village-based economy. The flourishing private mining and trading economy became an enclave within the self-sufficient, theocratic Mormon Commonwealth. Utah became a dualistic economy in which an imported non-Mormon capitalistic system was superimposed upon the collectivistic and exclusive system of the Latter-day Saints.

In an attempt to strengthen its cooperative sector and isolate it from the effects of the boom-and-bust cycles that typified the mining enclave, the Mormons inaugurated a protective campaign and established united orders, boards of trade, and tightly controlled cooperatives of many kinds. Locally built cooperative railroads were promoted, as were textile mills, clothing factories, tanneries, iron works, furniture factories, and wholesaling and retailing establishments. The economic base was broadened to locally owned industry, and Utah's economy became more diversified than that of other western states and territories.

The United States refused to permit the continuance of a theocratically directed closed society within its borders. The public opposed continuation of the practice of plural marriage; American democracy objected to the institutions of theocracy; and eastern free enterprises bridled at the restrictiveness implicit in the Mormon cooperative system. The passage of the Edmunds-Tucker Act in 1887 tolled the death knell of Utah's protective institutions, and the Latter-day Saints ultimately abandoned their planned theocratic kingdom. A new era was ushered in as Utah's unique institutions were abandoned and the territory gained statehood in 1896.

The Mormon Church sold nearly all its economic properties to eastern capitalists, who invested heavily in Utah mines, mills, smelters, and agricultural processing plants. The traditional Mormon sector accommodated to the national economy, and the state's economy became more highly commercialized and specialized. Although cash income increased, income and employment became more and more unstable. The economic fortunes of the state came to depend upon the decisions of centers of control that lay far outside the confines of the state. Utah's manufacturing relied on processing the raw materials produced locally by the agricultural and mining industries, which were then exported to the East. Required semiprocessed and finished goods were imported from the East. Utah's agriculture and mining were marginal, and the economy became dangerously vulnerable to fluctuations in the national economy. Consequently, Utah ultimately suffered relatively more, in terms of unemployment and decline in income, than almost any state in the Union during the great depression of the 1930s.

James B. Allen and Glen M. Leonard, *The Story of the Latter-day Saints* (1992); Leonard J. Arrington, *Great Basin Kingdom* (1958); Leonard J. Arrington and Dean May, *Building the City of God* (1976).

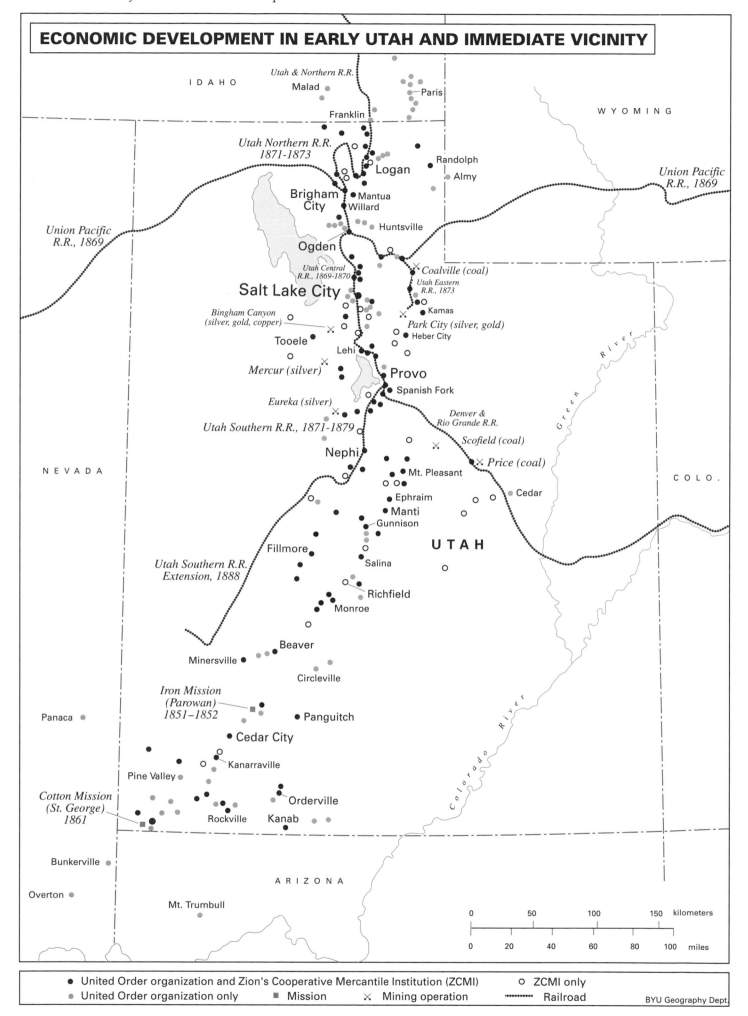

ECONOMIC DEVELOPMENT IN EARLY UTAH AND IMMEDIATE VICINITY

IDAHO

Utah & Northern R.R.

Malad

Paris

Franklin

Utah Northern R.R.
1871-1873

Randolph

Logan

Almy

WYOMING

Union Pacific
R.R., 1869

Brigham
City

Mantua
Willard

Huntsville

Union Pacific
R.R., 1869

Ogden

Utah Central
R.R., 1869-1870

Coalville (coal)

Utah Eastern
R.R., 1873

Salt Lake City

Kamas

Bingham Canyon
(silver, gold, copper)

Park City (silver, gold)

Heber City

Tooele

Lehi

Mercur (silver)

Provo

Spanish Fork

Green River

Eureka (silver)

Denver &
Rio Grande R.R.

Utah Southern R.R., 1871-1879

Scofield (coal)

Price (coal)

Nephi

Mt. Pleasant

Cedar

NEVADA

COLO.

Ephraim

Manti
Gunnison

U T A H

Fillmore

Salina

Utah Southern R.R.
Extension, 1888

Richfield

Monroe

Beaver

Minersville

Circleville

Iron Mission
(Parowan)
1851–1852

Panaca

Panguitch

Cedar City

Kanarraville

Pine Valley

Cotton Mission
(St. George)
1861

Orderville

Rockville

Kanab

Colorado River

Bunkerville

ARIZONA

Overton

Mt. Trumbull

| 0 | | 50 | | 100 | | 150 | kilometers |

| 0 | 20 | 40 | 60 | 80 | 100 | miles |

● United Order organization and Zion's Cooperative Mercantile Institution (ZCMI)   ○ ZCMI only

● United Order organization only   ■ Mission   ✕ Mining operation   ••••• Railroad

BYU Geography Dept.

BRIGHAM YOUNG'S TRAVELS IN THE WEST

Ronald K. Esplin

In the East, before 1848, Brigham Young had been a man on the move. On foot, by wagon, stage, or canal boat, in a few cases by train, steamer, or sail, he traveled thousands of miles several times from Ohio to Missouri and from Illinois to New York, and once across the Atlantic. After three trips across the Great Plains in 1847 and 1848, he established his residence in Salt Lake City and turned his back on the East forever. Even the ease and speed of travel on the transcontinental railroad after 1869 failed to entice him from his mountain retreat.

But the traveling did not stop. From 1847 to 1877, Brigham Young spent more time on the road than ever before. By horse and carriage, supplemented in the 1870s by rail, he traveled tens of thousands of miles. Several of the dozens of major treks were exploring expeditions—efforts to personally assess resources and judge the settlement potential of valleys, mountains, and deserts. Many involved important contacts with Indians. Most journeys were primarily pastoral in nature, undertaken with the express purpose of visiting and encouraging the widespread Saints in their villages and homes. Such visits enhanced community, unity, and loyalty; they helped people to persevere in difficult circumstances; and they demonstrated that each community was considered important. Whether Latter-day Saints lived 45 miles, 80 miles, or 300 miles from Salt Lake City, most could count on at least a yearly visit from President Young. During his visits he listened, observed, renewed friendships, counseled, instructed, comforted, motivated, scolded, strengthened, and blessed. So important were these visits to Young and to the settlers that even as he aged and his health declined, he continued his arduous travels. These trips were one key to his leadership and to the successful colonization of the Great Basin.

President Young prepared carefully for the longer journeys, and on the road he oversaw everything from itinerary to repairs. Other Church leaders accompanied him, along with family, friends, and invited guests—often several dozen. Young packed his carriage, which would lead the column, with items for emergencies, goods for the Indians, trinkets for the children, plus tools, rawhide, marbles—whatever he thought might be needed. Baggage wagons followed the carriages.

The arrival of the president's entourage in a settlement called for pageantry and celebration. Accounts of the 1864 journey south, for example, report that they were often met by an escort and then formed part of a grand procession into town. A brass band enlivened the reception as settlers lined the street. Either a public banquet or a more private feast usually followed. The centerpiece of the visit was the "meeting," in which visiting dignitaries instructed and encouraged the Saints. President Young's own ser-

mons on such occasions were always filled with practical advice. Then, in the larger and more distant towns, fiddlers accompanied merry dancers in a celebration that would last far into the night. Throughout the reception, people sought and received their personal "audience" with the visiting leader. This mixture of entertainment, instruction, and renewing of ties was memorable and vital for young colonies far from Salt Lake Valley.

The longest round trip south occurred in 1870. It included exploration beyond St. George into southeast Nevada and northwest Arizona and occupied 53 days. The more typical round-trip journey through the southern settlements required three to four weeks, but when pressed, as they were in 1871, Young's party covered the 300-plus miles from Salt Lake City to St. George in only eight days. As they returned through settlements recently visited, the pace often quickened, to 50 miles per day and occasionally more. Such journeys wearied human participants and taxed animals. Very often, spent horses were exchanged for fresh ones, and some died along the way. Of the 15 carriage loads that departed Salt Lake in 1864, only three returned with the same animals. That trip of 29 days covered 800 miles and included 37 settlements where the visitors delivered 124 discourses.

Brigham Young made nearly two dozen trips to Parowan, Cedar City, and beyond. After 1860, these always extended to St. George, the heart of Utah's temperate "Dixie" and Young's winter home in the 1870s. One leg of these longer journeys frequently included the Sanpete settlements around Manti, but Young also made nearly a dozen more "southern" trips only as far as Manti or Fillmore. Young made extended trips northward just as frequently. Of the more than 30 trips beyond Ogden, most reached Cache Valley (after 1860) and many proceeded north to settlements in southeastern Idaho (after 1864). He also made four dozen shorter trips north into Davis and Weber counties, another four dozen excursions south to some part of Utah County, several to settlements east of Salt Lake, and at least 16 west to Tooele and Grantsville. These, plus numerous day or overnight trips to the spread-out settlements of the Salt Lake Valley or into nearby canyons, added up to approximately 40,000 miles traveled in the region by Young between 1849 and 1877.

Leonard J. Arrington, *Brigham Young, American Moses* (1985), pp. 306–311; Leonard J. Arrington and Ronald K. Esplin, "Building a Commonwealth: The Secular Leadership of Brigham," *Utah Historical Quarterly* 45 (Summer 1977): 216–232; Gordon Irving, "Encouraging the Saints: Brigham Young's Annual Tours of the Mormon Settlements," *Utah Historical Quarterly* 45 (Summer 1977):233–251.

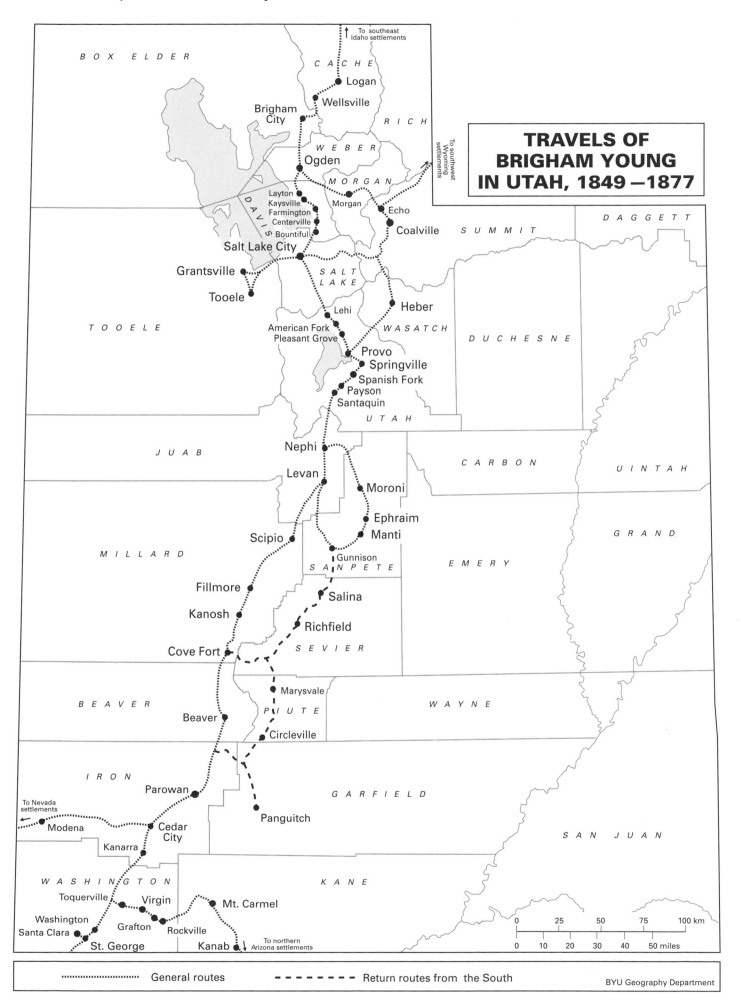

TRAVELS OF BRIGHAM YOUNG IN UTAH, 1849–1877

To southeast Idaho settlements

To southwest Wyoming settlements

BOX ELDER

CACHE

Logan

Wellsville

Brigham City

RICH

WEBER

Ogden

MORGAN

Morgan

Echo

Coalville

SUMMIT

DAGGETT

Layton
Kaysville
Farmington
Centerville
Bountiful

DAVIS

Salt Lake City

Grantsville

SALT LAKE

Tooele

TOOELE

Lehi

Heber

WASATCH

DUCHESNE

American Fork
Pleasant Grove

Provo
Springville
Spanish Fork
Payson
Santaquin

UTAH

Nephi

Levan

Moroni

Ephraim
Manti

CARBON

UINTAH

Scipio

Gunnison

SANPETE

EMERY

GRAND

Fillmore

Salina

Kanosh

Richfield

MILLARD

SEVIER

Cove Fort

Marysvale

WAYNE

Beaver

PIUTE

Circleville

BEAVER

Parowan

Panguitch

GARFIELD

SAN JUAN

To Nevada settlements

Modena

Cedar City

Kanarra

IRON

WASHINGTON

KANE

Toquerville

Virgin

Mt. Carmel

Washington

Grafton

Rockville

Santa Clara

St. George

Kanab

To northern Arizona settlements

0   25   50   75   100 km
0   10   20   30   40   50 miles

·········· General routes   – – – – – – Return routes from the South

BYU Geography Department

RELIEF SOCIETY (1884)

Maureen Ursenbach Beecher

In December 1866, Brigham Young assigned his plural wife Eliza R. Snow, already acknowledged leader of Mormon women, to reestablish the Female Relief Society as an integral part of every ward in the Utah-based Church. From its 1842 founding by Joseph Smith in Nauvoo, Illinois, the women's organization, considered by its members to have been organized after the order of heaven, was perceived as a partner organization to male priesthood quorums, under priesthood direction.

From 1842 to 1866, the Relief Society had led an interrupted existence. Dormant after 1844, it resurfaced in Utah in the 1850s and was acknowledged officially by the Church only to be disrupted during the Utah War. In delegating Snow to reinstate the society in 1866, Young set in motion an organizational whirlwind that would continue unabated until every Mormon settlement had its women's group.

At its half-century Jubilee in 1892, the Relief Society had risen from its peak in Nauvoo of 1,300 women to 17,002 members in 302 branches in Utah Territory and neighboring communities. Expansion into the eastern United States and overseas was by then well under way, but existing records are insufficient to trace the extent of membership abroad. The Relief Society Centenary in 1942 celebrated 115,000 members worldwide, and at its 1992 Sesquicentennial, the Relief Society claimed 3,100,000 members in 1,837 stakes with 18,810 wards or branches in 138 nations and territories.

Under Snow's leadership from 1866 to 1887, the society in the American West expanded to incorporate most Church programs that involved women and children. At general and local levels, the Relief Society sponsored the Young Ladies Mutual Improvement Association and Primary Association, both of which, with the Relief Society, endure to the present as regular parts of standard LDS ward organization.

During the decades of the 1870s and 1880s, Mormon women through their organizations fostered myriad pro-jects for community development: the *Women's Exponent*, a semimonthly tabloid-size newspaper; a silk industry and other cottage manufactures; cooperative stores and commission retailing outlets; a grain storage program; a movement for universal suffrage; and the Deseret Hospital. Local branches built Relief Society halls and granaries on property purchased with their own funds. More significantly, the women, through the Relief Society, provided the major share of each community's charity and welfare work as an integral part of their assignment.

The map shows the distribution of Relief Society organizations as compiled by then-secretary Emmeline B. Wells and published in 1884. The local units, numbering 295, were organized after the general Church pattern into 23 stakes, in 30 counties, in five states or territories. On the basis of the 1887 figures the local societies averaged 56 members each. As complete as Wells's compilation was, it did not record societies too remote to be included in stake organizations. Those in the Colorado communities of Ephraim and Manasseh, for example, and those in the Pacific and Europe, are not listed, nor is it possible to ascertain the extent of membership abroad. Significant here, however, is the evidence of the early spread of the society, well on its way to becoming the largest of its kind on earth.

Jill Mulvay Derr, Janath Russell Cannon, and Maureen Ursenbach Beecher, *Women of Covenant: The Story of Relief Society* (1992); Sarah M. Kimball, "Central Organization in Utah," *Women's Exponent* 20 (April 1, 1892): 144; "Relief Society: Names of Stake and Branch Presidents of the Relief Society of Latter-day Saints, In the Valleys of the Mountains" (broadside) (1884), LDS Church Archives; Eliza R. Snow, "The Relief Society" (1876) (holograph, Western Americana, University of Utah Libraries).

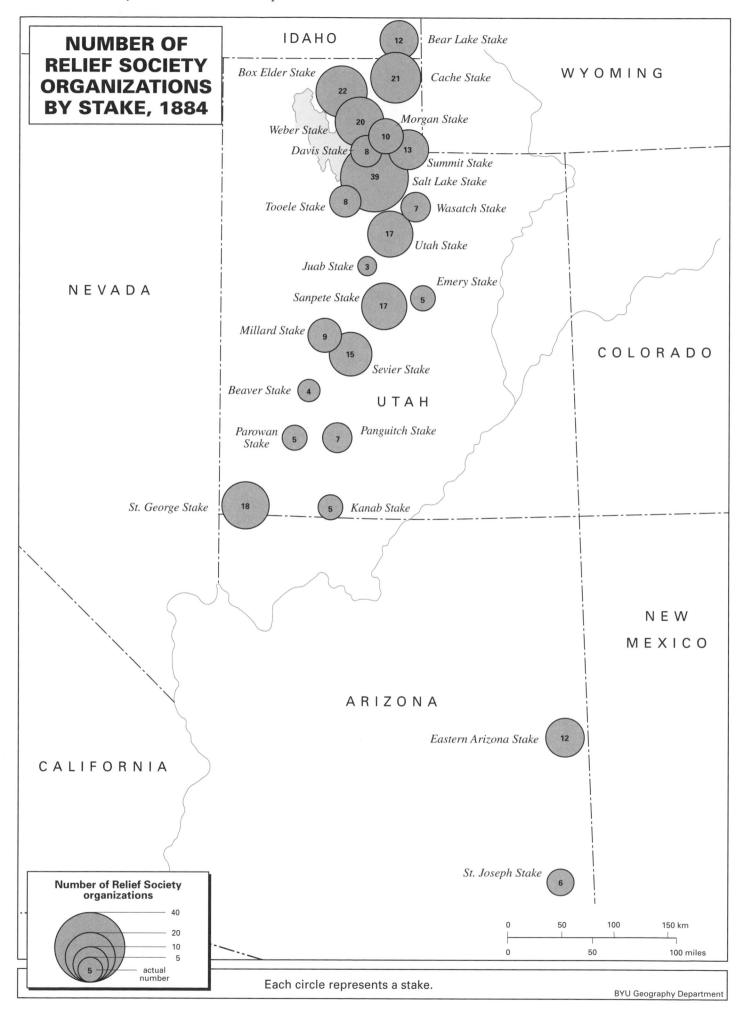

NUMBER OF RELIEF SOCIETY ORGANIZATIONS BY STAKE, 1884

IDAHO

WYOMING

NEVADA

UTAH

COLORADO

CALIFORNIA

ARIZONA

NEW MEXICO

Bear Lake Stake — 12
Box Elder Stake — 22
Cache Stake — 21
Morgan Stake — 10
Weber Stake — 20
Davis Stake — 8
Summit Stake — 13
Salt Lake Stake — 39
Tooele Stake — 8
Wasatch Stake — 7
Utah Stake — 17
Juab Stake — 3
Emery Stake — 5
Sanpete Stake — 17
Millard Stake — 9
Sevier Stake — 15
Beaver Stake — 4
Parowan Stake — 5
Panguitch Stake — 7
St. George Stake — 18
Kanab Stake — 5
Eastern Arizona Stake — 12
St. Joseph Stake — 6

Number of Relief Society organizations

40
20
10
5

5 — actual number

Each circle represents a stake.

0   50   100   150 km
0   50   100 miles

BYU Geography Department

ELIZA R. SNOW'S RELIEF SOCIETY TRAVELS (1880–1881)

Maureen Ursenbach Beecher

The phenomenal contribution that 19th-century Mormon women made to community development was facilitated largely through networks of female leaders who traveled widely from city to city and settlement to settlement. Meeting the assembled membership, the leading sisters from Church headquarters heard reports of local societies, reported activities of sister groups, made suggestions for new or expanded projects, and carried the official messages of the Prophet and the Apostles to the female membership of the Church.

Eliza Roxcy Snow (1804–1887) presided over all the women's organizations from 1866 to 1887. Her organizational genius, her secular and religious knowledge, her access to her Church president husband, Brigham Young, and her spiritual insight and direction gave her an additional authority to which Church members, male and female, responded enthusiastically.

Accompanied by one or two of the corps of leading sisters, Snow maintained an ambitious program of official visits throughout her administration. Between March 1880 and December 1881, for example, as illustrated by the adjacent map, she traveled throughout Utah territory with either Emmeline B. Wells or Zina D. H. Young. Railroads had by then made travel possible into Cache Valley and as far south as Nephi; for the rest of their trips the women used whatever carriages or wagons local Saints could provide.

"In company of Mrs. Z. D. H. Young, my 1st Coun[selor]. in R[elief]. S[ociety]. Central Board," wrote Eliza Snow, "I spent the Autumn and Winter of 1880–1 in St. George, officiating in the Temple for the dead, and visiting and organizing Associations in that interesting City, and adjacent country—having traveled one thousand m[ile]s. by team over jolting rocks and through bedded sand, occasionally camping out at night on long drives, before I started for home, and returned to Salt Lake City in March" (Eliza R. Snow, "Sketch of My Life"). The *Women's Exponent* reported that Snow herself "drove a horse and buggy the whole distance from Fayette to Levan, twenty-six miles, over the most fearful roads," though usually one of the local men handled the reins.

A major purpose of these visits was to organize Primary Associations for the children in the wards, though work in the recently dedicated St. George Temple and the furthering of ongoing Relief Society projects were also aims. "We welcome Sisters Eliza and Zina as our Elect Lady and her Counselor, and as Presidents of all the feminine portion of the human race," read the introduction of the two in meetings in Kanab, "although comparatively few recognize their right to this authority." Men and children as well as women attended meetings, remembering the events years later as significant moments. The sisters' testimonies of plural marriage, and of Joseph Smith's prophetic calling, accompanied by Snow's showing of the watch the Prophet had given her, were recorded by hearers.

The map indicates only those places specifically named in Church and personal records. Each extended tour included visits to places unnamed as well as those in which documented meetings were held. To simplify the map, the return from distant centers is shown as a straight line back to headquarters; however in most cases the women stopped along the return trip as well.

[For dates of Snow's travels, see appendix.]

Deseret News Weekly, vols. 29–30; A. Karl Larson and Katherine Miles Larson, *Diary of Charles Lowell Walker*, 2 vols. (1980); Minutes of local Relief Societies (holograph, LDS Church Archives); "Relief Society: Names of Stake and Branch Presidents of the Relief Society of Latter-day Saints," in *Valleys of the Mountains* (1884) (broadside, LDS Church Archives); Eliza R. Snow, "Sketch of My Life" (holograph, Bancroft Library, Berkeley, Calif.); *Women's Exponent*, vols. 8–10; Zina D. H. Young, Diary (November 9–13, 1880) (holograph, Special Collections, Harold B. Lee Library, Brigham Young University, Provo, Utah).

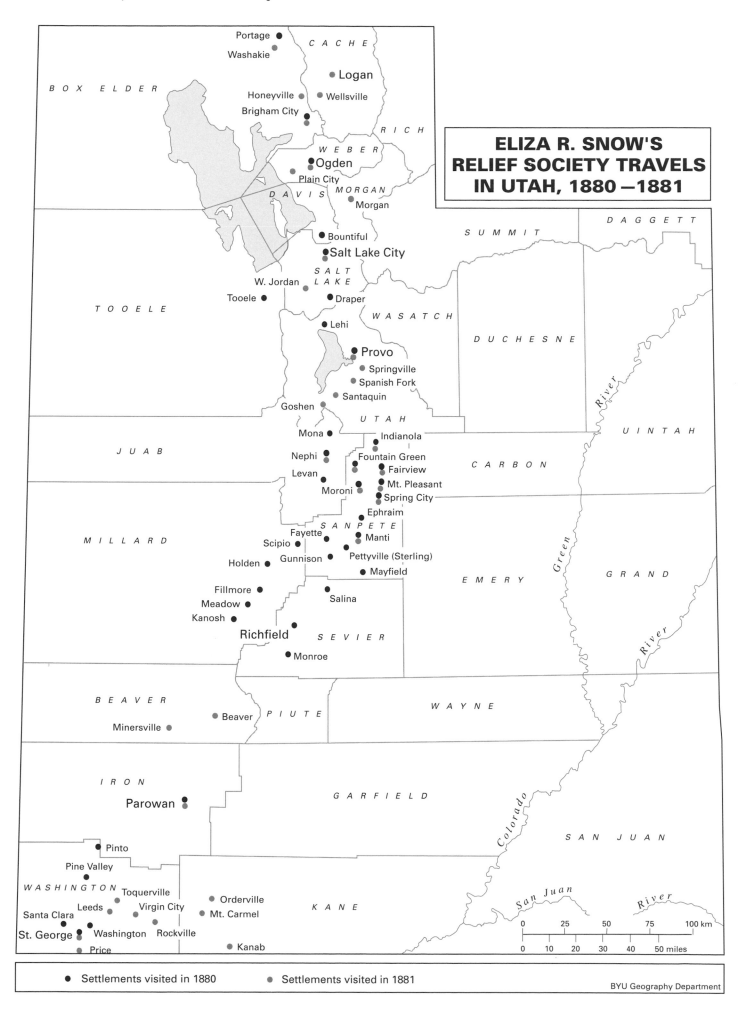

ELIZA R. SNOW'S
RELIEF SOCIETY TRAVELS
IN UTAH, 1880–1881

CACHE
Portage
Washakie
BOX ELDER
Logan
Honeyville
Wellsville
Brigham City
RICH
WEBER
Ogden
Plain City
MORGAN
DAVIS
Morgan
SUMMIT
DAGGETT
Bountiful
Salt Lake City
SALT LAKE
W. Jordan
WASATCH
Tooele
Draper
TOOELE
DUCHESNE
Lehi
UINTAH
Provo
Springville
Spanish Fork
Santaquin
Goshen
UTAH
Mona
Indianola
Nephi
Fountain Green
CARBON
Levan
Fairview
Moroni
Mt. Pleasant
Spring City
Ephraim
SANPETE
Fayette
Manti
Scipio
Gunnison
Pettyville (Sterling)
Holden
Mayfield
EMERY
GRAND
Fillmore
Salina
Meadow
Kanosh
MILLARD
Richfield
SEVIER
Monroe
BEAVER
PIUTE
WAYNE
Beaver
Minersville
SAN JUAN
GARFIELD
IRON
Parowan
Pinto
Pine Valley
WASHINGTON
Toquerville
Orderville
KANE
Leeds
Virgin City
Santa Clara
Mt. Carmel
St. George
Washington
Rockville
Price
Kanab

Green River
Colorado River
San Juan River

0   25   50   75   100 km
0 10 20 30 40 50 miles

● Settlements visited in 1880   ● Settlements visited in 1881

BYU Geography Department

107

CANADA

Richard E. Bennett

Within months of the organization of The Church of Jesus Christ of Latter-day Saints in upstate New York in 1830, Mormon missionaries were preaching their newfound gospel in nearby Canada (or British North America, as it was then known). In the 1830s and 1840s, some 2,500 Canadians joined the Church, many of whom gathered with other converts in Ohio, Missouri, Illinois, and eventually the Great Basin. Several of these Canadian converts, such as John Taylor, William Law, Mary Fielding, and Theodore Turley, figured prominently in the later rise of the Church. Geographically proximate to Palmyra, New York, and Kirtland, Ohio, these converts were gained as the result of early Mormon missionary forays into Upper Canada either following established Methodist preaching circuits, returning to Canada to teach family and friends, or responding to scattered invitations to preach. Brigham Young and his brother, Phineas, were instrumental in converting many former Methodists in the Kingston-Earnestown-Loughborough-Sydenham area in 1832 and 1833. Joseph Smith, Jr., converted the Freeman Nickerson family in the Mt. Pleasant area just west of Niagara Falls. Parley P. Pratt reaped a rich harvest of followers in the Toronto area in 1835. And John E. Page converted well over 1,000 people in 1836 and 1837 in the Portland-North Crosby-Boston Mills area in the Rideau Canal district north of Kingston. Fewer converts were realized in the provinces of New Brunswick, Nova Scotia, and Prince Edward Island, and fewer still in old Quebec (Lower Canada). By 1850, with so many departed, Mormonism in eastern Canada was but a memory.

Fifty years later, however, the scene shifted from eastern to western Canada and the approach had changed from one of plucking to one of planting. At a time when the Church was expanding in the Rocky Mountain West, while experiencing persecution because of its adherence to polygamy, the Canadian West looked particularly attractive. John Taylor, an English-born Canadian from Toronto who had converted 50 years earlier and who succeeded Brigham Young as president of the Church, at one point seriously considered moving Church headquarters from Salt Lake City to Victoria Island but settled, instead, on sending Charles Ora Card north to plant a new colony on safer British soil. Card scouted out a new settlement in southern Alberta in 1886, but did not select the Lee's Creek site, now Cardston, until 1887. Pursued by American marshals because of his adherence to plural marriage, Card and his original party—consisting of eight families with their cattle and household goods—were assisted over the St. Mary River and into Canada in June 1887 by a detachment of the North-West Mounted Police.

At that time the Canadian government, fearing possible American annexation of this southerly region of western Canada, was encouraging new settlements of every kind. Mormon communal skills and agricultural prowess, coupled with aid from Salt Lake City as well as from Ottawa, gave the early Cardston settlers a distinct advantage over neighboring settlers. Isolated but industrious, Mormons were gradually accepted into Canadian society. As the advantages of settling in Alberta became known, more Mormons moved northward, resulting in the founding of surrounding settlements south of Cardston. These included Aetna (1888), Mountain View (1890), Beazer (1891), Leavitt (1893), and Kimball (1897), all platted in characteristic grid pattern format common to other Mormon farm villages in the western United States. Cardston itself was laid out in square blocks, each containing 8.4 acres and subdivided into eight lots.

In 1898, with the Alberta government's decision to build an irrigation canal from the St. Mary River near the Montana border to the lower lands near Lethbridge, some 500 new Mormon settlers arrived. Well-known for their expertise in irrigating semi-arid regions, this second wave of settlers established new towns situated in newly irrigated farm country such as Magrath, Stirling, Caldwell, and Taylorville (all 1898), and Woodford (1900).

With the turn of the century, three other Mormon towns sprang into being—Orton (1901), Frankburg (1902), and Taber (1902)—as a result of the short-lived experimentation in sugar beet farming pioneered by Charles A. Magrath, Jesse Knight, and his son Raymond Knight. In 1906, with the Church's purchase of the 60,000-acre Cochrane Ranch northwest of Cardston, Glenwood (1908) and Hillspring (1910) were settled, marking the end of the early period of Mormon pioneering efforts in southern Alberta.

The Mormon presence in Canada has grown considerably since the early 19th century. In 1994 the Latter-day Saint population in Alberta numbers almost 60,000 (about half the total Mormon membership in Canada), the majority of whom have long since left the farm for opportunities in large urban centers such as Lethbridge, Calgary, and Edmonton. Meanwhile, thousands of other Alberta-born Mormon descendants have fanned out all across Canada, where they have played pivotal roles in the growth and reestablishment of the Church, often in those very regions that 150 years before had surrendered some of their best citizens to the message of Mormonism.

Richard E. Bennett, "A Study of The Church of Jesus Christ of Latter-day Saints in Upper Canada, 1830–1850" (Master's thesis, Brigham Young University, 1975); Lynn A. Rosenvall, "The Transfer of Mormon Culture to Alberta," in *Essays on the Historical Geography of the Canadian West*, Lynn A. Rosenvall and S. M. Evans, editors (1987), pp. 122–144; Brigham Young Card, "Charles Ora Card and the Founding of the Mormon Settlements in Southwestern Alberta, North-West Territories," *The Mormon Presence in Canada*, Brigham Y. Card et al., editors (1990), pp. 77–107.

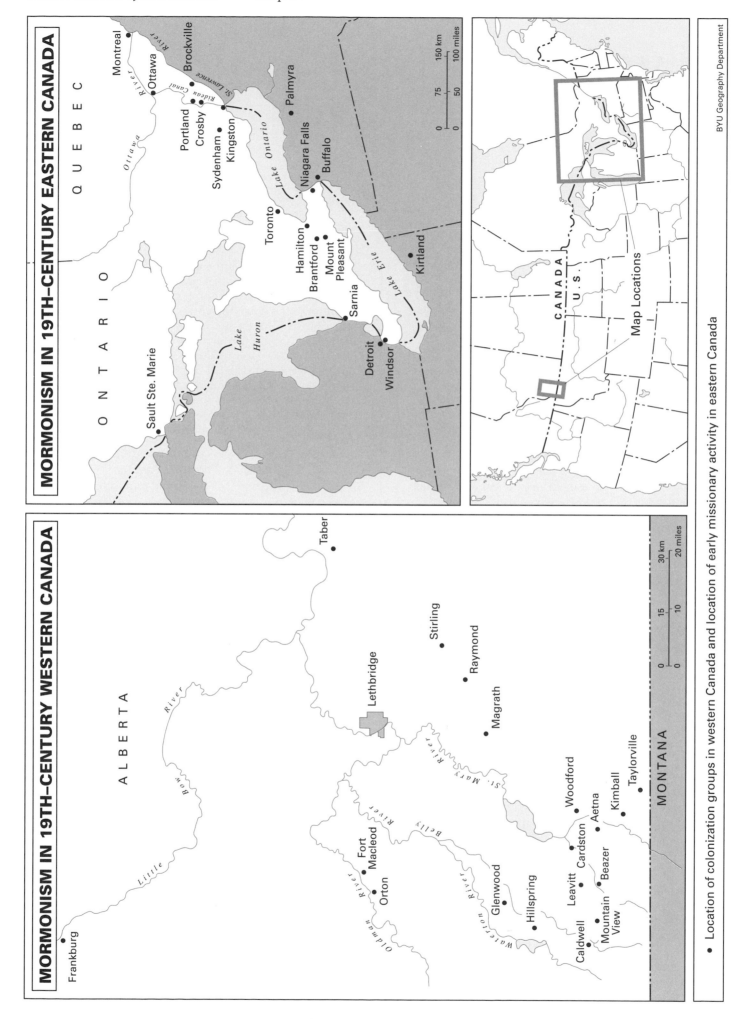

MORMONISM IN 19TH-CENTURY EASTERN CANADA

QUEBEC

ONTARIO

Montreal
Ottawa
Brockville
Portland
Crosby
Sydenham
Kingston
Palmyra
Niagara Falls
Buffalo
Toronto
Hamilton
Brantford
Mount Pleasant
Kirtland
Sarnia
Detroit
Windsor
Sault Ste. Marie

Lake Ontario
Lake Erie
Lake Huron
Ottawa River
St. Lawrence River
Rideau Canal

CANADA
U.S.
Map Locations

BYU Geography Department

MORMONISM IN 19TH-CENTURY WESTERN CANADA

ALBERTA

MONTANA

Frankburg
Taber
Stirling
Raymond
Lethbridge
Magrath
Fort Macleod
Orton
Woodford
Aetna
Kimball
Taylorville
Glenwood
Hillspring
Leavitt
Cardston
Beazer
Caldwell
Mountain View

Bow River
Little River
Oldman River
Belly River
Waterton River
St. Mary River

• Location of colonization groups in western Canada and location of early missionary activity in eastern Canada

MORMON COLONIES IN MEXICO

LaMond Tullis

In 1847, having been driven from their properties in the midwestern United States, the Mormons secured a new homeland in Mexico's Great Salt Lake Valley, later ceded to the United States in 1848 by the Treaty of Guadalupe Hidalgo as a consequence of the Mexican-American War. Within a year the Mormons were sending out colonizing companies throughout the Great Basin in order to establish suitable living sites for the tens of thousands of converts arriving annually. By 1875, the Mormons had explored western Canada and northern Mexico as possible colonization areas. Ten years later (1885) the first Mexican colony was established in Chihuahua (Colonia Juárez), followed soon by eight others—Dublán and Díaz (along with Juárez) on Chihuahua's central plateau; Cave Valley, Pacheco, García, and Chuichupa in Chihuahua's mountains; and Oaxaca and Morelos in the semitropical areas of Sonora.

Mormon leaders had long been interested in Mexico for theological and practical reasons. In 1875 they received positive reports about the Casas Grandes region of Chihuahua from an early Mormon exploring and missionary expedition. They established a mission in Mexico City in 1879 and proceeded to make important and helpful contacts with Mexican federal government officials. Both the knowledge of terrain and the contacts in Mexico served the Mormons well, for U.S. government opposition to plural marriage prompted a new exodus. The 1882 Edmunds Act penalized severely even those who merely believed in polygamy, and in 1887 the Edmunds-Tucker Act was passed, which shattered the Mormon Church's temporal foundation, abolishing every important Mormon institution including the Church's governing bodies and its schools.

In the early years, before the revolution of 1910 to 1917 that turned Mexico's politics and economics into utter chaos, the Mormon colonies in Chihuahua and Sonora prospered immensely. Within several years of their founding they became economically integrated, trading the goods, produce, and materials that each best produced. By establishing an irrigation system (some of which followed an ancient indigenous canal), farming and associated industries could flourish in the plateau colonies of Juárez and Dublán. The mountain colonies of Cave Valley, Pacheco, García, and Chuichupa were all situated in timbered areas of pine and oak where meadows and trees sustained cattle and timber industries. The semitropical Sonoran colonies of Oaxaca and Morelos, situated on the Bavispe River, yielded valuable produce. In 1892 the Juárez colonists built a canning factory for their abundant orchard fruit and tomatoes.

Concerning Colonia Juárez, the Mormons' flagship colony, Charles W. Kindrich of the U.S. State Department reported in 1899 that

> the gardens [there] are fragrant with flowers, and the blossoms of the peach, apricot, and plum trees glow in the pure air. Clear water from the *Acequia* along the hillside flows down the gutter of each cross street. Neat brick residences are nestled amid grapevines and pear trees. . . . From this valley the Mormons have extracted in ten years enough wealth to give them independence. . . . There is a gristmill, a furniture factory, and other industries in Colonia Juárez. There is an academy with five teachers and 400 pupils. It is the policy of the Mormons to erect school-houses before churches and temples. (*Review of Reviews* 19 (June 1899): 704)

Except for economic relationships, the colonies maintained a relatively isolated posture from the rest of Mexico. This isolation, the discipline required by a frontier existence, and the premium that Mormons placed on family life combined to produce some of the Church's most able families. Indeed, between 1885 and 1895, six of the Mormon Church's Twelve Apostles lived in the colonies, mostly in Juárez.

During their first 20 years, all the colonies received new residents frequently, most fleeing U.S. federal marshals or the atmosphere of persecution unleashed in the Great Basin by the antibigamy laws. Later, after 1890 and 1906, with the polygamy issue resolved by the Church renouncing it both in the United States and abroad, the Mexican colonies continued to attract newcomers, mostly for economic reasons.

The Mexican revolution of 1910 to 1917 ended all that. Revolutionaries and Mexican federal troops taxed and took, burned and looted. Mormons abandoned their colonies and fled back to the United States. After the revolution, some Mormon families returned to Mexico to try to reclaim their lands. Some were partially successful, but the Mormons' social experiment in Mexican isolation was finished. All the colonies except for Juárez and Dublán have been cut from their Mormon roots. In these two colonies, Anglo and Mexican Mormons and non-Mormons live side by side in a tenuous but relatively cooperative relationship, fully integrated into Mexico's national economy, polity, and society.

Edward A. Geary, "The Literary Image of the Mormon Colonies in Mexico," *Mormon Letters Annual* (1984): pp. 111–123; *The Mormon Colonies in Mexico: Commemorating 100 Years* (1985); Thomas Cottam Romney, *The Mormon Colonies in Mexico* (1938); LaMond Tullis, *Mormons in Mexico: The Dynamics of Faith and Culture* (1987).

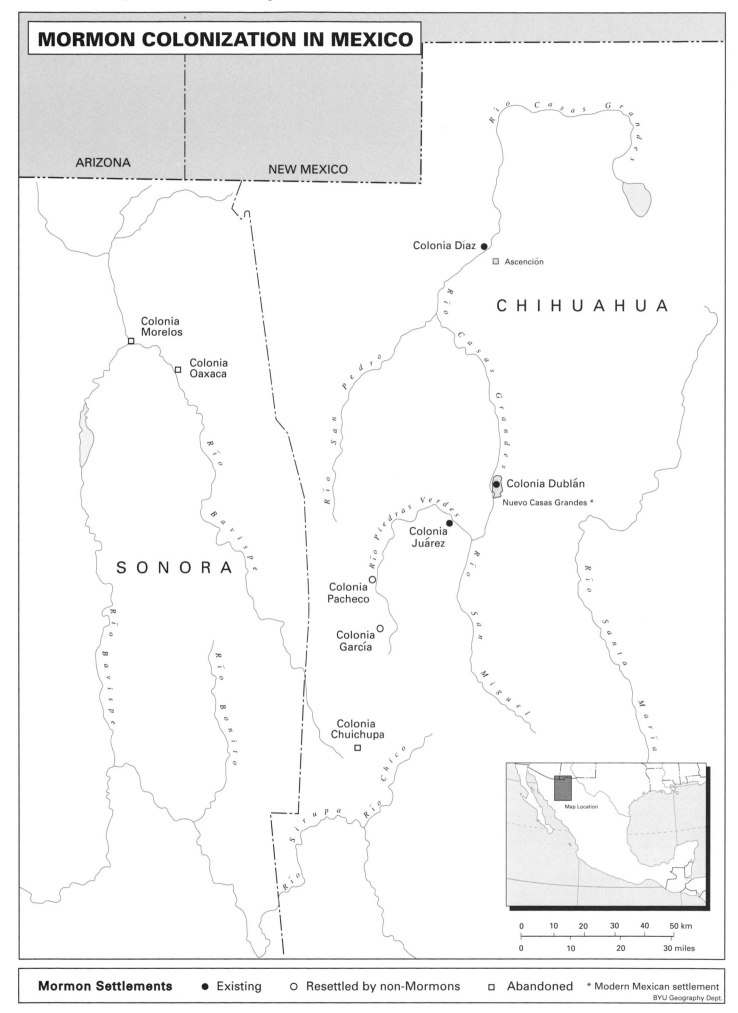

MORMON COLONIZATION IN MEXICO

ARIZONA

NEW MEXICO

Río Casas Grandes

Colonia Díaz ●

☐ Ascención

C H I H U A H U A

Río Casas Grandes

Colonia
Morelos ☐

Colonia
Oaxaca ☐

Río San Pedro

Río Bavispe

S O N O R A

Río Piedras Verdes

Colonia Dublán ●

Nuevo Casas Grandes *

Colonia
Juárez ●

Colonia
Pacheco ○

Río San Miguel

Río Santa María

Colonia
García ○

Río Bavispe

Río Bonito

Colonia
Chuichupa ☐

Río Chico

Río Sirupa

Map Location

0	10	20	30	40	50 km

0	10	20	30 miles

Mormon Settlements   ● Existing   ○ Resettled by non-Mormons   ☐ Abandoned   * Modern Mexican settlement

BYU Geography Dept.

INDIAN FARMS

Howard A. Christy

Mormons were uniquely motivated to reach out to their Native American brethren: they believed that they were brethren in fact—by blood and by birth, because the Book of Mormon told them so. Further, the Book admonished that they must seek out their ancient Lamanite brethren and bring them back to Christ.

The first mission to Native Americans occurred soon after the Church was organized, when in the fall of 1830 a group of missionaries trekked westward from New York to teach the gospel to any who would listen. They were largely unsuccessful, and the effort was abandoned until two decades later—after the exodus of the entire Church to the Great Basin. Once again, missionaries were sent out, and other, less religiously motivated, accommodations were attempted. For the first time, Mormons came face to face with Native Americans on a day-to-day basis as both groups competed for the same land and resources in the oases along Utah's Wasatch Front and elsewhere. At the earliest opportunity, Brigham Young, as territorial governor, ex officio superintendent of Indian affairs, and president of the Church, forthrightly and pragmatically addressed the serious problems that soon presented themselves between the two groups. He met with only limited success.

Relations were complicated, uneven, confused, and more often than not, tragic. The cultural gap between the two groups was very broad, and misunderstanding was deep. Leaders on both sides sought accommodation but were unable to succeed. Central to the dilemma was an irreconcilable disagreement as to how the bounties of the earth should be shared and controlled. On the one hand, the Mormon settlers immediately took ownership of the very limited usable land under the belief (shared by most Europeans) that it rightly belonged to those who could develop it to its fullest economic potential. On the other hand, Native Americans generally believed that the bounties of the earth were there for all to share—without the necessity for boundaries and individual ownership. Complicating this difference was an erroneous conviction (also shared by most Europeans) that Native Americans would easily become acculturated to European ways. Additionally, one of the most lamentable misfortunes of American history, the vulnerability of Native Americans to European diseases, had its effect in Utah soon after arrival of European settlers, and probably destroyed at the outset any chance for a successful cultural integration. By the time either side might have been able to accommodate the other, both disease and conflict had reduced the local Native Americans to a bitter remnant, whose members either emigrated or were forcibly removed to distant locales. For the most part, the two groups have lived separate existences ever since.

Still, efforts to accommodate were made for several decades, including the establishment by Mormons of missions and farms, and in several cases, dual-purpose farm missions (among Native Americans both nearby and distant). Beginning in 1850, lands were set aside near Mormon settlements, supplied with the necessary tools, equipment, seeds, and animals, and local natives were invited to move there and learn to till the soil and tend livestock under the tutelage of a resident Mormon farmer. The presumption was that once the Native Americans learned to farm, they would give up their traditional hunter-gatherer way of living and become acculturated to the European system of agriculture. At the same time, the gospel of Christ was extended to the native people, also with limited success.

Again, the effort largely miscarried. The farms were small, ill equipped, ill maintained, and sparsely attended, and, one by one, most were abandoned only a short time after they were established. Some were appropriated and operated by the federal government before being abandoned or absorbed into the reservation system, others were reabsorbed into the general Mormon agricultural landscape, and a few tiny outposts have survived into the present. Depending upon the wisdom and capabilities of the different individuals involved on both sides, some assistance, acquiescence, accommodation, and even love was achieved in one locale, while disagreement, lack of cooperation, resentment, hatred, and even bloodshed occurred in another.

If any historical process could qualify as being inevitable, it might be the failure of the three-centuries-long effort to achieve viable accommodation between the anciently established but relatively powerless Native Americans and the more recently established but much more powerful Europeans who ultimately came to dominate the American scene. Honorable intent notwithstanding, the Mormon Indian farm program was doomed to fail along with the larger enterprise of which it was a part.

Howard A. Christy, "Open Hand and Mailed Fist: Mormon-Indian Relations in Utah, 1847–1852," *Utah Historical Quarterly* 46 (Summer 1978): 216–235; Howard A. Christy, "The Walker War: Defense and Conciliation as Strategy," *Utah Historical Quarterly* 47 (Fall 1979):395–420; *Journal History of the Church*, passim, 1847–1880; William M. Rieske, *Utah Indian Farms and Reservations* [map] (1980).

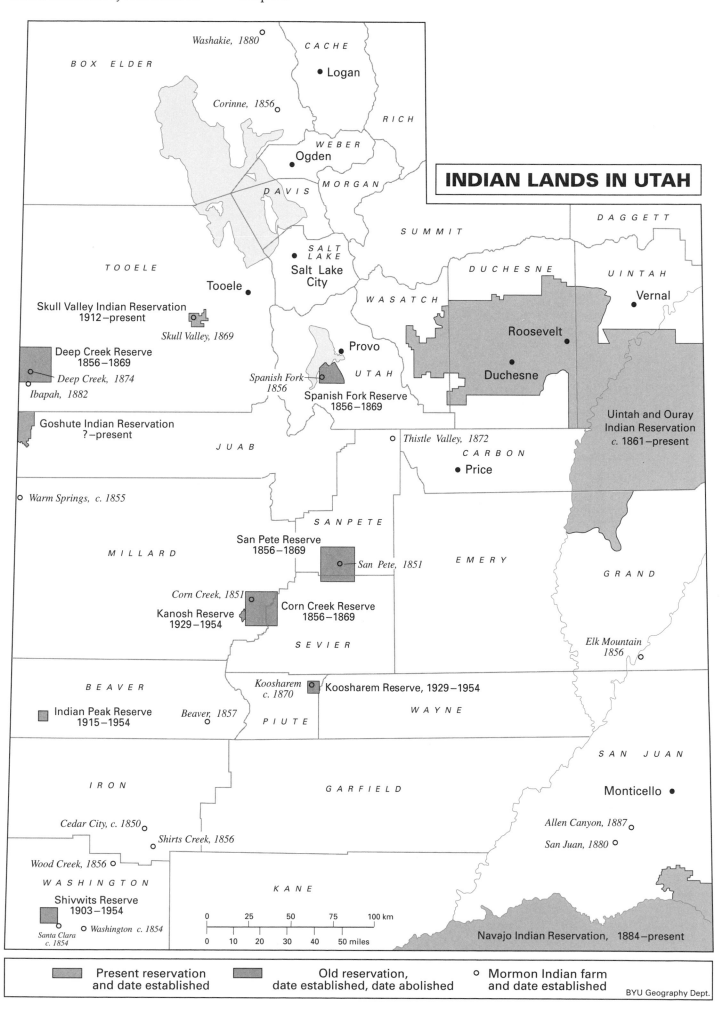

Washakie, 1880

CACHE

BOX ELDER

• Logan

Corinne, 1856

RICH

WEBER

Ogden

MORGAN

DAVIS

SUMMIT

DAGGETT

INDIAN LANDS IN UTAH

SALT LAKE

DUCHESNE

UINTAH

TOOELE

Salt Lake City

WASATCH

Vernal

Tooele

Roosevelt

Skull Valley Indian Reservation
1912–present

Skull Valley, 1869

Deep Creek Reserve
1856–1869

Deep Creek, 1874

Provo

Duchesne

Ibapah, 1882

Spanish Fork 1856

UTAH

Goshute Indian Reservation
?–present

Spanish Fork Reserve
1856–1869

Uintah and Ouray
Indian Reservation
c. 1861–present

JUAB

Thistle Valley, 1872

CARBON

• Price

Warm Springs, c. 1855

SANPETE

San Pete Reserve
1856–1869

EMERY

GRAND

MILLARD

San Pete, 1851

Corn Creek, 1851

Kanosh Reserve
1929–1954

Corn Creek Reserve
1856–1869

SEVIER

Elk Mountain
1856

Koosharem
c. 1870

Koosharem Reserve, 1929–1954

BEAVER

Indian Peak Reserve
1915–1954

Beaver, 1857

PIUTE

WAYNE

SAN JUAN

IRON

GARFIELD

Monticello •

Cedar City, c. 1850

Allen Canyon, 1887

Shirts Creek, 1856

San Juan, 1880

Wood Creek, 1856

WASHINGTON

KANE

Shivwits Reserve
1903–1954

| 0 | 25 | 50 | 75 | 100 km |

Santa Clara c. 1854

Washington c. 1854

| 0 | 10 | 20 | 30 | 40 | 50 miles |

Navajo Indian Reservation, 1884–present

Present reservation
and date established

Old reservation,
date established, date abolished

○ Mormon Indian farm
and date established

BYU Geography Dept.

ABANDONED SETTLEMENTS IN THE WEST

Lynn A. Rosenvall

During the latter half of the 19th century, the Mormons established nearly 500 settlements in an area covering seven western states and stretching from Mexico to Canada. Since abandoned settlements often leave little evidence of their past, it is difficult to determine which of these settlements still exist.

Research, however, indicates that 69 of the 497 communities (13.9 percent) that were founded in the West during the period of 1847 to 1900 have been abandoned. When the communities that were founded in the Midwest, Canada, and Mexico are included, the failure rate jumps to 16.4 percent or 88 out of a total of 537.

The year 1900 has been recognized as a practical terminal date for Mormon colonization, and on these maps only settlements that were *founded* prior to 1900 are shown. The year 1930, however, was selected as the closing date for abandoned settlements, and only settlements that *failed* before 1930 are included. The period of 1900 to 1930 provides a potential "failure zone" for settlements that were founded toward the end of the 19th century.

It is difficult to assign an exact abandonment date to many of these settlements because they were vacated over a period of time and because adequate records do not exist. For some settlements, the failure period could be before or after the given date, or both. Some of these sites, such as San Bernardino, Mormon Station, and Las Vegas, were reoccupied in later years by others.

Failure rates may appear to be high in light of the careful attention that Mormons gave to locating their settlements. On the other hand, one must consider the uninviting environment and the debilitating external factors that the inhabitants faced.

Abandoned settlements can be divided into two major groups: (1) settlements that failed because of pressures from outside forces over which the Mormons had little or no control, and (2) settlements that ceased to exist because of the inhabitants' volition. The first group failed because of such factors as Indian conflicts, the coming of Johnston's army (in the Utah War), Nevada tax problems, religious conflicts, and the Mexican Revolution. This group is the smallest—26 failures out of 497 settlements, or 5.2 percent. The second group, whose failures were due to environmental factors, were abandoned, in general, because of floods, inadequate water supply, and poor location. Fully 43 settlements (8.7 percent) ceased to exist because of environmental factors. This group is possibly the more important of the two, because by analyzing these settlements one can begin to judge the ability of Mormons to locate permanent settlements within some of the harsh environments of the arid West.

Because Mormons had to learn about their new surroundings by trial and error, one might expect that most of the failures would occur during the first few years. But, surprisingly, no settlements that were founded during the period 1847 to 1849 failed for reasons linked to the environment. The period with the highest failure rate was the decade of 1870 to 1879, when areas of the Colorado Plateau, mainly Arizona, were first settled. Moreover, by 1870 the most desirable areas of the Mormon region were occupied, and only marginal spots remained to be colonized.

Even at their zenith, the population of these 43 abandoned settlements, abandoned due to environmental factors, was notably small. Therefore, their effect on Mormon colonization was minimal. For example, the average peak population per settlement was approximately 100 persons. Consequently, fewer than 5,000 persons were affected. Some of these communities consisted of only three or four families at most, and the largest ones contained no more than about 400 persons.

Low population could have been a factor in the demise of some settlements. For example, large dams were often required to control the overflow of rivers, and these impoundments could not be readily built by a community consisting of 100 or fewer persons. Several settlements also suffered from low population because the removal of only a few families made the function of a community difficult or made the region undesirable to the remaining settlers.

Most colonists did not give up readily. In fact, only three communities were vacated within the first year of occupancy, and some settlements lasted as long as 60 years or more before their demise. The average lifetime of these 43 settlements was approximately 22 years. Such statistics attest to the tenacity of the Mormon colonizing venture. The significant aspect is not that 43 settlements failed for environmental reasons, but that the marginal nature of the areas colonized by the Mormons did not lead to a much higher failure rate.

Stephen L. Carr, *The Historical Guide to Utah Ghost Towns* (1972); Andrew Jensen, *Encyclopedic History of the Church of Jesus Christ of Latter-day Saints* (1941); Lynn A. Rosenvall, "Defunct Mormon Settlements: 1830–1930," in *The Mormon Role in the Settlement of the West*, Richard H. Jackson, editor (1978).

FORMER MORMON SETTLEMENTS

MONT.

ORE.

IDAHO

Snake River

Ft. Limhi •

WYO.

Morristown ○

Meadowville ○

● Ft. Bridger
● Ft. Supply

Iosepa ○

● Mt. Dell
● Mound City

Skull Valley ○

Palmyra ○
Ft. Saint Luke

Knightsville ●

NEV.

Georgetown ○

Juab ○

UTAH

COLO.

● Mormon Station
● Frankton

Prattville ○

Elephant ○ ● Giles
○ ○ Caineville

● Elk Mt.

Ephraim ●
○ Eastdale

Spring Valley ●

Ft. Sanford ●

Los Cerritos ○

Bloomington
Price
Tonaquint
Harrisburg
Mountain Dell
Duncan's Retreat
Adventure
Shonesburg

Clover Valley ○

Pinto

Dalton

Clifton ○

Hebron ○
Hamblin ○

Zion ●

Georgetown ○

Northrop

Paria ○
Adairville ○

La Plata ○

CALIF.

West Point ●
Mill Point ○
Simonsville

Pipe Springs

Scutumpah
Johnson

● Tuba City

Las Vegas ●

Junction City

Call's
Landing

Taylor
Brigham City ○ ○ ○ Obed

● Meadows

Sunset
Wilford ●

○ ○ Concho

● Pleasanton

N. MEX.

Adair ● Forest Dale

● San Bernardino

ARIZ.

Nephi ○

MacDonald ○

Rio Grande

Colonia San José ●

● Colonia Díaz

Colonia Oaxaca ○ ● Colonia Morelos

PACIFIC
OCEAN

MEXICO

Cave Valley ○ ● Galeana

| 0 | 100 | 200 | 300 | 400 | 500 km |

| 0 | 100 | 200 | 300 miles |

Causes of extinction: ○ Environmental factors ● External factors

BYU Geography Department

POLYGAMY

Martha S. Bradley

In some measure it was rumors of plural marriage that led to the assassination of the Prophet Joseph Smith and the eventual removal of the Saints from Nauvoo. Although it would not be until 1852 that apostle Orson Pratt would publicly announce before a general conference of the Church the doctrine of plural marriage, Joseph Smith was sealed to his first plural wife as early as 1835. In Nauvoo, Joseph introduced some of his most trusted associates to the doctrine, was himself sealed to several additional wives, and permitted others to do likewise.

As the Mormons traveled west, their plural families joined together as groups, sometimes for the first time. Brigham Young encouraged these family organizations, or "kingdoms," to unite into companies for the journey into the far West. After leaving Mt. Pisgah and arriving in Winter Quarters, Zina Diantha Huntington Jacobs Young lived for the first time with her sister wives, women like Eliza R. Snow, who was sealed to Brigham Young after Joseph Smith's death.

Polygamy spread throughout the Great Basin with virtually all colonization efforts, although to say polygamy existed everywhere is a misleading conclusion. While it is likely that polygamists lived in most Mormon towns, plurality was much more popular in some places than in others. For example, the incidence of plural marriage was higher in southern settlements such as St. George and Santa Clara than in communities north of Salt Lake City such as Bountiful or Utah's gentile capital, Ogden, which had the lowest incidence of plural marriage.

It was a decade after the 1852 Pratt address that the federal government passed its first antibigamy law—the Morrill Act—prohibiting plural marriage in the territories. Because the country was in the midst of the Civil War, the law was left unenforced, and Mormons continued to practice plural marriage openly. During the 1870s, however, federal pressure to conform to the law increased and the 1879 *Reynolds v. United States* case confirmed the constitutionality of the Morrill Act.

From that point forward, Presidents Rutherford B. Hayes, James A. Garfield, and Chester A. Arthur publicly condemned the practice. In response to this and an overwhelming public outcry against the practice, Congress passed the Edmunds Act in 1882 and subsequently a strengthened version in 1887 known as the Edmunds-Tucker Bill. In addition to making polygamy a felony, these laws destroyed the temporal power of the Church by disincorporating it and calling for the escheat of Church properties. In response to these pressures, many polygamous members of the Church went into hiding in what became known among Mormons as the underground. Mormon society was completely disrupted as husbands, wives, and often children moved to surrounding states and territories like Afton, Wyoming, or Franklin, Idaho. Quickly it became apparent that the threat of arrest was just as real outside Utah, and Mormons looked elsewhere for refuge.

Colonization efforts increased in the 1870s and 1880s largely in reaction to the pressure caused by the antipolygamy legislation. In less than three years, from 1876 to 1879, more than 100 new settlements were founded outside Utah, in Arizona, Nevada, Wyoming, and Colorado. Havens for polygamists on the run, these settlements expanded Mormon influence throughout the region.

Although the first expedition to Mexico was in 1875, it was not until the mid-1880s that serious colonization efforts began, spurred by intense pressure created by the Edmunds Act of 1882. By the end of 1885, hundreds of Mormon colonists poured into Chihuahua in northern Mexico, encouraged to do so by Church leaders.

By the time that Utah became a state (1896), more than 3,000 Saints lived in eight polygamous colonies in Mexico—six in Chihuahua and two in Sonora. The Mormon settlements were scattered across the varied terrain of northern Mexico and included the plateau colonies of Juárez, Dublán, and Díaz; the mountain colonies of Cave Valley; Pacheco, García, and Chuichupa (all in the state of Chihuahua); and in Sonora, the semi-tropical colonies of Oaxaca and Morelos. Throughout this period Mexican statutes prohibited polygamy, but the government did not actively prosecute Mormons.

In September 1886, after hearing that Charles Ora Card was planning to travel to Mexico to escape prosecution for polygamy, Church president John Taylor advised him to go instead to British Columbia to find a site for a Mormon settlement. Taylor was sure that there the Mormons would find "British justice." The Church organized the Cardston Ward of the Cache Stake in 1895, and by 1891 there were 359 Mormons in Cardston and the surrounding area. After the 1890 Manifesto, plural marriage lingered longest in isolated communities, like the Mexican colonies, and in areas on the periphery of Mormon centers.

Lowell C. Bennion, "The Incidence of Mormon Polygamy in 1880: 'Dixie' versus Davis Stake," *Journal of Mormon History* 11(1984): 27–42; Brigham Y. Card, *The Mormon Presence in Canada* (1990); Kate B. Carter, comp., *Treasures of Pioneer History* (1953), 2:80–83; Larry M. Logue, *A Sermon in the Desert: Belief and Behavior in Early St. George, Utah* (1988); Richard VanWagoner, *Mormon Polygamy: A History* (1986), p. 189.

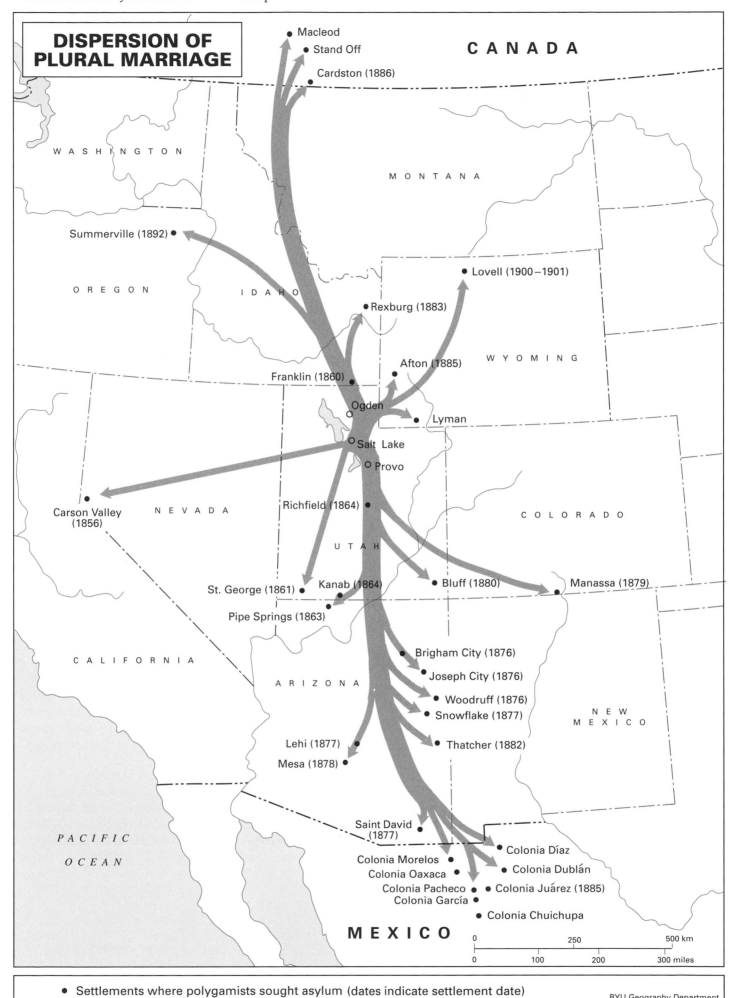

DISPERSION OF PLURAL MARRIAGE

CANADA

Macleod

Stand Off

Cardston (1886)

WASHINGTON

MONTANA

OREGON

IDAHO

Summerville (1892)

Lovell (1900–1901)

Rexburg (1883)

Afton (1885)

WYOMING

Franklin (1860)

Ogden

Lyman

Salt Lake

Provo

Carson Valley (1856)

NEVADA

Richfield (1864)

COLORADO

UTAH

St. George (1861)   Kanab (1864)   Bluff (1880)   Manassa (1879)

Pipe Springs (1863)

CALIFORNIA

Brigham City (1876)

ARIZONA

Joseph City (1876)

Woodruff (1876)

Snowflake (1877)

NEW MEXICO

Lehi (1877)   Thatcher (1882)

Mesa (1878)

Saint David (1877)

PACIFIC OCEAN

Colonia Díaz

Colonia Morelos

Colonia Oaxaca   Colonia Dublán

Colonia Pacheco   Colonia Juárez (1885)

Colonia García

Colonia Chuichupa

MEXICO

0   250   500 km

0   100   200   300 miles

• Settlements where polygamists sought asylum (dates indicate settlement date)

BYU Geography Department

GENTILES IN UTAH

Philip F. Notarianni

The term *gentile* is often used to describe individuals or groups, not of the Mormon faith, who immigrated to Utah. The main impetus for non-Mormon settlement resulted from U.S. military activity and the growing economic diversity and industrialization that began in the mid-nineteenth century. Of particular importance were the railroad and mining industries.

With the 1849 California gold rush, Jewish merchants entered to help supply migrating prospectors. The U.S. Army sent soldiers into Utah territory to establish Camp Floyd in 1857. In 1862, Col. Patrick Connor and the Third California Volunteers entered the Salt Lake Valley and established Fort Douglas.

In 1869, when the Transcontinental Railroad joined at Promontory, Utah, non-Mormon merchants and former Union Army officers established the town of Corinne, which quickly became the early gentile capital of Utah. Corinne was founded on the Union Pacific Railroad line as a freight center to serve Montana mines and trails. The town fought Mormons politically and economically.

Colonel Connor's soldiers had prospected the mountains surrounding Salt Lake Valley. With rail transportation appearing in the 1860s, effective commercial mining for precious metals began in the 1870s. With the influx of non-Mormon laborers, accompanying service industries arrived, as well as needed institutions such as social and fraternal organizations.

Irish railroad men, fresh from working on the transcontinental railroad, flocked to mining towns, as did Chinese. Based on prospecting done by Connor's men in the 1860s, mining towns near Salt Lake City sprang up, dotting not only Salt Lake, but Tooele, Summit, Juab, Utah, and Beaver counties. With camps and towns came more people.

Religious diversity accompanied ethnic diversity. Evangelical Protestants were among the first Gentiles to organize. Episcopalians began activity in 1867 under Daniel Sylvester Tuttle. Tuttle's philosophy was peaceful coexistence with Mormons. St. Mark's Cathedral began in 1870, and by 1880, Episcopalians had founded Rowland Hall School.

Rev. Edward Bayless brought Presbyterianism to Corinne in 1870, followed by churches in Salt Lake City, Alta, and Mount Pleasant. Many Scandinavian converts to Mormonism lived in Sanpete County, and Presbyterian ministers began work to return them to Protestantism. Schools again proved important, especially during the 1877–1884 period, when Wasatch Academy opened in Mount Pleasant. Presbyterian congregations were founded in Bingham Canyon (1875), American Fork (1876), Manti (1878), Ogden (1878), Brigham City (1878), Logan (1878), Springville (1880), and Payson (1883).

In 1868, Rev. A. N. Fisher of the Methodist Church visited Salt Lake City. By 1870, Methodist activity began, again in railroad and mining towns. Park City boasted a Methodist church in 1891. The Women's Home Missionary Society, inaugurated in 1880, was active in Salt Lake City, Ogden, Moroni, Spanish Fork, Richfield, Elsinore, Grantsville, Ephraim, Mount Pleasant, and Spring City. In 1895, Utah Methodists numbered 1,440.

Catholicism in Utah is traced originally to the Franciscan Spanish missionaries Dominguez and Escalante, who journeyed into the Utah area in 1776. In 1873, Rev. Lawrence Scanlan, who came to symbolize Irish influence, arrived in Utah to establish the effective foundations of Catholicism. Scanlan's first missionary efforts were directed toward Salt Lake City and Ogden (1875), then Silver Reef (1879), Park City (1881), Frisco (1881), and Eureka (1885). The Diocese of Salt Lake City was established in 1891 with 8,000 members in 15 churches.

Another group to enter Utah was the Baptists. George W. Dodge established the first congregation in 1871, which lasted until 1875. In 1881, Rev. Dwight Spencer began the Ogden Baptist Church, completing a building in 1882. He created a congregation in Salt Lake City in 1883, finishing a building in 1884. From 1884 to 1900, 5 preaching stations and 13 churches existed in the area. A Swedish Baptist church opened in 1891, and about 1892, members of Utah's black community established the Calvary Baptist Church. By 1896, Baptists counted 478 members, 4 schools, and 9 churches in Utah.

Lutherans arrived to proselyte, particularly among Scandinavian Mormons. Congregations were located in Salt Lake City (1882), Mount Pleasant (1888), Ogden (1889), and Santaquin (1894). Most were organized by language, including Norwegian, German, Icelandic, and Danish.

Jewish merchants had arrived in the late 1840s. Julius and Isabell Brooks came to Salt Lake City in 1853, and in 1857, Samuel Auerbach and Samuel Kahn ventured to Camp Floyd. In 1870, Congregation B'nai Israel began in Salt Lake City, and another congregation formed in Ogden in 1890.

In 1881, coal was discovered in what later became Carbon County. New gentile groups flocked to meet labor demands. Finns settled in Scofield, while Italians and southern Slavs were recruited to work in Scofield, Winter Quarters, and Castle Gate. Before 1910, Greek and Japanese miners and railroad workers also arrived, followed by African Americans and Mexican immigrants. Industrialization brought a growing diversity to Utah's population.

Robert J. Dwyer, *The Gentile Comes to Utah: A Study in Religious and Social Conflicts (1862–1890)* (1941); Klaus D. Gurgel, "Churches and Church Membership Patterns," in *Atlas of Utah* (1981), pp. 140–149; T. Edgar Lyon and Glen M. Leonard, "The Churches in the Territory," in Richard D. Poll, Thomas G. Alexander, Eugene E. Campbell, and David E. Miller, editors, *Utah's History* (1989), pp. 317–335; Helen Z. Papanikolas, editor, *The Peoples of Utah* (1976).

GENTILE (NON-MORMON) SETTLEMENTS IN UTAH

BOX ELDER

CACHE

• Promontory

• Logan

• Corinne

• Brigham City

RICH

• Lucin

WEBER

• Ogden

Wahsatch

△ Buel City

MORGAN

DAVIS

• Salduro

• Morgan

• Echo

△ Grass Creek

△ Coalville

SUMMIT

DAGGETT

• Wendover

SALT LAKE CITY

□ Ft. Douglas

Ft. Thornburgh □

○ Grantsville

△ Park City

Bingham Canyon

SALT LAKE

△ Alta

DUCHESNE

Vernal ○

Tooele ○

Copperfield

WASATCH

Ft. Duchesne □

Ophir △

Camp Floyd

Forest City

American Fork

Roosevelt ○

TOOELE

Mercer

Provo

Topliff △

○ Springville

Duchesne ○

Scranton △

• Spanish Fork

Dividend

Payson

Eureka

UTAH

Tintic △ Mammoth

Silver City

Scofield △

Castle Gate

JUAB

Winter Quarters △

• Helper

Joy △

Price ○

CARBON

UINTAH

△ Ibex

Mt. Pleasant

△ Hiawatha

Moroni ○

△ Mohrland

Spring City

○ Ephraim

GRAND

○ Manti

○ Castle Dale

MILLARD

SANPETE

EMERY

Sego △

Green River •

• Thompson

Cisco •

SEVIER

Temple Mtn. △

Basin △

Sulphurdale △

Kimberly

Newhouse △ △

△

Frisco

△ Alunite

WAYNE

• Milford

△ Shantie

PIUTE

△ Stateline

Parowan

IRON

△

GARFIELD

• Modena

SAN JUAN

△ Iron City

WASHINGTON

KANE

Silver Reef △

0   25   50   75   100 km

0 10 20 30 40 50 miles

Gentile Origins   • Railroad   △ Mining   □ Military

BYU Geography Department

PIONEER PROPERTY IN SALT LAKE CITY

Glen M. Leonard

The Latter-day Saints left Nauvoo, Illinois, in 1846 with clear memories of a contest between competing land agents. In the Salt Lake Valley, Brigham Young established an orderly land distribution system to limit the profit motive. Each family received without cost a 1.25-acre city plot, one of eight in each 10-acre block. Men with plural wives could claim additional lots. Farm plots south of Ninth South were 5, 10, and 20 acres. Settlers agreed not to divide or sell their property, a provision not long enforced.

With the initial survey launched on August 3, 1847, members of the Quorum of the Twelve Apostles selected their city lots near the temple block. Brigham Young eventually built his office and homes east of a corner reserved for the Deseret Store and Tithing Office. Heber C. Kimball claimed the next block north, while Willard Richards, the other counselor in the First Presidency, picked lots just south of Temple Square. Other General Authorities built nearby. Together these Church officials owned most of eight blocks surrounding Temple Square. Recorder Thomas Bullock charged a $1.25 recording fee, but owners received legal title only after the U.S. government established a land office in 1873.

Other 1847 pioneers, wintering in the log fort on Block 48, waited a year for building lots. After Church leaders returned from Winter Quarters in September 1848, they allocated city lots through a lottery. The 1847 migration had numbered 2,000 immigrants; the arriving 1848 migration would double that number. The city expanded to meet growing needs. To supplement the useful lots in the 113 blocks of Plot A (22 blocks on the northern hillside were not assigned), Church leaders immediately added Plot B with 63 blocks to the east. Surveys in 1849 and 1850 added 24 blocks to the west (Plot C) and 240 smaller, four-lot blocks (18 of them set aside for a cemetery) on the slopes to the northeast (Plot D). Only one-third of Brigham Young's pioneer party of July 1847 received lots in Plot A; many of them settled elsewhere in the expanding city or in other communities (some single men were not ready to claim lots). Returning Mormon Battalion veterans who claimed lots in Plot A settled mostly in the northernmost tiers or west and south of the fort. So did a few of the Mississippi Saints, but most of that 1847–1848 immigrant company settled ten miles away, on a plot created for them at the mouth of Big Cottonwood Canyon.

City lots were intended for residential use, with space enough for a home, garden, orchard, and small outbuildings. Tradesmen and merchants were expected to operate their businesses on their residential lots, but soon a concentrated business district developed. Settlers built the first public buildings on the temple block—boweries (temporary shelters), tabernacles, public works shops housing carpenters, stonemasons, and blacksmiths, and the Endowment House. Commercial and public buildings appeared outside Temple Square beginning with the Council Hall and nearby mercantile store and post office on Main Street. Soon, other merchants established operations in an emerging commercial district between First and Third South.

With Brigham Young's death in 1877, the Church claimed property held in his name as trustee-in-trust. This included the temple block and commercial and administrative properties to the south and east. Other land surrounding Temple Square gradually moved to LDS Church ownership, especially since the 1950s. Today the Church, through various entities, holds title to nearly 90 acres downtown. Included are several apartment complexes and two shopping malls (ZCMI Center and Crossroads Plaza) with related office towers and parking plazas, all developed by the Church-owned Zions Securities Corporation. Salt Lake County uses Church land under the Salt Palace complex for one dollar a year. With the expansion of church holdings in the 20th century, the same central blocks originally owned largely by Mormon leaders are now under Church control.

Looking ahead to needs of the community and an international Church in a new century, LDS leaders have carefully planned their downtown property. The plan maintains a central corridor of Church office buildings east and west of Temple Square. It looks to more multi-unit housing complexes east and north of that corridor and confirms a commercial use for the district south of South Temple. The master plan guarantees that the buildings of Church headquarters and Temple Square will have a compatible surrounding neighborhood in the vibrant north portion of downtown Salt Lake City.

Leonard J. Arrington, *Brigham Young: American Moses* (1985), pp. 146–147, 168–171; John S. McCormick, *The Historic Buildings of Downtown Salt Lake City* (1982); Nicholas G. Morgan, Sr., *Pioneer Map: Great Salt Lake City* (1950); Michael Phillips, "City, LDS Church Team Up to Create a Shangri-La in S.L.," *Salt Lake Tribune*, June 19, 1992.

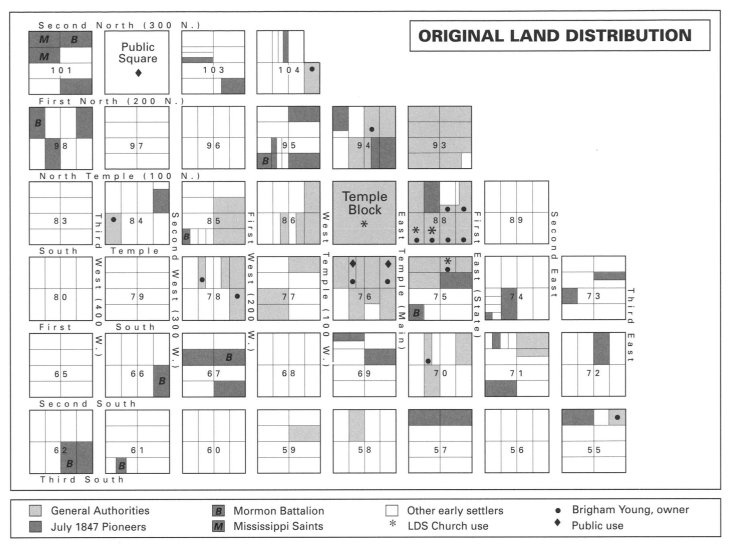

ORIGINAL LAND DISTRIBUTION

| | General Authorities | | **B** | Mormon Battalion | | □ | Other early settlers | | ● | Brigham Young, owner |
| | July 1847 Pioneers | | **M** | Mississippi Saints | | ✳ | LDS Church use | | ◆ | Public use |

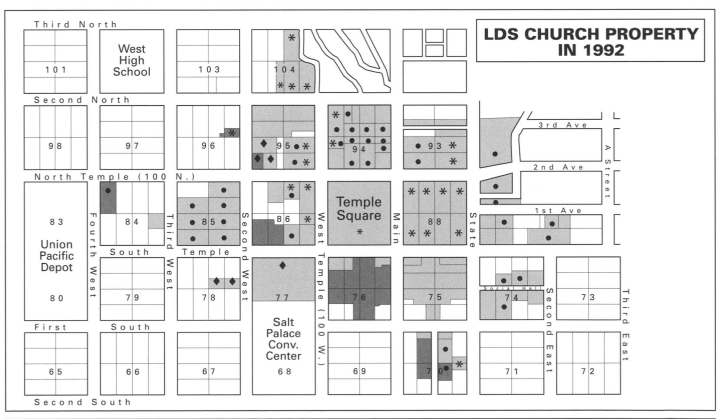

LDS CHURCH PROPERTY IN 1992

| | LDS Church property | | ✳ | LDS Church use | | ● | Parking lot or vacant lot |
| | Owned by Church (with others) | | ◆ | Government use | | | |

BYU Geography Department

MEMBERSHIP GROWTH BY STATES AND COUNTRIES

J. Matthew Shumway

Since its organization, The Church of Jesus Christ of Latter-day Saints has undergone both dramatic increases in membership and changing geographic distribution of its members. It is possible to divide the historical growth and distribution of the Church into four periods based on geographic location.

The early period from 1830 to 1850 can be characterized as a period of rapid growth and migratory movement of the Church. Membership increased from 6 in 1830 to 16,865 in 1840. During this time the main body of the Church moved from upstate New York to Ohio and Missouri, ultimately uniting in Illinois. There the Church continued its rapid growth, almost doubling in size between 1840 and 1845. Such growth was necessary for its survival, but it also frightened many local nonmembers, and by 1845 the Church was forced out of Illinois. This time most members settled in the midst of the Rocky Mountains in what later became Utah. By 1850, Church membership had tripled to 51,839.

The consolidation of the Utah Church characterized the second growth and location period. Between 1850 and 1900, Church membership increased from 51,839 to 283,765, at an average annual growth of approximately 4 percent. During this time the Church encouraged new members to immigrate to the United States and to migrate to Utah. In 1850, only 39 percent of Church members were located in the United States. However, this changed to 90 percent by 1900 as Utah and surrounding states became home to the majority of members. In 1860, 97 percent of Church members in the United States lived in Utah. This concentration peaked in 1870 at 98 percent and then gradually declined to 72 percent by 1900, leaving the Great Basin region home to most members.

A third distinctive period occurred between 1900 and 1950. This was an era of relatively slow growth and slow geographic diffusion from Utah to surrounding states. Church membership went from 283,765 in 1900 to 1,111,314 in 1950, for an average annual growth rate of 2.2 percent, approximately one-half of the 4-percent growth rate during the previous half century. In 1900, 90 percent of the Church's members lived in the United States and 72 percent of these lived in Utah. By 1950, 90 percent of its members were still found in the United States, but only 46 percent of them lived in Utah. The states surrounding Utah contained another 21 percent, while the Pacific states had approximately 14 percent of the Church's membership. Thus, of total Church membership in the United States, 91 percent lived in the western United States. Obvious reasons for slower growth during this time were the two world wars, which reduced both areas where missionaries could proselyte and the number of missionaries available.

Since the end of World War II, the Church has again experienced very rapid growth, averaging almost 5 percent annually. Three factors make this growth particularly important. First, the rate of growth is measured against a larger and increasing base population of Church members, thus representing very large absolute growth. Total Church membership increased from 1,111,314 in 1950 to 8,406,895 by the end of 1993. Second, the majority of new members shifted from children of members, who are baptized at eight years of age, to convert baptisms, although this varies widely among geographic regions. Third, during this time the majority of growth took place outside the United States. By the end of 1992, only 53 percent of Church members resided in the United States, with only 16.5 percent living in Utah. For rates of growth, the fastest growing world regions are Africa (13 percent), Mexico and Central America (12 percent), South America (10 percent), and Asia (9 percent). For absolute growth, the newest members of the Church are coming from South America, Mexico and Central America, the western United States, and the eastern United States. If current regional growth trends continue, the demographic makeup of Church members will be dramatically different in the future. The biggest changes will be in the United States, Canada, and Europe, regions that will likely decline from around 40 percent in the year 2000 to 22 percent by 2010 and only 11 percent of Church membership by 2020. On the other hand, Mexico, Central America, and South America should increase from around 46 percent in the year 2000 to 62 percent in 2010 and 71 percent of all Church membership by 2020.

This internationalization of Church membership represents the Church's attempt to fulfill its divinely inspired mission to spread its gospel to "every nation, and kindred, and tongue, and people" (D&C 133:37).

Deseret News 1993–1994 Church Almanac (1992); Tim B. Heaton, "Vital Statistics," in *Encyclopedia of Mormonism*, Daniel H. Ludlow, editor (1992) 4:1518–1531; Rodney Stark, "The Rise of a New World Faith," *Review of Religious Research* 26 (1984):18–27.

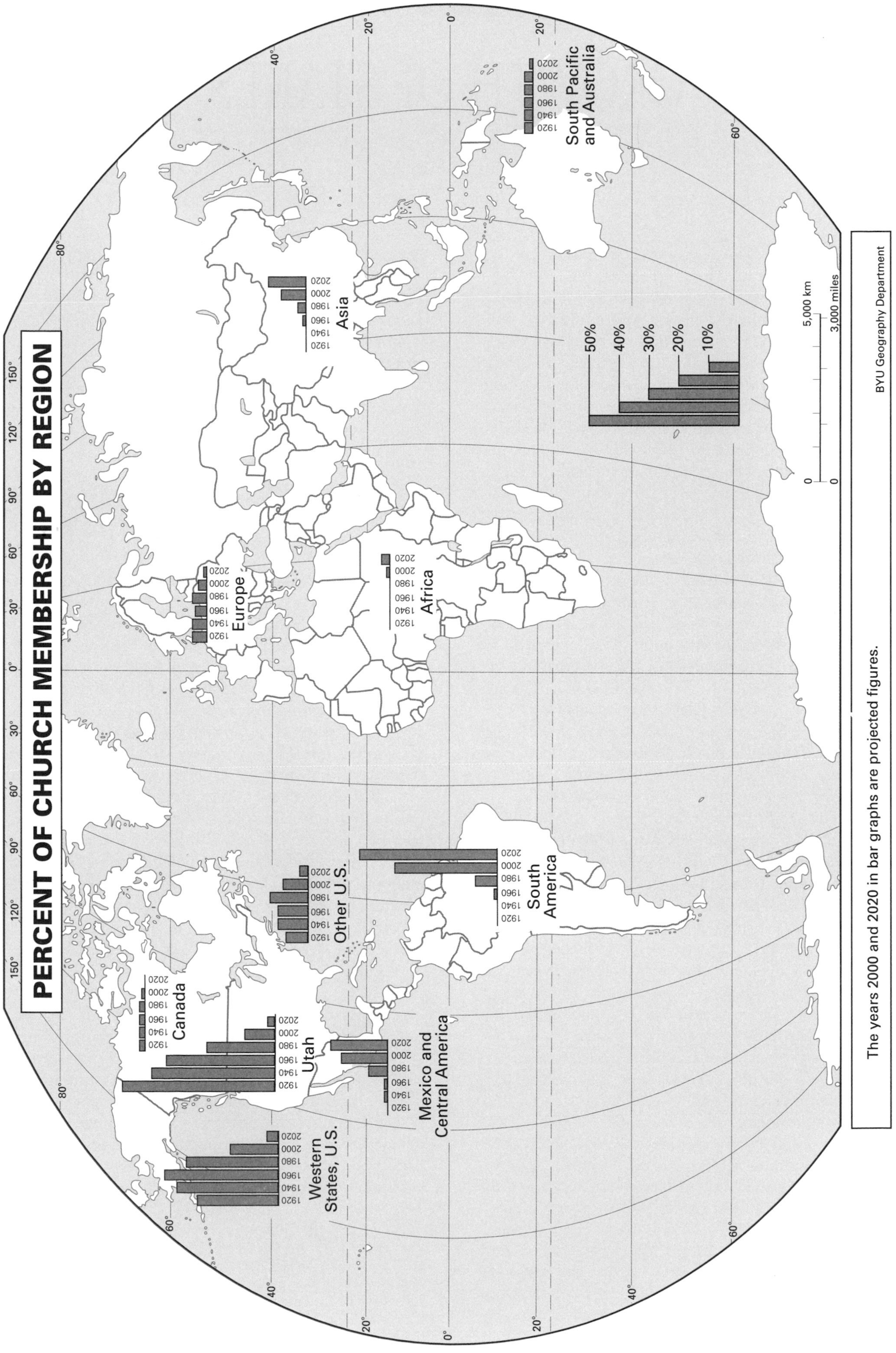

PERCENT OF CHURCH MEMBERSHIP BY REGION

South Pacific
and Australia

2020
2000
1980
1960
1940
1920

Asia

2020
2000
1980
1960
1940
1920

Europe

2020
2000
1980
1960
1940
1920

Africa

2020
1980
1960
1940
1920

50%
40%
30%
20%
10%

5,000 km

3,000 miles

0

Canada

2020
2000
1980
1960
1940
1920

Other U.S.

2020
2000
1980
1960
1940
1920

Utah

2020
2000
1980
1960
1940
1920

Mexico and
Central America

2020
2000
1980
1960
1940
1920

South
America

2020
2000
1980
1960
1940
1920

Western
States, U.S.

2020
2000
1980
1960
1940
1920

The years 2000 and 2020 in bar graphs are projected figures.

BYU Geography Department

123

GROWTH OF STAKES

Dale J. Stevens

A stake in The Church of Jesus Christ of Latter-day Saints is an administrative unit encompassing five to 12 wards or congregations. A stake is organized after the local population of an area reaches approximately 3,000 members and there are sufficient numbers to assume leadership roles in the ward and stake offices. Otherwise, in areas where Church membership is limited, members belong to branches and are under the jurisdiction of a mission. The stake or mission is an administrative level of Church organization between the wards or branches and Church headquarters. The function of the stake is to guide and direct the local affairs of the Church. A stake is led by a stake presidency consisting of a president, two counselors, and a 12-member high council of high priests.

The term *stake* symbolically represents the tent pegs holding in place the tent of God's covering over the Church. Isaiah 54:2 refers to stakes, or pegs, firmly holding the curtains around the tabernacle or sanctuary and seat of the Lord. The stake serves a similar purpose in the Church today.

The first stake was organized in 1832 in Kirtland, Ohio, with Joseph Smith as the stake president. The second stake was organized in Clay County, Missouri, in 1834. Before the Saints were forced to move from their settlements in Ohio, Illinois, and Missouri, ten stakes had been organized. No stakes were organized during the troubled years 1841 to 1846. Upon arrival in the Salt Lake Valley in 1847, the Salt Lake Stake was established.

Between 1847 and 1877, stake organization was not given as much emphasis as during earlier and later periods. Their main function during this time was to host conferences, to instruct ward leaders, and to discharge disciplinary actions that were brought before the stake high councils. The general trend was that directions to ward bishops came directly from general Church authorities. During this period, seven stakes were organized in Utah, as well as one in San Bernardino, California, one in St. Louis, Missouri, and one in Carson Valley, Nevada.

A major restructuring of Church organization was begun in 1877 by Brigham Young. He declared that all stakes were equal and autonomous and that the Salt Lake Stake held no authority over other stakes. Members of the Quorum of the Twelve Apostles were released as stake presidents and several of the largest stakes were divided. Quarterly stake conferences were instituted, to be presided over by a visiting General Authority. Stake presidencies were to be involved in overseeing the wards in their stake and to call local priesthood leaders to be home missionaries. The stake thus became the major governing unit between the wards and Church headquarters. Between 1847 and 1880, twenty-three stakes were organized. Although most were in Utah, stakes functioned in

Arizona and Idaho, while the San Bernardino, St. Louis, and Carson Valley stakes had been discontinued. The first stakes organized outside of the United States were in 1895 in Cardston, Alberta, Canada, followed by one in Colonia Juárez, Mexico. The following illustrates the growth of stakes to the beginning of 1993. In October of 1993 there were 1,956 stakes in over 50 separate countries of the world.

1840	10	1900	43	1960	319
1850	1	1910	62	1970	537
1860	7	1920	83	1980	1,218
1870	9	1930	104	1990	1,784
1880	23	1940	134	1993	1,956
1890	32	1950	180		

As of October 1993, there were stakes in every state and in the District of Columbia in the United States and in seven provinces in Canada. There were 18 countries in Latin America that had stakes, 15 in Europe, 7 in the South Pacific, 5 in Asia, and 3 in Africa.

Although ward meetinghouses have always been the focus of most Church functions, many stakes also constructed stake tabernacles or large assembly halls between 1852 and 1956. Approximately 70 tabernacles were constructed during that period to be used for the quarterly stake conferences and other cultural events. Many of these tabernacles are still used for stake conferences, musical concerts, and other functions. Currently in most stakes, a large stake house, which also serves as a meetinghouse for two to four wards, houses stake offices and provides facilities for stake conferences and other stake events. A typical stake in Utah with ten wards has a stake house and two or three other ward meeting buildings.

Aside from the traditional functions of the stake, some stakes have been instrumental in testing and adopting programs that have become church-wide in application. Among them are the seminary program for high school students, youth drama, social and sports programs, family home evening, the Church welfare program, and others. Today stakes hold conferences twice a year. Along with the usual administrative responsibilities, stake presidencies issue temple recommends, ordain worthy men to priesthood offices, and assume other functions formerly performed by general Church authorities.

Stan L. Albrecht, "Stakes," in *Encyclopedia of Mormonism*, Daniel H. Ludlow, editor (1992) 3:1411–1414; Richard O. Cowan, *The Church in the Twentieth Century* (1985); *Deseret News 1993–1994 Church Almanac* (1992); Crystal Wride Jensen, "The Geographical Landscape of Tabernacles in the Mormon Cultural Region" (Master's thesis, Brigham Young University, 1992).

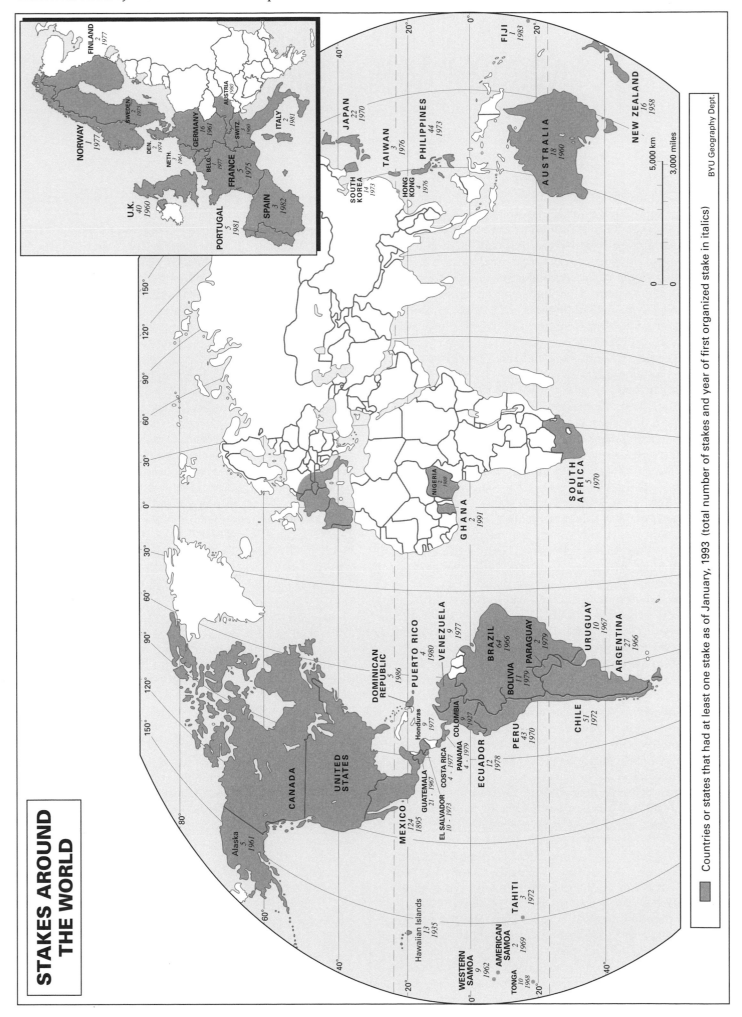

STAKES AROUND
THE WORLD

Countries or states that had at least one stake as of January, 1993 (total number of stakes and year of first organized stake in italics)

BYU Geography Dept.

5,000 km

3,000 miles

Inset map:

FINLAND
2
1977

NORWAY
1
1977

SWEDEN
5
1975

DEN.
2
1974

NETH.
3
196?

U.K.
40
1960

BELG.
1
1977

GERMANY
16
1961

AUSTRIA
1
1980

SWITZ.
5
1960

FRANCE
5
1975

ITALY
2
1981

PORTUGAL
5
1981

SPAIN
3
1982

Main map labels:

JAPAN
22
1970

TAIWAN
3
1976

SOUTH
KOREA
4
1973

HONG
KONG
4
1976

PHILIPPINES
44
1973

FIJI
1
1983

NEW ZEALAND
16
1958

AUSTRALIA
18
1960

NIGERIA
2
1988

GHANA
2
1991

SOUTH
AFRICA
5
1970

CANADA

UNITED
STATES

Alaska
5
1961

MEXICO
124
1895

GUATEMALA
21
1967

EL SALVADOR
10 - 1973

Honduras
9
1977

COSTA RICA
4 - 1977

PANAMA
4 - 1979

DOMINICAN
REPUBLIC
5
1986

PUERTO RICO
4
1980

VENEZUELA
9
1977

COLOMBIA
12
1977

ECUADOR
12
1978

PERU
43
1970

BRAZIL
64
1966

BOLIVIA
11
1979

PARAGUAY
2
1979

URUGUAY
10
1967

ARGENTINA
27
1966

CHILE
51
1972

Hawaiian Islands
13
1935

TAHITI
3
1972

WESTERN
SAMOA
9
1962

AMERICAN
SAMOA
2
1969

TONGA
10
1968

DAVID O. McKAY'S WORLDWIDE TRAVELS

Lavina Fielding Anderson

In the fall of 1920, David O. McKay, 47 years old and an apostle since age 32, was sent on an extraordinary mission by LDS Church president Heber J. Grant. He was accompanied by Hugh J. Cannon, the indefatigable and cheerful president of Liberty Stake in Salt Lake City. Their odyssey spanned 12 months, more than 61,000 miles, and 15 missions; they met with more than 300 missionaries and uncounted members, friends, and public officials. According to Hugh J. Cannon's summary, they had traveled 23,777 miles on land and 37,869 by water, on 24 separate oceangoing vessels.

This year-long voyage by the young apostle was unquestionably influential in two ways: first, 40 years before the Church was ready for extensive international growth, it gave McKay an international outlook and a keen sense of the need for representing members of the Church far from its center core; and second, it confirmed his already strong passion for face-to-face contact in collecting information, working out problems, and dealing with the press about the image of the Church.

McKay had been the first apostle to visit most of the countries on his itinerary. Over the next 34 years, he continued to travel widely, as an apostle, as a member of the First Presidency, and, after 1951, as president of the Church. His international travels had begun with his mission to Scotland (1897–1899). From 1922 to 1924, he served as president of the European Mission, conducting a conference nearly every weekend and traveling repeatedly to virtually every city of any size in Great Britain, Wales, the Netherlands, France, Switzerland, Germany, Denmark, Sweden, and Norway. He and his wife also accompanied Mae Booth to visit her missionary husband, Joseph Booth, in Aleppo, Syria. After his return to the United States, he maintained a heavy schedule of stake conferences, including, most years, an extensive mission tour that took him away from home for weeks at a time: the Eastern States Mission (1925); the Southern States Mission (1926); Alberta, Canada (1927); the Central States Mission (1927); Eastern Canada (1929); Idaho (1930, 1931); Washington, D.C. (1930); and Montana (1931), until he became a member of the First Presidency in 1935.

His first major presidential tour took him to Europe in 1952, where in 64 days his party visited nine countries, some of them more than once, selected temple sites in England and Switzerland, and held at least 49 public meetings. This itinerary included Scotland, England, Switzerland, the Netherlands, Denmark, Sweden, Finland, Germany, Switzerland (again), France, Wales, England (again), and Scotland (again). In 1953, he returned to Europe to dedicate the London Temple site, combining it with mission tours that covered 16,600 miles in 21 days. The groundbreaking services for the London Temple (1955), the dedication of the Swiss Temple and the Tabernacle Choir tour of Europe (1955), and the dedication of the London Temple (1958) all furnished reasons to return. In 1954, he became the first president of the Church to visit South Africa, South America, and Central America, an ambitious 35,000-mile undertaking that began in London.

McKay was an extraordinary ambassador for the Church. According to one of his sons who acted as his secretary during one of these strenuous tours, McKay spoke spontaneously and freely in his public address, easily weaving in local allusions and adapting "the rhythms of his speech to convenient units for translations." Courteous and charming in his numerous press interviews and conferences, he easily disarmed hostile reporters.

> Father's stamina was extraordinary. He seldom got more than six or seven hours of sleep a night, . . . thought nothing of making up time by missing a meal or even two and had a remarkable ability to move from public presentation to intimate counseling sessions without losing his intense focus. He was never inattentive nor distracted, no matter how fatigued. . . . He understood intuitively that his visit was the experience of a lifetime for the Saints and willingly . . . [shook] hands for hours with entire congregations after nearly every conference (McKay, 220–221).

The result of such tours was a spurt in the callings of local leaders, a vigorous building program, and the growth of Church schools, stakes, and temples around the world. This travel was a foundation for spiraling Church growth during the entire last half of the 20th century.

Francis M. Gibbons, *David O. McKay: Apostle to the World, Prophet of God* (1986); David Lawrence McKay, *My Father, David O. McKay*, Lavina Fielding Anderson, editor (1989).

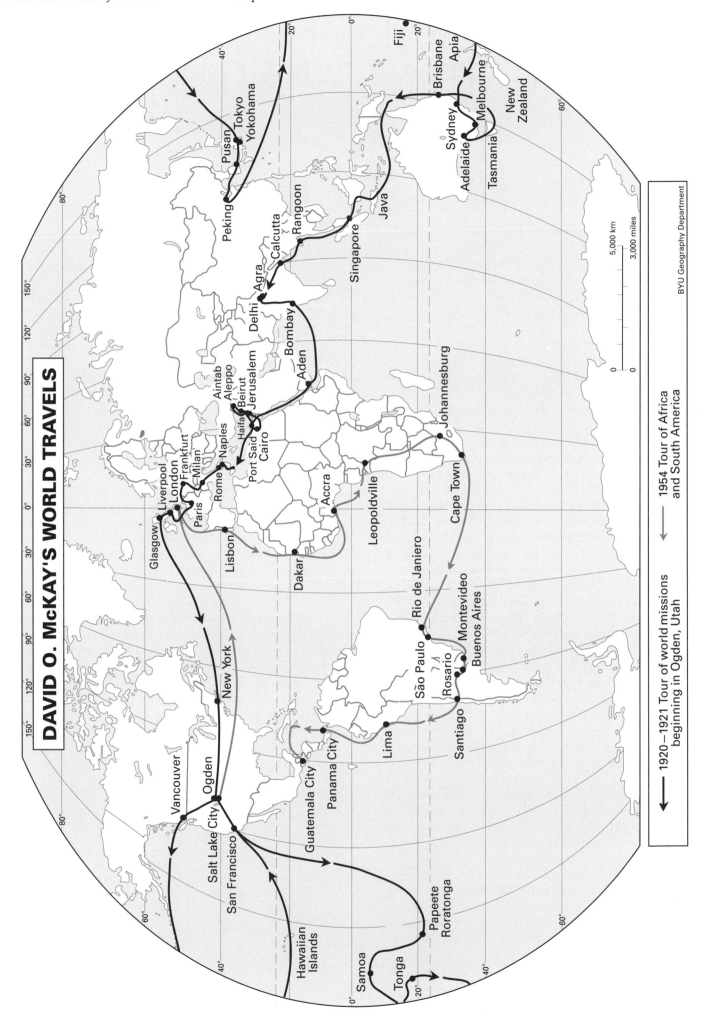

DAVID O. McKAY'S WORLD TRAVELS

Fiji

Brisbane
Apia
Sydney Melbourne
Adelaide New
Tasmania Zealand

Tokyo
Yokohama
Pusan
Peking

Rangoon
Calcutta
Java
Singapore

Delhi Agra
Bombay
Jerusalem Aden
Aintab
Aleppo
Beirut
Haifa
Port Said
Cairo

Johannesburg

Glasgow
Liverpool
London
Frankfurt
Milan
Paris Rome Naples
Lisbon

Accra

Leopoldville

Cape Town

Dakar

Rio de Janiero

São Paulo
Rosario
Montevideo
Buenos Aires

Santiago

Vancouver

Salt Lake City
Ogden
San Francisco

New York

Guatemala City

Panama City

Lima

Papeete
Roratonga

Hawaiian
Islands

Samoa
Tonga

1920–1921 Tour of world missions beginning in Ogden, Utah

1954 Tour of Africa and South America

5,000 km
3,000 miles

BYU Geography Department

SAINTS OF THE WESTERN STATES (1990)

Lowell C. Bennion

Since 1940, the American share of the LDS Church's world membership has shrunk to almost half—from about 90 to 50 percent. The western states' share of U.S. Saints has declined much less, despite the creation of LDS stakes throughout the East. About 80 percent of American Mormons reside in the 13 western states (including Alaska and Hawaii), with most of them (nearly 80 percent) living in the eight intermountain states. Moreover, neither percent has changed much during the past 20 years of rapid worldwide Church growth. Thus, in both 1970 and 1990, Utah counted roughly twice as many Mormons as California.

How can one explain American Mormons' strong preference for the West, particularly the Great Basin Kingdom? Any complete answer would require mapping rates of natural increase, migration, and conversion, for some combination of such factors has enabled that region to maintain its preponderance of U.S. Saints. Arizona alone, with 200,000 LDS in 1990, had as many as the northern states of the East combined. The North has offered transplanted intermountain Mormons far less employment than the southern states, which recorded 430,000 LDS (55 percent in Texas, Florida, and the Washington, D.C., area).

While LDS leaders have tried for a century to stop the Gathering to Zion, they have never quite succeeded, not even by building temples outside Mormon country. The pining for Zion attitude persists, affecting not only converts but born-in-the-Church members. Many intermountain Mormons who take jobs on the Pacific coast or east of the Rockies eventually return. Converts overseas, in the eastern United States, and even in the far West often join them, seeking a safer and more Mormon environment. If the Wasatch Front seems too crowded, they gather to a small town in rural Utah or an LDS ward in a neighboring state.

The 1990 western Saints map may remind some readers of the classic "Mormon Culture Region" described by D. W. Meinig (1965). As his maps demonstrate so well, the spatial configuration of Mormondom keeps changing in myriad ways. By comparing his 1965 map and the 1990 map, one can detect both continuity and change. Meinig's *core area* remains centered on the four-county Wasatch Front, which contains more than 75 percent of both Utah's total and LDS populations, and which now spills over into all adjoining counties. Within the core, Provo and Orem—at the southern end—have eclipsed the railroad hub of Ogden to the north, intensifying the rivalry between Mormondom's Mecca (Salt Lake City) and Medina (Provo). Most rural counties of Utah and southeastern Idaho, Meinig's *domain*, have a population whose LDS percent runs even higher than Utah's and the Wasatch Front's average of just under 72. The exceptions naturally catch the eye. In Summit County (east of Salt Lake City), Mormons hold a bare majority (53 percent) because the old mining town of Park City has attracted flocks of non-Mormon skiers and artists. Even more surprising is the minority position of Mormons in Utah's southeast corner, where the percent falls lower than in certain *sphere* (10–50 percent LDS) counties of Nevada, Idaho, and Wyoming. A century ago, Francis A. Hammond, the leader of Utah's San Juan Mission, often despaired of forming strong wards among the region's cowboys and Navajos. One cannot help but wonder why his successors never fared much better.

Delineating an outer boundary for the sphere proves problematic because Latter-day Saints become much more dispersed and less visible away from the domain. In all but one county of the Mormon sphere, the LDS Church represents the largest single denomination. Its number one status reflects the fact that in every western state except New Mexico, only 30 to 50 percent of the total population professes any church affiliation. Since 1965, the sphere has expanded in all directions but most notably into western Wyoming and southwestern Idaho and across eastern Nevada. As new LDS temples in Boise, Las Vegas, Denver, and along the Pacific Coast indicate, most major metropolitan areas of the West now have sizable LDS populations (100,000 in Los Angeles County alone). Ironically, most western Mormons have become urban while most of the counties that constitute their culture region have remained rural.

Atlas of Utah (1981), especially the section "Churches and Church Membership," pp. 140–143; Lowell C. Bennion and Dean R. Louder, "Mapping Mormons across the Modern West," in *The Mormon Role in the Settlement of the West*, Richard H. Jackson, editor (1978), pp. 135–169; Martin B. Bradley et al., *Churches and Church Membership in the United States, 1990* (1992); Francis A. Hammond, *Journals: 1852–1900*, half in Special Collections, Harold B. Lee Library, Brigham Young University, Provo, Utah, and half in the Historical Department, LDS Church Archives, Salt Lake City; D. W. Meinig, "The Mormon Culture Region: Strategies and Patterns in the Geography of the American West, 1847–1964," *Annals of the Association of American Geographers* 55, no. 2 (1965):191–220.

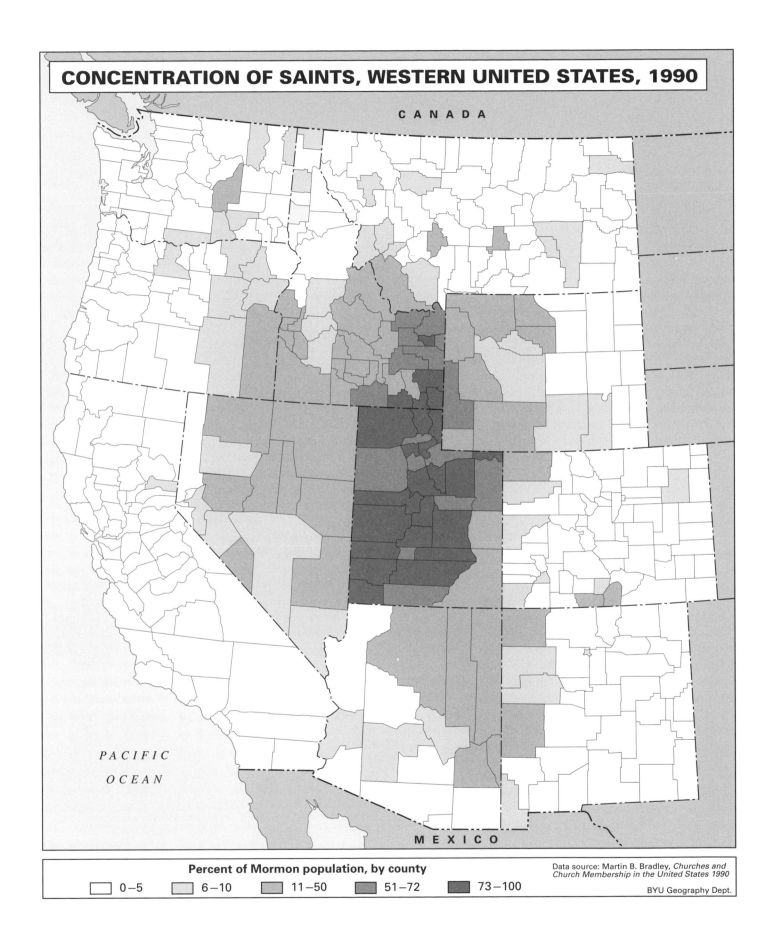

CONCENTRATION OF SAINTS, WESTERN UNITED STATES, 1990

Percent of Mormon population, by county

0–5	6–10	11–50	51–72	73–100

Data source: Martin B. Bradley, *Churches and Church Membership in the United States 1990*

BYU Geography Dept.

DISTRIBUTION OF WORLD MEMBERSHIP (1992)

J. Matthew Shumway

In 1950, membership of The Church of Jesus Christ of Latter-day Saints was at 1,111,314. Of this total, 951,400 (87 percent) were living in North America. By 1993, there were 8,406,895 members of the Church, but only 56 percent of these members were living in North America. Thus, much of the growth in Church membership in the past 40 years has taken place outside of the United States and Canada. As a consequence, the Church has restructured its administrative procedures. Such administrative restructuring was necessary for the Church to provide all of its members with similar facilities, programs, and resources. Out of this administrative restructuring came a new Church geography.

The Church is administratively organized both functionally and spatially. Its functional organization consists of three types of structures: first, ecclesiastical, based on the priesthood; second, auxiliary organizations for different groups in the Church; and third, professional services. Church spatial organization consists of a hierarchy of geographic units (going from smallest to largest): *branches*, generally less than 200; *wards*, with anywhere from 200 to 800 members; *stakes*, a group of approximately six to 10 wards; *regions*, a group of stakes; and *areas*, which consist of a group of regions. Areas constitute the newest geographic unit and represent the major international division of Church spatial organization.

The basic fundamental units of the Church have always been the branch, ward, and stake. Most members' direct experience with the Church is at these ecclesiastical and geographical levels. However, due to the rapid growth of the Church, a number of administrative changes have occurred. In 1967, stakes were organized into regions for the first time, and in 1975, regions were organized into areas. At that point in time, the area as a unit was simply a collection of regions that reported directly back to Church headquarters. In 1984, however, area presidencies were called to administer the new and larger geographical units. Area presidencies are made up of General Authorities from the First and Second Quorums of the Seventy with the responsibility to administer all Church programs within their assigned areas.

In 1992, there were 23 Church areas that spanned the entire world. There are three areas in Utah, six in North America outside of Utah, two in Mexico, one in Central America, one in Brazil, two other areas in the rest of South America, one in the Pacific, one in the Philippines and Micronesia region, two other areas in the rest of Asia, three in Europe, and one in Africa. The number of Church areas by world region generally reflects the relative concentration of Church members in the various world regions. The area boundaries do not reflect rates of growth within areas. Thus, as has been the case in the past, the number and boundaries of Church areas will certainly change.

Although the direct Church experience of most members is at the ward and stake levels, in order for the Church to deal effectively with its burgeoning worldwide growth, changes in its administration have been required. Administrative changes have facilitated the ability of the Church to ensure doctrinal consistency and to coordinate Church practices and policies that are essential to the gospel while still allowing cultural variation. The Church is no longer a Utah church nor an American one. As such it has had to find a way simultaneously to maintain doctrinal purity and to allow cultural variation to exist. The Church has been able to do this by maintaining functional linkages through which Church doctrine, programs, and policy can flow, and by creating geographical units, with increasing numbers of Church leaders called from these areas, in order to allow cultural variation to exist. The second problem that this arrangement alleviates is the increasing demand put on General Authorities by the growth of the Church. By reorganizing spatially, the Church has been able to decentralize some administrative functions to Church areas, region and stakes that were formerly the responsibility of Church leaders in Salt Lake City.

Although members can expect organizational changes in the future, the flexibility introduced by the present administrative system enables the Church to prepare for continued growth and expansion.

"Area Presidencies Called as Church Modifies Geographical Administration," *Ensign* 14, no. 8 (1984):75; Perry H. Cunningham, "Area, Area Presidency," in *Encyclopedia of Mormonism*, Daniel H. Ludlow, editor (1992) 1:65–66; William C. Hartley, "Organizational and Administrative History," in *Encyclopedia of Mormonism*, Daniel H. Ludlow, editor (1992) 3:1035–1044; Lee T. Perry, Paul M. Bons, and Alan L. Wilkins, "Contemporary Organization," in *Encyclopedia of Mormonism*, Daniel H. Ludlow, editor (1992) 3:1044–1049.

AREAS AND MEMBERSHIP OF THE CHURCH

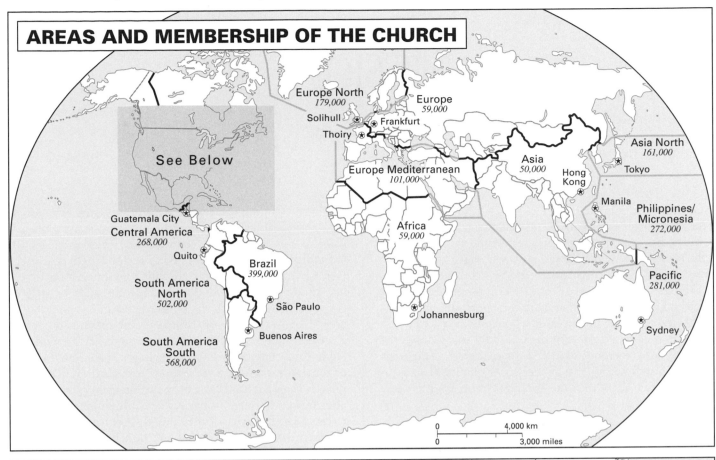

Europe North
179,000

Europe
59,000

Solihull

Frankfurt

Thoiry

Europe Mediterranean
101,000

Asia
50,000

Asia North
161,000

Hong Kong

Tokyo

Manila

Philippines/
Micronesia
272,000

Guatemala City
Central America
268,000

Africa
59,000

See Below

Quito

Brazil
399,000

South America
North
502,000

São Paulo

Johannesburg

Pacific
281,000

Buenos Aires

South America
South
568,000

Sydney

0   4,000 km
0   3,000 miles

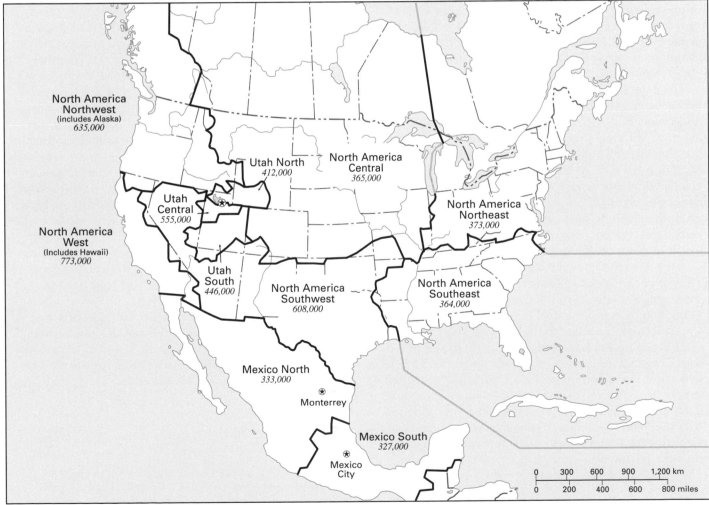

North America
Northwest
(includes Alaska)
635,000

Utah North
412,000

North America
Central
365,000

Utah
Central
555,000

North America
Northeast
373,000

North America
West
(Includes Hawaii)
773,000

Utah
South
446,000

North America
Southwest
608,000

North America
Southeast
364,000

Mexico North
333,000

Monterrey

Mexico South
327,000

Mexico
City

0   300   600   900   1,200 km
0   200   400   600   800 miles

⊛ Area headquarters (Salt Lake City is the headquarters for all areas in the United States and Canada.)

BYU
Geography
Department

MISSIONS

David F. Boone

Missionary work is the lifeblood of The Church of Jesus Christ of Latter-day Saints. Organized in 1830, the Church has grown steadily since that time through the efforts of thousands of missionaries who have given their time and energy, at their own expense, to share Church teachings and a unique way of life with others. Frequently today an individual Church member can readily trace his or her genealogy to an ancestor who came into the Church as a consequence of the Church's missionary program. As of December 31, 1992, there were 276 missions in the Church within 146 of the world's nations and territories. Within these missions 46,025 missionaries served full-time.

A *mission* is a geographical and cultural designation for an area of the world where missionary activity is conducted by Latter-day Saints. It is a basic component for future growth of Church organization in a specific locale. For example, when missionary work begins within a country, Church leaders organize a mission by calling a mission president and two counselors to preside over other Church members and representatives in the area.

The names of the missions have traditionally reflected their general locale in order to distinguish them from other proselyting regions of the world. For example, the first mission formally organized in the Church after its founding in April 1830 was the British Mission, established in July 1837. At the outset, mission designations included immense geographical regions because the numbers of proselyting missionaries were small, and as a result, the ability to proselyte individuals within those regions was limited. Following the organization of the British Mission, the next earliest mission organizations were the Eastern States Mission in the United States (1839) and the Society Islands Mission (1844), the latter comprising virtually all of the islands of the South Pacific.

In 1846, Latter-day Saints left the boundaries of the United States in an effort to find a place where they could live in peace and implement their religious practices. They located in the Great Basin and soon began to branch out into adjoining regions. During the next several decades, the Church colonized settlements from Canada in the north to Mexico in the south and from California to Texas. Whenever Church members settled in a new region, a part of their efforts often went to proselyting the local inhabitants. For a period of about ten years (1847–1857) the desired peace sought by the Latter-day Saints was realized, and consequently organized missionary efforts grew dramatically in terms of both the numbers of missionaries who served and new geographical areas where gospel teachings were introduced.

As the Church has grown in numerical strength and in social acceptability, the commitment to missionary work has also increased. As an accompanying consequence, individuals who were converted in various regions of the world became a part of the growing missionary effort because of their newfound faith. Thus the addition of converts to the Church has perpetuated a continual growth and expansion of Church membership and hence a continuing spread of the gospel throughout the world. Additional consequences have included the strengthening of the members who were distant from Church headquarters and a diminishing of their reliance upon missionaries from other regions because local members were able to carry out the work of the Church themselves. In time, the increased growth has enabled the Church to assign full-time missionaries to other areas that were not strong in spiritual or numerical strength.

In 1978, Church President Spencer W. Kimball gave the challenge and set the standard for future growth of missions in a landmark address. He said, among other things, that "it seems clear to me—indeed, this impression weighs upon me, that the Church is at a point in its growth and maturity when we are at last ready to move forward in a major way. . . . We have paused on some plateaus long enough. Let us resume our journey forward and upward."

Further prophetic direction came in 1980 during an area conference in Rochester, New York, when President Kimball admonished Church members to become better prepared individually, and stated, "We have already asked you and we now repeat that request, that every family, every night and every morning, in family prayer and in secret prayers, too, pray to the Lord to open the doors of other nations so that their people, too, may have the gospel of Jesus Christ."

Since these declarations, almost 100 missions have been organized worldwide. A third of the new missions were created in South and Central America, 18 percent were organized in Asian countries, and 16 percent were organized in other, non–U.S. countries.

Richard O. Cowan, *The Church in the Twentieth Century* (1985); *Deseret News 1993–1994 Church Almanac* (1992); "Let Us Move Forward and Upward," *Ensign* (May 1979):82; "Statistical Report 1992," F. Michael Watson, *Ensign* (May 1993):22; *The Teachings of Spencer W. Kimball* (1982), pp. 176 and 584.

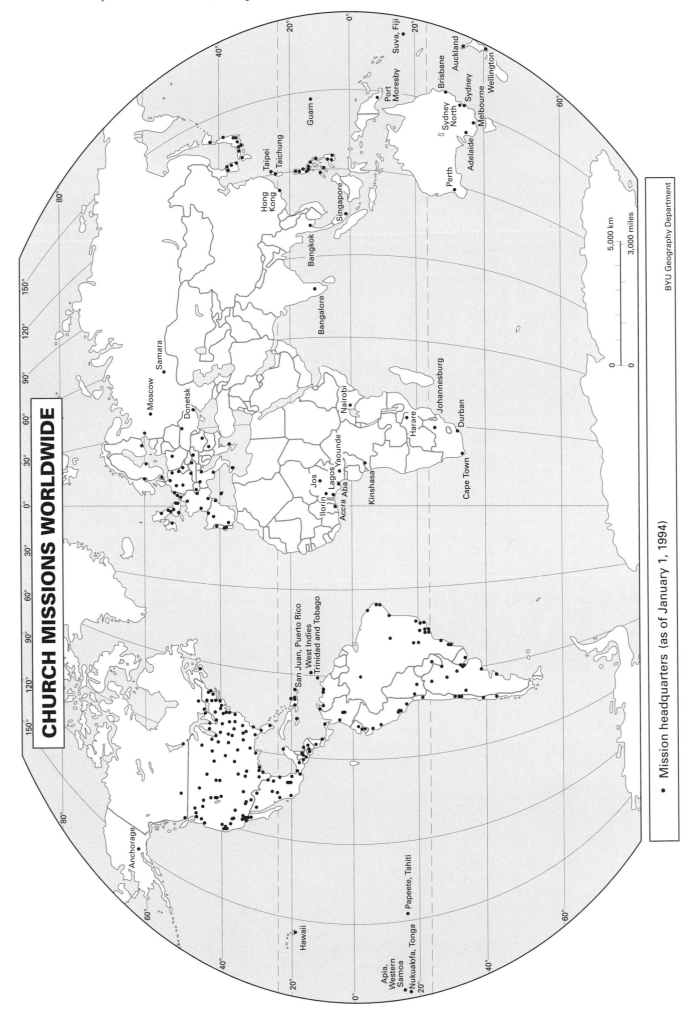

CHURCH MISSIONS WORLDWIDE

BYU Geography Department

5,000 km
3,000 miles

• Mission headquarters (as of January 1, 1994)

Guam

Taipei
Taichung

Hong Kong

Singapore

Bangkok

Bangalore

Port Moresby

Suva, Fiji

Brisbane
Auckland
Sydney North
Sydney
Wellington
Melbourne
Adelaide

Perth

Moscow
Samara

Donetsk

Nairobi

Johannesburg
Durban

Harare

Cape Town

Jos
Lagos
Ilorin
Accra Aba
Yaounde
Kinshasa

San Juan, Puerto Rico
West Indies
Trinidad and Tobago

Anchorage

Hawaii

Papeete, Tahiti

Apia, Western Samoa
Nukualofa, Tonga

CHURCH MISSIONS IN NORTH AMERICA

CANADA

Vancouver
Calgary
Winnipeg
Halifax
Tacoma
Seattle
Spokane
Montreal
Portland
Billings
Toronto East
Manchester
Boston
Eugene
Boise
Rapid City
Minneapolis
Toronto
Detroit
Rochester
New York North
Hartford
Pocatello
Milwaukee
Lansing
Pittsburgh
New York
Morristown
Roseville
Utah Ogden
Des Moines
Chicago
Cleveland
Harrisburg
Philadelphia
Santa Rosa
Utah SLC
Omaha
Peoria
Columbus
D. C. North
Sacramento
Utah Provo
Denver North
Indianapolis
Charleston
D. C. South
Oakland
San Jose
Fresno
Denver
Independence
St. Louis
Louisville
Richmond
Las Vegas
Knoxville
Raleigh
ATLANTIC OCEAN
Ventura
Arcadia
Albuquerque
Tulsa
Nashville
Charlotte
Los Angeles
San Bernadino
Riverside
Oklahoma City
Little Rock
Atlanta
Columbia
Anaheim
Carlsbad
Phoenix
Birmingham
San Diego
Tempe
Macon
Tijuana
Tucson
Fort Worth
Dallas
Jackson
Jacksonville
PACIFIC OCEAN
Hermosillo
Houston
Baton Rouge
Tallahassee
Chihuahua
San Antonio
Houston East
Tampa
Corpus Christi
Ft. Lauderdale
Torreón
Monterrey North
Monterrey South
León
Tampico
CUBA
HAITI
Santiago
Santo Domingo West
DOM. REP.
Mazatlán
MEXICO
Kingston
Santo Domingo East
Guadalajara
Mexico City N.
Mexico City E.
Mexico City S.
Veracruz
Mérida
JAMAICA
Port-au-Prince
Puebla
BELIZE
Guatemala City North
Guatemala City Central
Guatemala City South
Oaxaca
Tuxtla Gutierrez
Quezaltenango
GUATEMALA
HONDURAS
San Pedro Sula
Tegucigalpa
EL SALVADOR
Managua
NICARAGUA
Panama City
San Salvador West
San Salvador East
San José
COSTA RICA
PANAMA

45°
30°
15°
30°
15°
105°
90°

0 500 1,000 1,500 km
0 500 1,000 miles

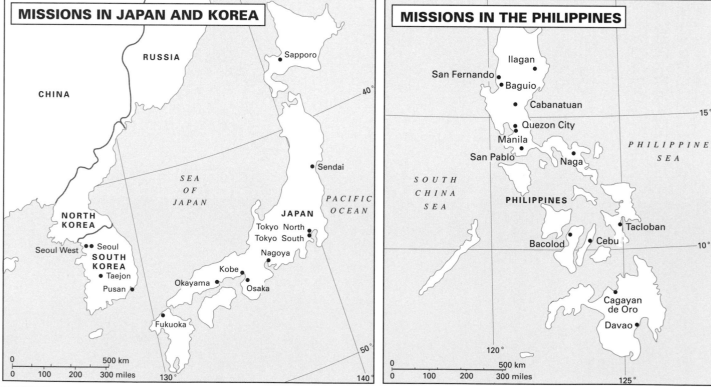

MISSIONS IN JAPAN AND KOREA

RUSSIA
Sapporo
CHINA
40°
NORTH KOREA
Sendai
Seoul West
Seoul
SOUTH KOREA
SEA OF JAPAN
JAPAN
Tokyo North
Tokyo South
Taejon
Nagoya
PACIFIC OCEAN
Pusan
Kobe
Okayama
Osaka
Fukuoka
130°
140°
50°

0 500 km
0 100 200 300 miles

MISSIONS IN THE PHILIPPINES

Ilagan
San Fernando
Baguio
Cabanatuan
15°
Quezon City
Manila
PHILIPPINE SEA
San Pablo
Naga
SOUTH CHINA SEA
PHILIPPINES
Tacloban
Bacolod
Cebu
10°
Cagayan de Oro
Davao
120°
125°

0 500 km
0 100 200 300 miles

• Mission headquarters (as of January 1, 1994)

BYU Geography Department

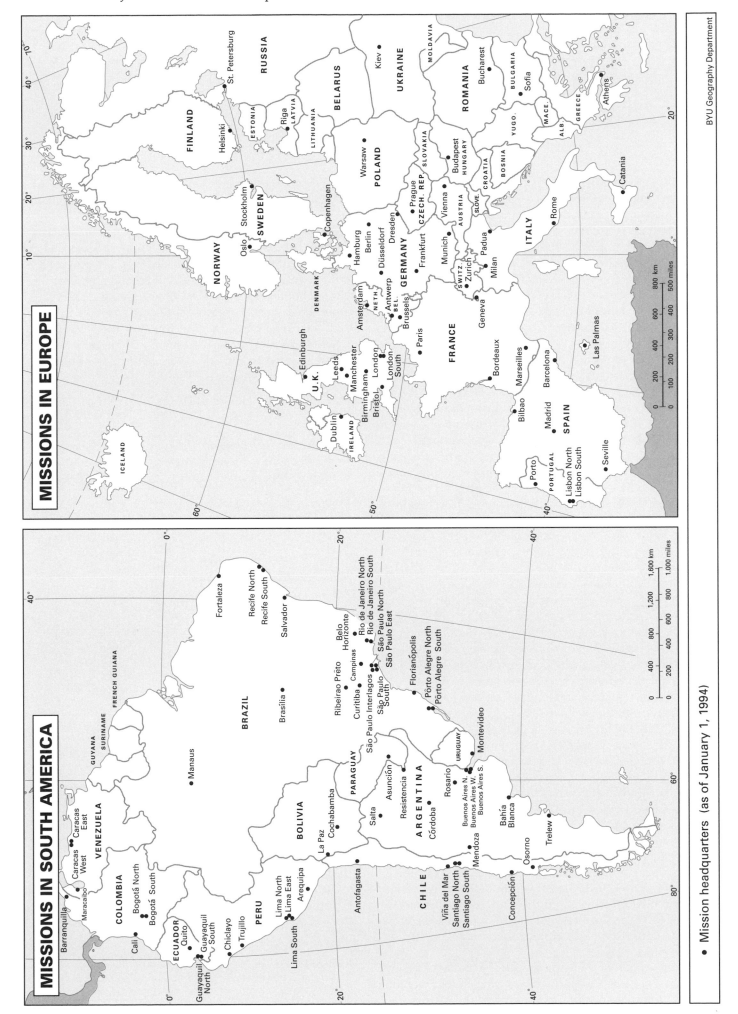

MISSIONS IN EUROPE

ICELAND

FINLAND
Helsinki

NORWAY
Oslo

SWEDEN
Stockholm

RUSSIA
St. Petersburg

ESTONIA
LATVIA
Riga
LITHUANIA

BELARUS

POLAND
Warsaw

UKRAINE
Kiev

MOLDAVIA

ROMANIA
Bucharest

BULGARIA
Sofia

DENMARK
Copenhagen

Hamburg
Berlin
Dresden
Düsseldorf
GERMANY
Frankfurt

Amsterdam
NETH.
Antwerp
BEL.
Brussels

Prague
CZECH. REP.
SLOVAKIA

Vienna
AUSTRIA
SWITZ.
Zurich
SLOVE.

Budapest
HUNGARY

CROATIA
BOSNIA
YUGO.
MACE.
ALB.

GREECE
Athens

ITALY
Padua
Milan
Munich
Rome
Catania

U.K.
Edinburgh
Leeds
Manchester
Birmingham
Bristol
London
London South

IRELAND
Dublin

Paris
FRANCE
Geneva
Bordeaux
Marseilles

SPAIN
Bilbao
Barcelona
Madrid
Seville
Las Palmas

PORTUGAL
Porto
Lisbon North
Lisbon South

0 100 200 300 400 500 miles
0 200 400 600 800 km

MISSIONS IN SOUTH AMERICA

VENEZUELA
Caracas East
Caracas West
Maracaibo

GUYANA
SURINAME
FRENCH GUIANA

COLOMBIA
Barranquilla
Bogotá North
Bogotá South
Cali

ECUADOR
Quito
Guayaquil North
Guayaquil South

PERU
Chiclayo
Trujillo
Lima North
Lima East
Lima South
Arequipa

BRAZIL
Manaus
Fortaleza
Recife North
Recife South
Salvador
Brasília
Belo Horizonte
Ribeirao Prêto
Campinas
Curitiba
São Paulo Interlagos
São Paulo South
São Paulo North
São Paulo East
Rio de Janeiro North
Rio de Janeiro South
Florianópolis
Pôrto Alegre North
Porto Alegre South

BOLIVIA
La Paz
Cochabamba

PARAGUAY
Asunción

ARGENTINA
Salta
Resistencia
Córdoba
Rosario
Buenos Aires N.
Buenos Aires W.
Buenos Aires S.
Mendoza
Bahia Blanca
Trelew

URUGUAY
Montevideo

CHILE
Antofagasta
Viña del Mar
Santiago North
Santiago South
Concepción
Osorno

0 200 400 600 800 1,000 miles
0 400 800 1,200 1,600 km

• Mission headquarters (as of January 1, 1994)

BYU Geography Department

MISSIONARY TRAINING CENTERS

David F. Boone

One of the constants in The Church of Jesus Christ of Latter-day Saints since before its organization in 1830 has been its missionary emphasis. An important corollary has been an interest in improving both the techniques and the preparation of the Church's missionaries. Early efforts to introduce such changes were slow and deliberate, but as the number of missionaries has increased, the need for training of Church representatives has become more pronounced.

Early missionaries had little formal training except what they might have received from parents, extended family, or Church leaders. In addition, most of the elders were sent to missions that reflected their national origin or that required language skills they possessed. Thus, Scandinavian natives or those of Anglo-Saxon extraction were more likely to serve in northern European missions. Most went to their assigned missions without sufficient financial support, on the model of the ancient twelve Apostles. In doing so, many depended on the hospitality of the local citizenry and preached extemporaneously on the street or wherever they would be heard.

Fewer opportunities for such hospitality were available in the 20th century as more and more people moved to urban areas. Also, the number of missionaries seeking hospitality increased. Accordingly, the techniques of the missionary work changed.

During the administration of LDS President David O. McKay (1951–1970), the number of missionaries rose from approximately 5,000 to over 13,000. In 1961, the Language Training Institute was established at Brigham Young University in Provo, Utah. Originally, only the Spanish language was taught. The Institute experienced success, and, recognizing other missionaries' need for preparation in foreign languages, it expanded its operation in 1963 to create the Language Training Mission, which increased not only the amount of instruction but also the number of languages taught. Classes were held daily at Brigham Young University, and missionaries were encouraged to speak only in their assigned foreign languages in an effort to facilitate learning. In addition to the Language Training Center, where Spanish, Portuguese, Italian, French, German, Dutch, and Scandinavian languages were taught, another center specializing in Polynesian languages was opened at the LDS Church College in Hawaii.

In 1978 each training facility was renamed a missionary training center. In 1993, fifteen training centers were in operation worldwide. All of the Church's missionary training centers are located adjacent to or in close proximity to a Latter-day Saint temple in accordance with Church policy.

The expansion of the language studies and other training of prospective missionaries has involved other factors such as the costs of operation, not only to the Church, but also to the families of the missionaries, who are usually responsible for travel and boarding costs during the missionaries' training period. One reason for locating missionary training centers throughout the world is to encourage missionary participation at a reasonable cost.

The number of missionaries continues to rise, and the training center in Provo has needed to acquire new properties, expand its present site, and use neighboring church buildings for classes. Other training centers around the world are not as busy as the Provo site; in fact, few are in operation year round or used to capacity when they are open. Approximately 75 percent of the Church's potential missionary force receives its orientation and preparation in the Provo facility.

Mission training facilities (1993)

Asia

Japan Missionary Training Ctr.	Tokyo, Japan
Korea Missionary Training Ctr.	Seoul, South Korea
Philippine Missionary Training Ctr.	Manila, Philippines

Europe

England Missionary Training Ctr.	New Chapel (near London), England

Mexico and Central America

Guatemala Missionary Training Ctr.	Guatemala City, Guatemala
Mexico Missionary Training Ctr.	Unidad Aragón, Mexico

North America

Provo Missionary Training Ctr.	Provo, Utah

Pacific

New Zealand Missionary Training Ctr.	Hamilton, New Zealand
Samoa Missionary Training Ctr.	Apia, Western Samoa
Tonga Missionary Training Ctr.	Nukualofa, Tonga

South America

Argentina Missionary Training Ctr.	Buenos Aires, Argentina
Brazil Missionary Training Ctr.	São Paulo, Brazil
Chile Missionary Training Ctr.	Santiago, Chile
Columbia Missionary Training Ctr.	Bogotá, Columbia
Peru Missionary Training Ctr.	Lima, Peru

Richard O. Cowan, "Missionary Training Centers," in *Encyclopedia of Mormonism*, Daniel H. Ludlow, editor (1992) 2:913–914; Jay E. Jensen, "The Effect of Initial Mission Field Training on Missionary Proselyting Skills" (Ph.D. thesis, Brigham Young University, 1988).

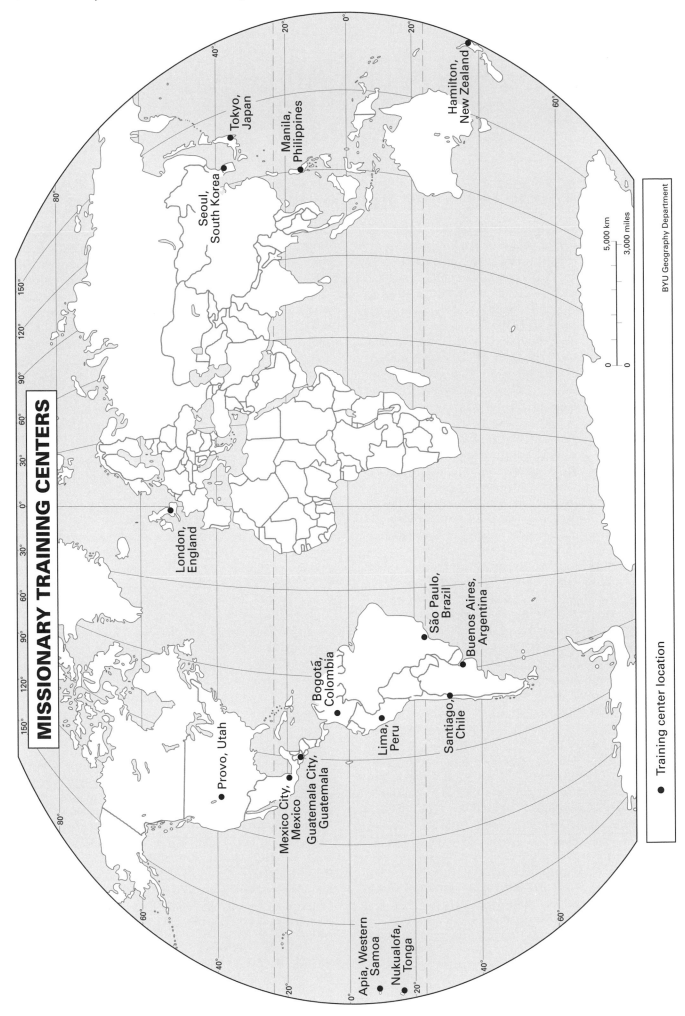

MISSIONARY TRAINING CENTERS

Tokyo, Japan

Manila, Philippines

Hamilton, New Zealand

Seoul, South Korea

London, England

São Paulo, Brazil

Buenos Aires, Argentina

Bogotá, Colombia

Provo, Utah

Lima, Peru

Santiago, Chile

Mexico City, Mexico

Guatemala City, Guatemala

Apia, Western Samoa

Nukualofa, Tonga

5,000 km

3,000 miles

BYU Geography Department

● Training center location

HISTORIC SITES AND TOURISM

Lloyd E. Hudman

Two types of LDS historical sites can be recognized: those that consist of historical markers only, and those that include visitors' centers. Historical markers provide travelers with some specific information about LDS Church history at that site, such as campsites for the pioneer movement west and for the Mormon Battalion. The second type have important historical events associated with them and visitors' centers have been established to explain the importance of the site for LDS Church history.

Salt Lake Temple Square is the site of the Salt Lake Temple and the adjoining Tabernacle. With nearly 5 million annual visitors it attracts more than four times the number of people that visit all other visitors' centers combined.

Nauvoo, Illinois, Visitors' Center was opened September 4, 1971, to tell the story of the founding and occupancy of Nauvoo from 1841 to 1846. The restoration of many of its buildings has developed Nauvoo into an important attraction with over 150,000 visitors annually. Near Nauvoo is the Carthage Jail, opened on October 27, 1963, which receives only one-fourth the number of Nauvoo visitors. It was the site of the incarceration and assassination of Joseph Smith and his brother Hyrum by a mob on June 27, 1844.

The third major historical site, attracting nearly 100,000 annual visitors, is the Hill Cumorah Historical Center at Manchester, New York. It was created in 1937 adjacent to Hill Cumorah, the burial site of early American ancient records whose translation by Joseph Smith became known as the Book of Mormon. Each year, in the summer, a pageant presents the story of the Book of Mormon.

Near Hill Cumorah are three significant sites. The Joseph Smith Home in Manchester, New York, where Joseph Smith lived from 1825 until 1829, is most visited of the three, attracting approximately 83,000 visitors. It was here Joseph Smith received the First Vision in the Sacred Grove. The E. B. Grandin Press Building in Palmyra, New York, is the site of the first printing of the Book of Mormon in 1830 and attracts nearly as many visitors as the Joseph Smith Home. The Peter Whitmer Farm Historical Site at Waterloo, New York, was the site of the formal organization of The Church of Jesus Christ of Latter-day Saints. It attracts about half the visitors of the Joseph Smith Home and the Grandin Press.

Utah LDS historical sites with large numbers of visitors benefit from their location in Utah, attracting between 60,000 and 250,000 visitors. The Beehive House in Salt Lake City, Utah, was the home of Brigham Young; the Brigham Young Winter Home in St. George, Utah, was built in 1874 and restored in 1976; the Jacob Hamblin Home in Santa Clara, Utah, was the home of the first permanent Mormon missionary to the local Indians; the St. George Tabernacle in St. George, Utah, was constructed of red sandstone between 1863 and 1876 and resembles a New England church. One additional site, at Cove Fort, Utah, attracts nearly 60,000 visitors yearly and is illustrative of the pioneer period.

An important center of Mormon history and current tourism is Missouri. Two centers and a number of monuments exist there. The Independence Visitors' Center attracted approximately 55,000 visitors in 1992. This center tells the story of the Church movement and gathering in Independence. It stands near the temple block site, which was dedicated by the Prophet Joseph Smith in 1831 for the building of a temple. It is land that was appointed and consecrated as the City of Zion, and therefore holds importance in the future of the Church. The second visitors' center, the Liberty Jail, is where the Prophet Joseph Smith and five others were incarcerated for four and one-half months, from November 1838 to April 1839. The Prophet received three significant revelations while here (D&C 121, 122, and 123). The jail was restored in a cutaway design, and a center was dedicated September 15, 1963.

Other visitors' centers located near Mormon Church historical sites are visited less frequently because of their location and brief role in Church history. For instance, the Joseph Smith Birthplace at Sharon, Vermont, is noted by a 38.5-foot polished granite monument and attracted nearly 40,000 visitors in 1992.

In Kirtland, Ohio, the Newel K. Whitney Store attracted over 20,000 visitors last year. It stands near the Kirtland Temple and was a place of important events in early Church history. The nearby John Johnson Home receives slightly over one-third of the visitors to the Newel K. Whitney Store, where Joseph Smith lived from 1831 to 1832 and received many revelations contained in the Doctrine and Covenants.

Winter Quarters, near Omaha, was an important campsite during the pioneer migration west and attracts nearly 50,000 visitors a year. The San Diego Mormon Battalion Center at San Diego, California, tells the story both of the Mormon Battalion in the early days of the territory and of the apostasy and restoration of the gospel. It attracts approximately 30,000 visitors annually.

W. C. Anderson, *The New Guide Book to Mormon History for Family Travel* (1988); Richard H. Jackson, G. Rinschede, and J. Knapp, "Pilgrimage in the Mormon Church," in *Pilgrimage in the United States*, G. Rinschede and S. M. Bharddwaj, editors (1989), pp. 27–61; Stanley B. Kimball, *Historic Sites and Markers along the Mormon and other Great Western Trails* (1988); R. D. Oscarson and Stanley B. Kimball, *The Travelers' Guide to Historic Mormon America* (1976).

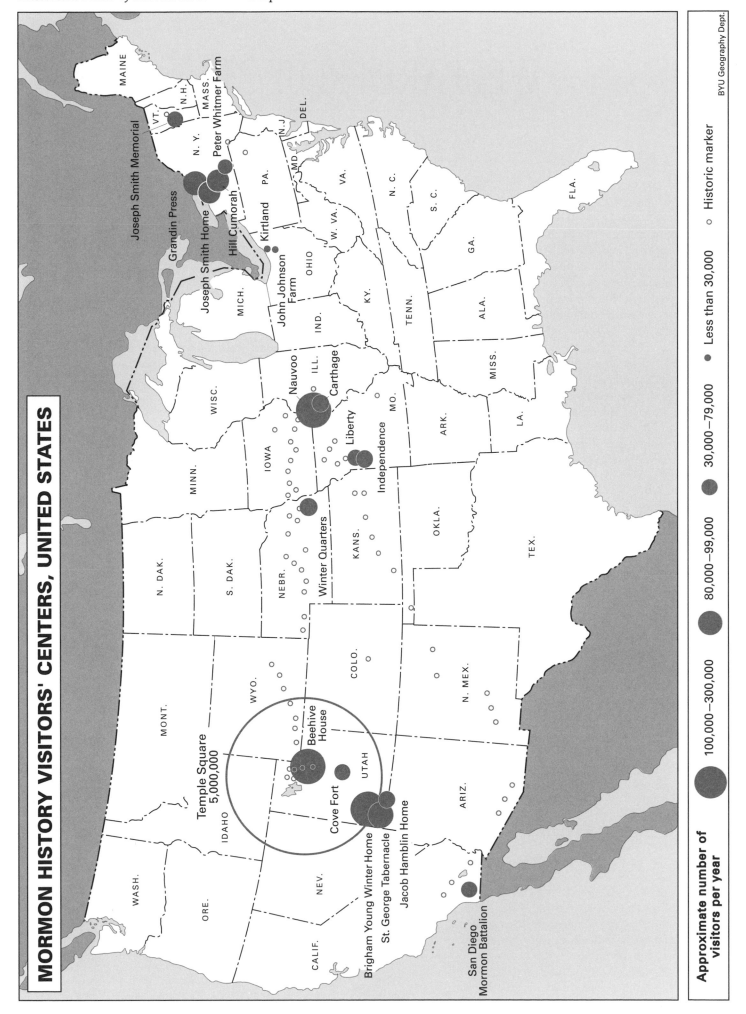

MORMON HISTORY VISITORS' CENTERS, UNITED STATES

MAINE

N.H.

VT.

MASS.

Joseph Smith Memorial

N.Y.

Peter Whitmer Farm

Grandin Press

Joseph Smith Home

Hill Cumorah

Kirtland

PA.

DEL.

N.J.

MD.

W. VA.

VA.

N. C.

S. C.

GA.

FLA.

John Johnson Farm

OHIO

IND.

KY.

TENN.

ALA.

MISS.

MICH.

WISC.

Nauvoo

ILL.

Carthage

IOWA

Liberty

Independence

MO.

ARK.

LA.

MINN.

Winter Quarters

KANS.

OKLA.

TEX.

N. DAK.

S. DAK.

NEBR.

WYO.

Beehive House

COLO.

N. MEX.

ARIZ.

MONT.

Temple Square 5,000,000

UTAH

Cove Fort

IDAHO

Brigham Young Winter Home

St. George Tabernacle

Jacob Hamblin Home

WASH.

ORE.

NEV.

CALIF.

San Diego Mormon Battalion

BYU Geography Dept.

○ Historic marker

● Less than 30,000

● 30,000−79,000

● 80,000−99,000

● 100,000−300,000

Approximate number of visitors per year

WELFARE PROJECTS

Garth L. Mangum

Efforts of The Church of Jesus Christ of Latter-day Saints to enhance the economic well-being of its members span the Church's entire history. Geography has also been a relevant element. The concept of gathering in the 19th century encouraged converts to gather first to Ohio, then to Missouri, Illinois, and the Intermountain West. Members needed relocation assistance and sustenance upon arrival.

Resettlement needs became apparent first in 1831, when Joseph Smith consolidated the 200 original New York Saints with 300 converts in and around Kirtland, Ohio. The settled Ohio members were asked to share their lands under a concept called the law of consecration and stewardship. Few complied, but enough did to make the temporary gathering viable.

Later in 1831, when a gathering place was designated in Jackson County, Missouri, no LDS residents lived there. Incoming Mormons could only share their liquid capital and tools, while members elsewhere were to donate monies for purchasing lands. When conflicts with non-LDS residents resulted in expulsion from Missouri, Church leaders purchased lands in and around Nauvoo, Illinois, and adjacent Montrose, Iowa, so that members could become self-sufficient. Driven later to the Mountain West (1846–1847), the Church again found sustenance for the trek and organized the infrastructure for transportation, communication, and irrigation throughout the Mormon settlements in the West.

During the early 20th century, Latter-day Saints, like other Americans, began urbanizing. Welfare attention shifted to social work. When agriculture and mining overexpanded during World War I, depressing farm and metal prices, the area became vulnerable to the Great Depression. The chief victims were in Salt Lake City, the major urban center. Though poor, farm families could eat, but farmers often could not pay for harvesting. Stake presidents in the Salt Lake City area organized work crews to harvest crops, taking foodstuffs in pay. Owners of warehouses donated space for storage and food processing. Women organized to can food and make clothing. Ward bishops distributed commodities among their poor, insisting that all able-bodied persons work. Distant stakes began similar activities and, by 1936, the approaches were sanctioned in a Church-wide centralized program. Although World War II prosperity reduced needs, the Church purchased farms and added other processing facilities. At the end of the war, the Church sent massive amounts of produce to Europe.

Convinced of the need for strategic reserves, as well as for work and service opportunities, the Church expanded production activities to over 500 farms—90,000 acres by 1960—with processing and storage facilities, all in the western United States and Canada. During the 1970s, farms and other facilities were established throughout the United States. Holdings in 1990 consisted of 199 agricul-tural production projects, 51 canneries, and 63 grain storage facilities feeding into 113 central, regional, and branch storehouses. In 1990, the cumulative size of Church farms included over 51,000 acres of cropland and 71,000 acres of grazing land in 1990. Another 50,000 acres were reclaimable for production should the need arise.

However, with increasing urbanization, the welfare program was moving in other directions. In 1938, Deseret Industries was established to employ handicapped and other difficult-to-employ members in rehabilitating donated clothing, furniture, and household effects. Forty-eight Deseret Industries stores now operate in the western United States. As long ago as the depression of the 1890s, the Church had established an employment center in Salt Lake City. The Church currently operates 104 employment centers throughout the world, 34 staffed by professionals and the remainder operated by volunteers. Volunteer employment specialists in every stake and ward seek to identify both members needing placement and jobs available from LDS employers.

With the stresses of urban life, personal welfare is no longer just an economic issue. LDS Social Services, with over 60 offices throughout the United States and Canada, and a few in Great Britain, Australia, and New Zealand, complements the counseling efforts of the LDS lay clergy.

In the 1990s, the central thrust came to be provident living, emphasizing literacy and education, career development, financial and resource management, home production and storage, physical health, and social, emotional, and spiritual strength.

Further, there are three areas of current experimentation. First, because Church membership has exploded, mostly in less developed countries, experiments are under way to develop programs abroad. Current emphasis is on employment preparation and placement, but microenterprise and small-plot agriculture development are promising possibilities. Second, the rise in Church membership in U.S. inner cities has sparked experiments to develop viable urban programs. Finally, the Church is extending itself to the nonmember needy in the United States and abroad through a Humanitarian Service program.

Throughout all of this development, the objectives have remained constant: (1) provide short-term help to the needy, (2) help members become self-sufficient, and (3) pursue the ultimate goal of achieving a Zion Society where there are no rich and no poor because all dwell in righteousness (Pearl of Great Price, Moses 7:18).

Leonard J. Arrington, Feramorz Y. Fox, and Dean L. May, *Building the City of God: Community and Cooperation among the Mormons* (1976); Garth L. Mangum, "Welfare Services," in *Encyclopedia of Mormonism*, Daniel H. Ludlow, editor (1992) 4:1554–1558; Garth L. Mangum and Bruce D. Blumell, *The Mormons' War on Poverty* (1993).

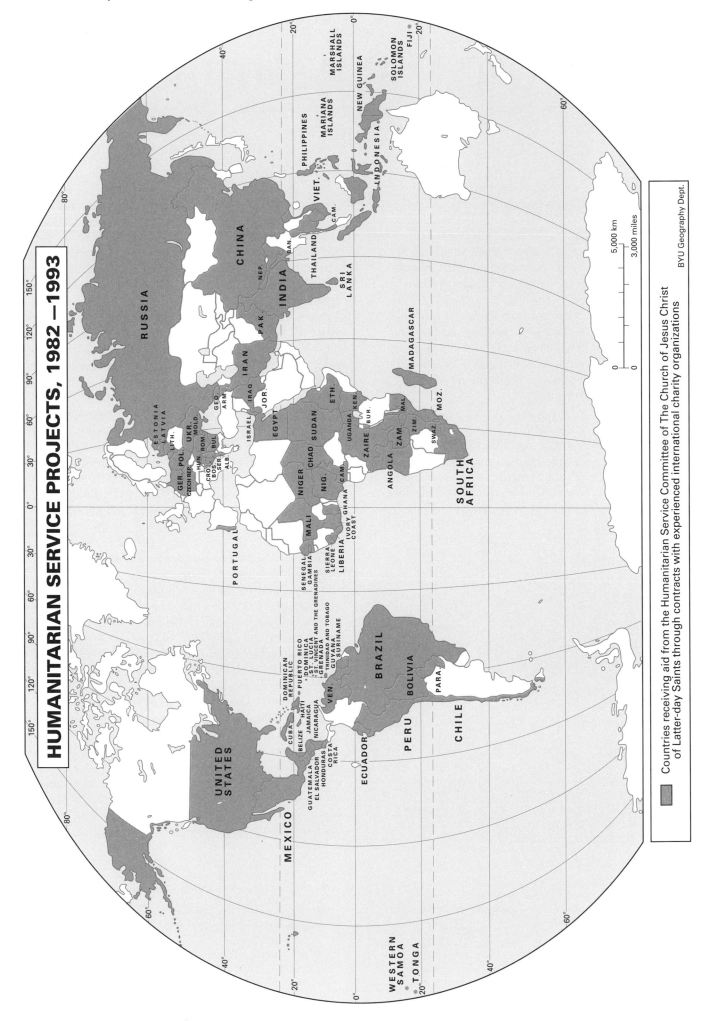

HUMANITARIAN SERVICE PROJECTS, 1982–1993

Countries receiving aid from the Humanitarian Service Committee of The Church of Jesus Christ of Latter-day Saints through contracts with experienced international charity organizations

BYU Geography Dept.

EDUCATIONAL INSTITUTIONS

Leon R. Hartshorn

In June 1831, Joseph Smith received a revelation calling Oliver Cowdery and W. W. Phelps "to do the work of printing and of selecting writings for schools . . . that little children may also receive instruction" (D&C 55:4). In this connection, the Doctrine and Covenants also contains passages that form the basis for Mormon attitudes toward education.

On July 4, 1838, at the cornerstone ceremony for a temple in Far West, Missouri, Sidney Rigdon, then a member of the First Presidency, indicated the nature of the educational plans of the Church and the very close connections between religion and education:

> This building [temple] is designed for the double purpose of a house of worship and an institution of learning. . . . Next to the worship of our God, we esteem the education of our children and of the rising generation. For what is wealth without society or society without intelligence. And how is intelligence to be obtained?—by education. What is religion without intelligence; an empty soul. (Moffitt, 5–6)

In 1840, Joseph Smith began his quest to open a university in Nauvoo, and on January 15, 1841, he issued the following proclamation: "The University of Nauvoo will enable us to teach our children wisdom, to instruct them in all the knowledge and learning, in the arts, science and learned professions" (*History of the Church* 4:269). Although Smith's dream was never completely realized, its organization would later become the groundwork for the University of Deseret, later renamed the University of Utah.

During the exodus under Brigham Young, consideration was given to the future education of Mormon youth in the isolated West. In a general epistle written to the Twelve Apostles near Council Bluffs, Iowa, December 23, 1847, President Young said:

> It is very desirable that all Saints should improve every opportunity of securing at least a copy of every valuable treatise on education—every book, map, chart, or diagram that may contain interesting, useful and attractive matter, to gain the attention of children, and cause them to love to learn to read; and also every historical, mathematical, philosophical, geographical, geological, astronomical, scientific, practical, and all other variety of useful and interesting writings, maps, etc., . . . for the benefit of the rising generation. (*Millennial Star*, 10:85)

During the journey to the West, educational classes were conducted in the camps. Within three months after Church members arrived in the Salt Lake valley, formal elementary classes began. Because adequate secondary public education was not available for the youth in the growing western colonies, Brigham Young Academy was founded in 1875. It was the first of 33 academies established in five western states, Canada, and Mexico. Of these academies, 11 closed shortly after opening, and only 22 schools actually had buildings. The schools offered basic academic subjects as well as vocational and cultural skills, including agriculture, mechanics, homemaking, music, and art. Because students were involved in numerous debates, plays, athletic competitions, and music recitals, the academies also became social centers for communities. As the number of public high schools increased, Church academies closed. By 1934, all the academies either were closed or had been turned over to the state to become junior colleges, except four: Brigham Young University, Ricks College, LDS Business College, and Juárez Academy in Colonia Juárez, Mexico.

As the Church has spread, it has continued the practice of providing education for its members. Schools have been built in Mexico, Chile, Paraguay, Bolivia, Peru, Indonesia, Hawaii, Samoa, Tonga, Tahiti, New Zealand, Kirabati, and Fiji. The majority have been closed as public education has become available. Enrollments in 1993 for Church universities and colleges are: Brigham Young University—30,724; Ricks College—8,217; BYU Hawaii—2,033; and LDS Business College—869. The total secondary and elementary school enrollment was 9,189 in 1992. The BYU Jerusalem Center for Near Eastern Studies, dedicated in 1989, had an enrollment of 171 in 1993.

In recent years, the Board of Education of the Church and the Board of Trustees for Church colleges and universities has been the First Presidency, six members of the Quorum of the Twelve Apostles, a member of the Presiding Bishopric, and the presidents of the Relief Society and the Young Women of the Church.

M. Lynn Bennion, *Mormonism and Education* (1939); Clark V. Johnson, *Mormon Education in Mexico: The Rise of the Sociedad Educativa y Cultural* (1977); John Clifton Moffitt, *The History of Public Education in Utah* (1946); Harvey Taylor, *The Story of LDS Church Schools* (1971).

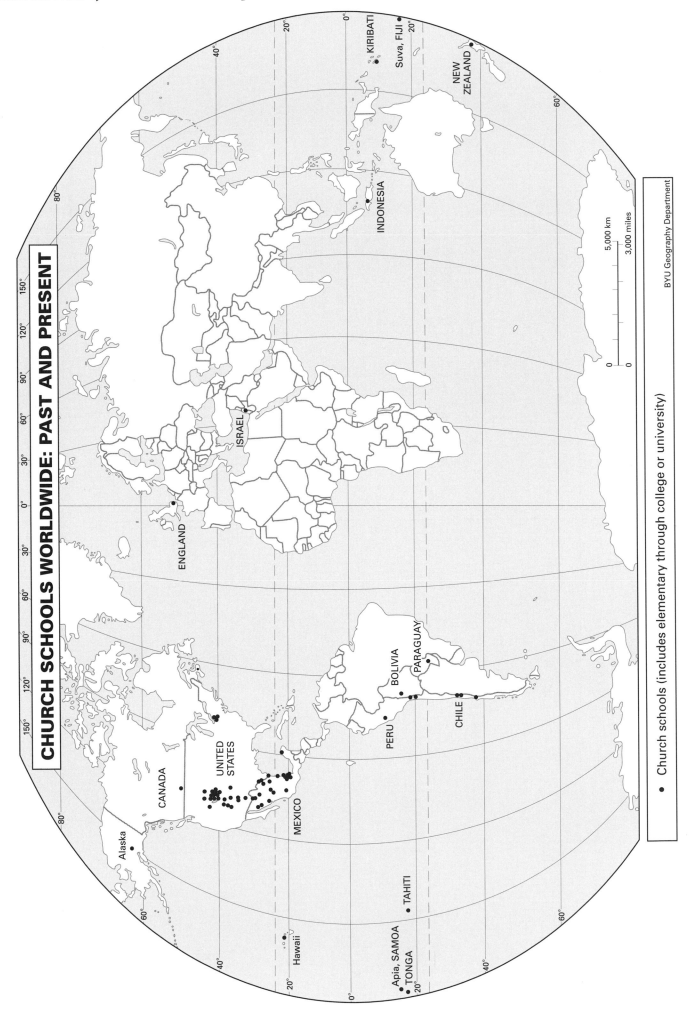

CHURCH SCHOOLS WORLDWIDE: PAST AND PRESENT

• Church schools (includes elementary through college or university)

BYU Geography Department

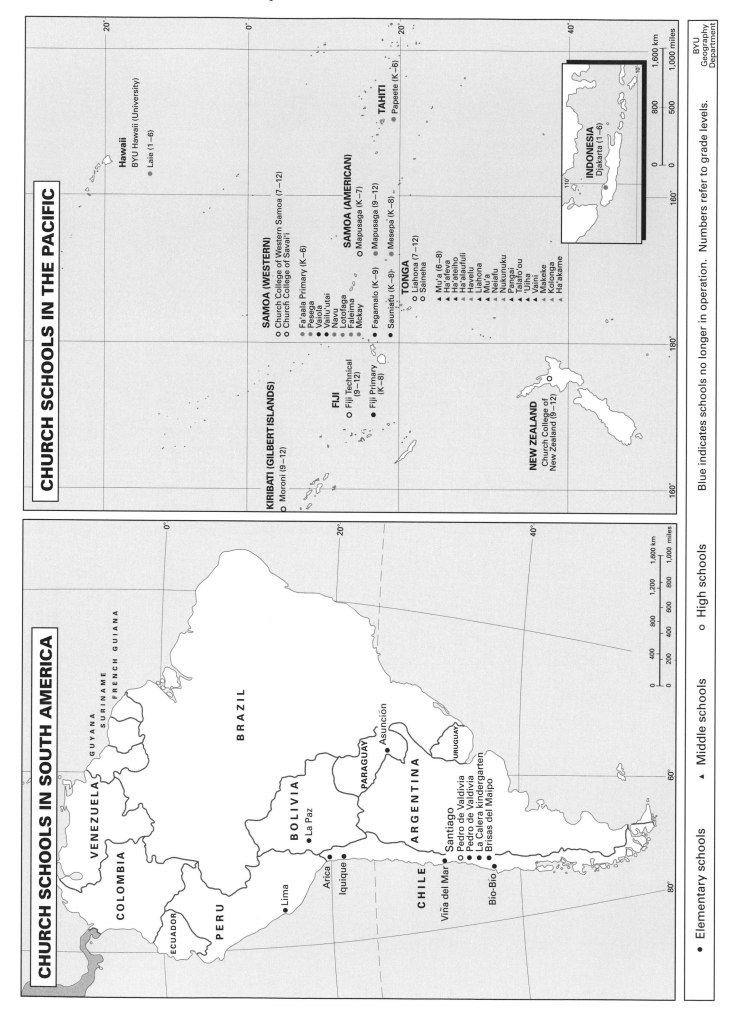

CHURCH SCHOOLS IN THE PACIFIC

Hawaii
BYU Hawaii (University)
● Laie (1–6)

SAMOA (WESTERN)
○ Church College of Western Samoa (7–12)
○ Church College of Savai'i
● Fa'aala Primary (K–6)
● Pesega
● Vaiola
● Vailu'utai
● Navu
● Lotofaga
● Faleima
● Mckay

SAMOA (AMERICAN)
○ Mapusaga (K–7)
● Mapusaga (9–12)
● Mesepa (K–8)

TAHITI
● Papeete (K–6)

TONGA
○ Liahona (7–12)
○ Saineha
▲ Mu'a (6–8)
▲ Ha'afeva
▲ Ha'ateiho
▲ Ha'alaufuli
▲ Havelu
▲ Liahona
▲ Mu'a
▲ Neiafu
▲ Nukunuku
▲ Pangai
▲ Talafo'ou
▲ 'Uiha
▲ Vaini
▲ Makeke
▲ Kolonga
▲ Ha'akame

KIRIBATI (GILBERT ISLANDS)
○ Moroni (9–12)

FIJI
○ Fiji Technical (9–12)
● Fiji Primary (K–8)
● Fagamalo (K–9)
● Sauniatu (K–8)

NEW ZEALAND
Church College of
New Zealand (9–12)

INDONESIA
Djakarta (1–6)

1,600 km
1,000 miles
800
500

Blue indicates schools no longer in operation.   Numbers refer to grade levels.

BYU
Geography
Department

CHURCH SCHOOLS IN SOUTH AMERICA

COLOMBIA
VENEZUELA
GUYANA
SURINAME
FRENCH GUIANA
ECUADOR
PERU
BRAZIL
BOLIVIA
● La Paz
● Lima
● Arica
● Iquique
PARAGUAY
Asunción
URUGUAY
ARGENTINA
CHILE
● Santiago
○ Pedro de Valdivia
● Pedro de Valdivia
● La Calera kindergarten
● Brisas del Maipo
● Viña del Mar
● Bio-Bio

1,600 km
1,000 miles
1,200   800
600   800
400   400
200   200
0   0

● Elementary schools   ▲ Middle schools   ○ High schools

144

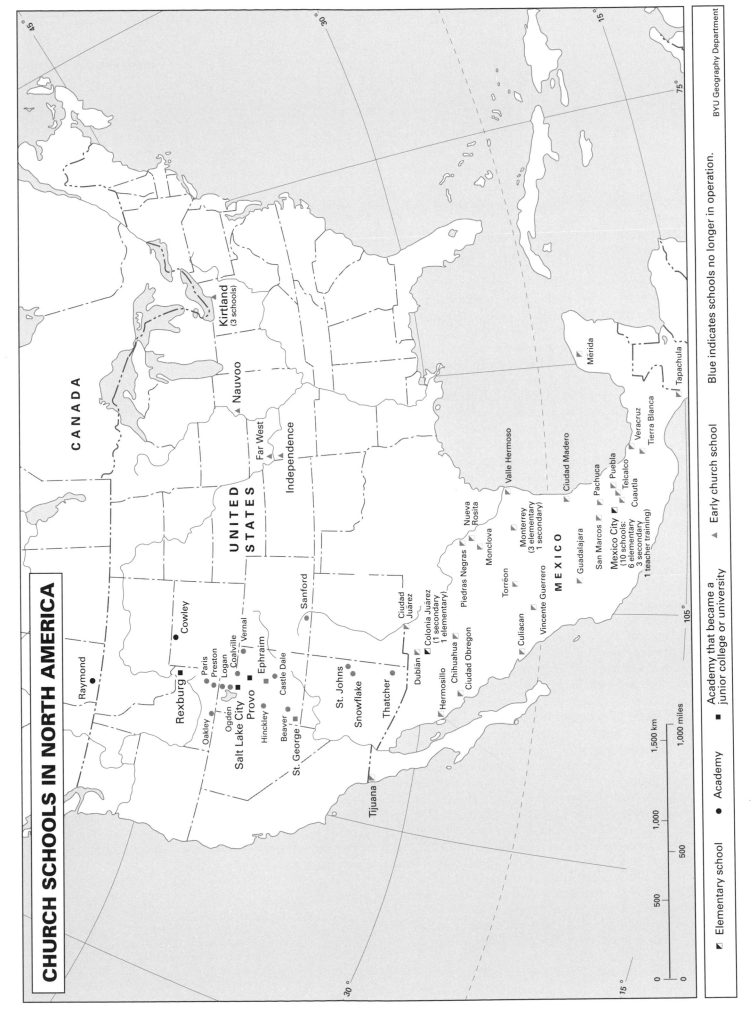

CHURCH SCHOOLS IN NORTH AMERICA

CANADA

UNITED STATES

Kirtland
(3 schools)

Nauvoo

Far West

Independence

Raymond

Cowley

Rexburg
Oakley
Paris
Preston
Logan
Coalville
Vernal
Ogden
Salt Lake City
Provo
Hinckley
Beaver
Castle Dale
Ephraim
St. George

Sanford

St. Johns
Snowflake
Thatcher

Ciudad Juárez

MEXICO

Tijuana

Colonia Juárez
(1 secondary
1 elementary)

Dublán
Hermosillo
Chihuahua
Ciudad Obregon

Culiacan

Torreón

Piedras Negras

Nueva Rosita

Monclova

Vincente Guerrero

Valle Hermoso

Monterrey
(3 elementary
1 secondary)

Ciudad Madero

Guadalajara

San Marcos
Pachuca
Puebla
Telcalco
Cuautla
1 teacher training

Mexico City
(10 schools:
6 elementary
3 secondary
1 teacher training)

Veracruz
Tierra Blanca

Mérida

Tapachula

1,500 km
1,000 miles

0   500   1,000   1,500

0   500   1,000

■ Elementary school   ● Academy   ■ Academy that became a junior college or university   ▲ Early church school   Blue indicates schools no longer in operation.

BYU Geography Department

ETHNIC MAKEUP IN THE 20th CENTURY

Jessie L. Embry

Since the 1950s, the LDS Church has experienced its most rapid growth, and membership even within the United States has become less European American. Because membership records do not include notations of ethnic background, it is impossible to know precisely how dramatic the ethnic shifts have been. It is clear, however, that the LDS Church faces a multicultural challenge.

This dilemma is new for the Mormon Church. In the early 20th century, most converts were Americans or Europeans. Even though some European converts immigrated to the United States, they gave up their language and much of their culture and became Americans as well as Mormons. To assist in the assimilation process, the Church supported ethnic branches and newspapers, but these features were deemed temporary until the members could learn English and fit into the geographical congregations.

During World War I, local public opinion against foreign languages forced some of the ethnic branches to be discontinued. But with increased immigration during the 1920s, new foreign-language branches and newspapers were established. In 1923, 30 foreign congregations met in 21 stakes: 2 Swedish, 13 Scandinavian, 2 Danish, 9 German, and 4 Mexican. But the Church began discouraging immigration to the United States during the 1920s. Church-sponsored ethnic newspapers lost readership; all four—German, Danish-Norwegian, Swedish, and Dutch—were discontinued in 1935.

With the outbreak of World War II, the First Presidency announced that all of the foreign language branches, except the Mexican branch in Salt Lake City, would be discontinued. Following the war there was a new influx of German-speaking immigrants, and monthly German meetings started again in Cache Valley, Utah. Attendance eventually dropped off and the gatherings were permanently discontinued during the 1950s.

After the war there was a renewed interest in ethnic groups. This time going further than merely setting up branches to serve Mormon immigrants, the Church inaugurated regional missions in Utah and Idaho to preach to non-Mormons. As a result of these activities and a concern for non-English-speaking members, the Church organized Japanese, Dutch, Swedish, Danish, Norwegian, and two Native American branches in Salt Lake City during 1962 and 1963. Salt Lake stakes also organized French, Mandarin, and Cantonese Sunday schools. At the same time, Native American branches were organized in the Southwest Indian Mission, which had been created in 1942 to serve the Navajo and Hopi peoples. By the late 1960s, the mission had 57 Native American branches. In 1964, the Church created another Indian mission in Rapid City, South Dakota. Spanish-speaking branches were also organized in the Spanish-American Mission in the southwest United States.

Ethnic branches continued throughout the 1960s. However, during the early 1970s, Church leaders questioned the policy of sponsoring separate branches and missions. In 1972, Church leaders sent out a letter that many stakes interpreted to mean that they should absorb the ethnic groups. In the same year, the Southwest Indian Mission was also dissolved. At first, some missionaries in the three geographical missions—Colorado, Arizona, and Arizona–New Mexico—continued to learn Navajo and work exclusively with Native Americans. By 1980, however, the mission president in the Rapid City, South Dakota, mission informed his missionaries that they were not called strictly to an Indian mission. The idea of separate branches and missions for ethnic and foreign-language-speaking members started to vanish.

With the introduction of the Basic Unit plan in 1977, however, the idea of ethnic branches returned. Several factors influenced the formation of new branches. Increasing numbers of Southeast Asians immigrating to the United States, a growing Church population in largely black sections of American cities as a result of increased missionary efforts following the priesthood revelation in 1978, and a desire by ethnic groups such as Tongans, Samoans, Hispanics, and Native Americans to worship in their own language and with members of similar backgrounds led to separate congregations. Branches representing these ethnic groups can be found throughout the United States. The map shows branches and wards whose primary language is not English. There were at least 405 foreign-language branches in the United States in 1992. There are other ethnic branches that are more difficult to identify because the meetings are conducted in English. Native American and African American branches, for example, would not show up in such a listing. For example, while there are only two Navajo units listed for the Chinle Stake in Arizona, created in 1990, most of the stake's members are Native Americans.

Dealing with multicultural groups creates a dilemma for the Mormon Church. While the Doctrine and Covenants states, "Every man shall hear the fullness of the gospel in his own tongue, and in his own language," the Church has encouraged integration so that members can become "fellow citizens with the saints" (Ephesians 2:19). These dissimilar ideals have led to the changing policy toward ethnic branches. This continues to be an unresolved issue for the Church.

Jessie L. Embry, "Ethnic Groups and the LDS Church," *Dialogue: A Journal of Mormon Thought* 25 (Winter 1992):81–97; Jessie L. Embry, "Little Berlin: Swiss Saints of the Logan Tenth Ward," *Utah Historical Quarterly* 56 (Summer 1988):222–235; Richard L. Jensen, "Mother Tongue: Use of Non-English Languages in The Church of Jesus Christ of Latter-day Saints in the United States, 1850–1983," *New Views of Mormon History: A Collection of Essays in Honor of Leonard J. Arrington*, Davis Bitton and Maureen Ursenbach Beecher, editors (1987), 273–303.

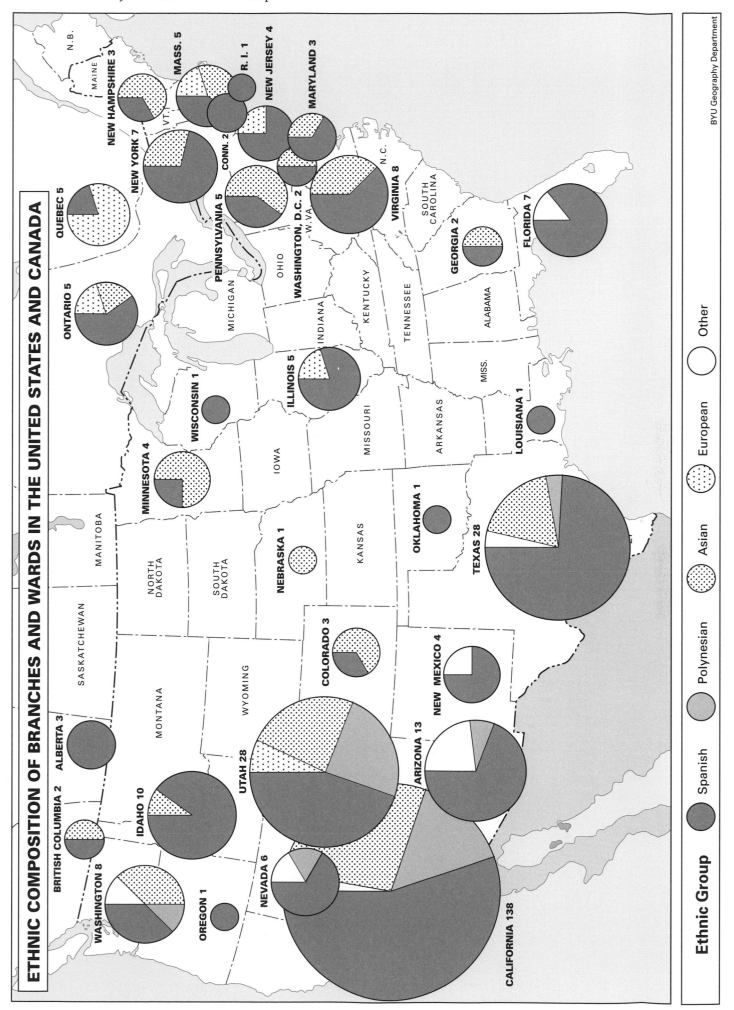

ETHNIC COMPOSITION OF BRANCHES AND WARDS IN THE UNITED STATES AND CANADA

BYU Geography Department

Ethnic Group

Spanish Polynesian Asian European Other

147

UTAH VOTING PATTERNS IN THE 20th CENTURY

Jean Bickmore White

In recent years, there has been a tendency to consider Utah a solidly Republican state, ostensibly because of the strong conservative tendencies of the state's Mormon majority. A longer view of the state's voting patterns shows that Utah has moved from one major party to the other, often following national trends. In the 25 presidential elections since statehood in 1896, Utah has voted for the losing candidate only five times, in 1896, 1912, 1960, 1976, and 1992. In three of those elections, however (1960, 1976, and 1992), Democrats were elected to statewide offices or congressional seats, illustrating Utahns' tendency to split tickets between parties. On three occasions, 1912 (Theodore Roosevelt), 1924 (Robert La Follette), and 1992 (Ross Perot), minor-party candidates polled a substantial number of votes, preventing the state winner from gaining a majority. Other minor-party candidates have had little success in statewide elections in Utah.

During the first decade of the 20th century, Utah clearly was a Republican state, reflecting efforts of Mormon Church leaders during the 1890s to establish a two-party system in Utah Territory. Until 1891 there had been two territorial political parties, the People's party, controlled by the Mormon Church, and the non-Mormon Liberal party. In a move toward statehood, the People's party was dissolved in 1891, and Church leaders worked to establish a two-party system along national lines. In national politics, Mormons had appeared to favor the Democratic party during the territorial period, so it was necessary to encourage some members to become Republicans. Some Church leaders, including Joseph F. Smith (later president), George Q. Cannon, and John Henry Smith, also wanted to show a substantial Republican vote during the early 1890s to gain national Republican support for statehood. This tilt toward the Republicans was furthered by that party's tariff policies; it also reflected national Republican strength, which persisted until the election of Woodrow Wilson in 1912. In 191,6 Utahns voted for Wilson and elected their first Democrat and non-Mormon governor, Simon Bamberger, a wealthy Jewish mining entrepreneur. Through the 1920s, Utah and the nation swung to the Republicans, keeping Republican apostle Reed Smoot, a dominating political figure at home, in the U.S. Senate. During this same period, however, Utahns twice elected Democrat (and non-Mormon) George Dern as governor.

The national embrace of the New Deal was matched in Utah from 1932 to 1950, the only period of Democratic dominance of virtually every major office since 1896. The Republican era that started with Dwight Eisenhower in 1952 was reflected in Utah. With the exception of Lyndon Johnson in 1964, Utahns have voted for Republican presidential candidates since 1952 and have not elected a Democratic U.S. senator since 1970. The governor's office is a different matter. Held by Republicans from 1949 to 1965, it was occupied by Democrats Calvin Rampton and Scott Matheson for the next 20 years, then won back by Republican Norman Bangerter in 1984. In elections for governor since statehood, Utahns have voted Republican 13 times and Democratic 12 times.

Utah's votes for the U.S. House of Representatives tend to be tied less to national trends than to local interests and personalities. Utah's First District, largely rural except for Ogden and Provo (until 1982), was carried by a Democrat from 1970 until 1980 and since then has been held by a Republican. The Second District, consisting largely of Salt Lake City, has had more Republican than Democratic incumbents since 1972, but is considered a swing district. The Third District seat, created in 1982 with Utah County as a core, is considered strongly Republican, but was won by a Democrat in 1990 and 1992.

The issue of Mormon Church influence on Utah politics is persistent. Church presidents were criticized for endorsing presidential candidates in 1912 and 1936; the favored Republican candidate in 1936 did not carry the state. Church policy in recent years has been to maintain strict neutrality in political campaigns; nevertheless most of Utah's highest officials and over 85 percent of its legislators are Mormons. Although sensitive to charges that they unduly influence political decisions, Church leaders reserve the right to speak out on what they consider to be moral issues. Abortion in most circumstances is opposed; the placing of MX missiles in Utah in the 1970s was opposed, as was a measure (overwhelmingly defeated) to allow county option voting on pari-mutuel betting in 1992. Church leaders support laws that discourage but do not prohibit consumption of alcohol, perhaps recalling that in 1933 Utah voted—over Church opposition—to end the nation's experiment with prohibition. Mormon Church leaders' influence in Utah elections undoubtedly will continue to be an issue.

Thomas G. Alexander, "Political Patterns of Early Statehood, 1896–1919," pp. 409–428; Frank H. Jonas, editor, *Politics in the American West* (1968), especially Frank H. Jonas, "Utah: The Different State," pp. 327–329; Richard D. Poll, editor, *Utah's History* (1978), especially Gustive O. Larson, "Government, Politics, and Conflict," pp. 243–274; F. Ross Peterson, "Utah Politics Since 1945," pp. 515–530.

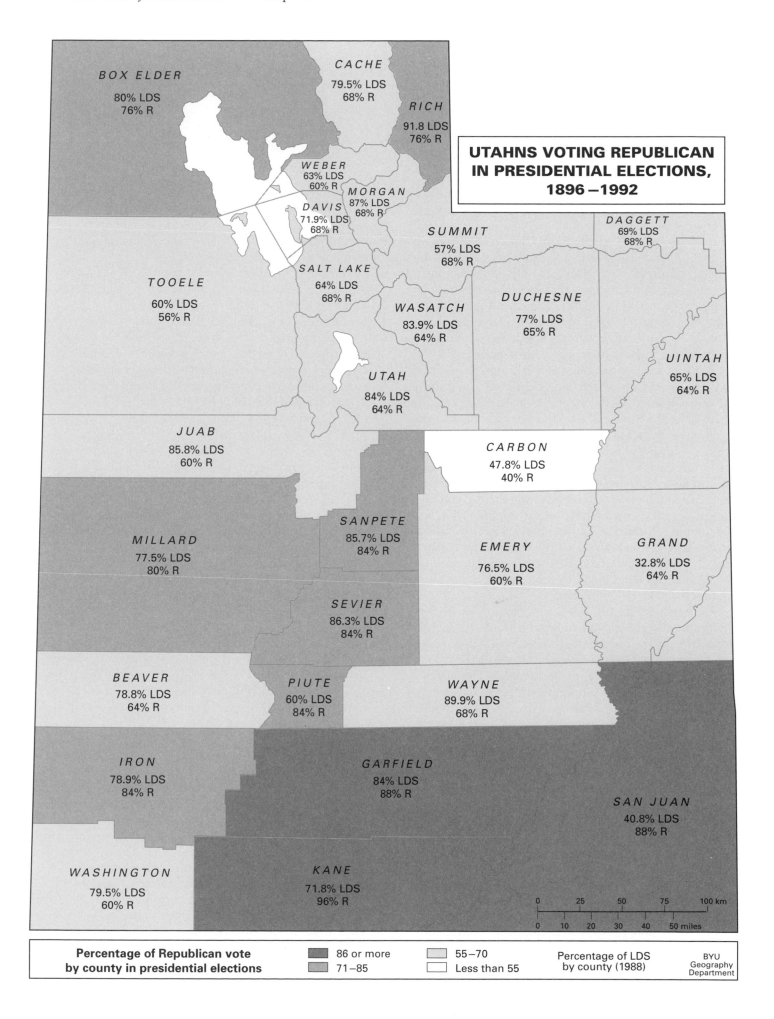

BOX ELDER
80% LDS
76% R

CACHE
79.5% LDS
68% R

RICH
91.8 LDS
76% R

WEBER
63% LDS
60% R

MORGAN
87% LDS
68% R

DAVIS
71.9% LDS
68% R

UTAHNS VOTING REPUBLICAN IN PRESIDENTIAL ELECTIONS, 1896–1992

SUMMIT
57% LDS
68% R

DAGGETT
69% LDS
68% R

TOOELE
60% LDS
56% R

SALT LAKE
64% LDS
68% R

WASATCH
83.9% LDS
64% R

DUCHESNE
77% LDS
65% R

UINTAH
65% LDS
64% R

UTAH
84% LDS
64% R

JUAB
85.8% LDS
60% R

CARBON
47.8% LDS
40% R

MILLARD
77.5% LDS
80% R

SANPETE
85.7% LDS
84% R

EMERY
76.5% LDS
60% R

GRAND
32.8% LDS
64% R

SEVIER
86.3% LDS
84% R

BEAVER
78.8% LDS
64% R

PIUTE
60% LDS
84% R

WAYNE
89.9% LDS
68% R

IRON
78.9% LDS
84% R

GARFIELD
84% LDS
88% R

SAN JUAN
40.8% LDS
88% R

WASHINGTON
79.5% LDS
60% R

KANE
71.8% LDS
96% R

| 0 | 25 | 50 | 75 | 100 km |
| 0 | 10 | 20 | 30 | 40 | 50 miles |

| Percentage of Republican vote by county in presidential elections | ▓ 86 or more | ░ 55–70 | Percentage of LDS by county (1988) | BYU Geography Department |
| | ▒ 71–85 | □ Less than 55 | | |

TEMPLES

Richard O. Cowan

Temples occupy an important place in the spiritual lives of Latter-day Saints. Unlike the Church's thousands of meetinghouses worldwide that are open to the public, temples are entered only by those Church members who are recommended as worthy by local ecclesiastical leaders. Sacred ceremonies performed only in temples include the endowment instructions that emphasize the requirements for returning to God's presence and sealings that unite families for eternity. In temples, Latter-day Saints may also be baptized vicariously for deceased persons and receive these higher ordinances in their behalf.

The first temple, dedicated at Kirtland, Ohio, in 1836, consisted principally of two large auditoriums, one above the other. It served as the meetinghouse and spiritual headquarters for the Saints. Although remarkable divine manifestations occurred in this structure, it was abandoned when the Mormons were forced to leave northeastern Ohio. During the 1830s, the Saints dedicated sites for two other temples at Independence and Far West, Missouri, but persecution prevented construction there. Temple ordinances were inaugurated during the early 1840s, and the temple dedicated at Nauvoo, Illinois, in 1846 included a baptismal font and other facilities designed for these sacred ceremonies. Once again, the Saints were compelled to abandon this temple, and soon afterward, it was burned by a mob and leveled by a tornado.

Cornerstones for the Salt Lake Temple were laid in 1853, but completion and dedication would come 40 years later. In the meantime, three other Utah temples were completed. The St. George Temple (1877) followed the basic pattern of earlier temples. The Logan Temple (1884), and Manti Temple (1888), however, replaced each lower auditorium with a series of rooms painted with murals to provide a setting for the instructions of the endowment. The Salt Lake Temple (1893) followed this new pattern and also provided special council rooms for general Church leaders. This six-spired structure has become perhaps the most widely recognized symbol of Mormonism.

The four temples dedicated during the first half of the 20th century reflected the Saints' geographical expansion. For the first time, the temples were not in the same state as Church headquarters: Laie, Hawaii (1919); Cardston, Alberta (1923); Mesa, Arizona (1927); and Idaho Falls, Idaho (1945). These omitted the upper auditorium and retained only the rooms for temple ordinances.

Thirteen more temples were completed during the next three decades. Three temples outside the United States were dedicated during the 1950s: in Switzerland in 1955, and in New Zealand and London in 1958. Rather than having the traditional series of muraled rooms, these three temples employed motion pictures to present the endowment in a single lecture room. Hence these structures were smaller, ranging from 34,000 to 38,000 square feet—less than half the size of most other temples. Further-more, the films facilitated presentation of temple instructions in multiple languages.

Two of the Church's largest temples went into service during this period: the 190,000 square-foot Los Angeles Temple (1956), and the 160,000 square-foot Washington, D.C., Temple (1974). Each of these temples incorporated a large "solemn assembly" hall on its upper floor. Other U.S. temples also provided multiple ordinance rooms where more than one group could receive the endowment instructions simultaneously. These included Oakland (1964), Ogden and Provo (1972), and Seattle (1980). The Jordan River Temple (1981) became the second in the Salt Lake Valley. Temples in other areas included São Paulo, Brazil, completed in 1978, Tokyo, in 1980, and Mexico City (the fifth largest temple built by the Church), in 1983.

The 1980s brought an explosion in planning and temple construction. Typically, only one new temple was announced at a time. Between 1980 and 1984, however, 22 new temples were planned, in Atlanta, Boise, Chicago, Dallas, and Denver in North America; and elsewhere in Argentina, Chile, Peru, Ecuador, Colombia, Guatemala, Tahiti, Tonga, Samoa, Australia, Korea, Taiwan, the Philippines, South Africa, and Sweden. Germany (after unification) became the only country outside of the United States or Canada to have two temples. All of these were much smaller structures, ranging from 7,500 to 29,000 square feet—about the size of local meetinghouses. In 1992, plans were also announced for temples in Hong Kong and Preston, England, and in 1993, for one in Madrid, Spain.

Beginning in 1984, nine larger temples (50,000 to 100,000 square feet) were planned for areas of Latter-day Saint growth in North America: Portland, Oregon; Las Vegas; Toronto; San Diego; Orlando; Bountiful, Utah; St. Louis; Hartford, Connecticut; and a second temple in Utah Valley, just south of Salt Lake City.

When all the temples that have been announced go into service, there will be a total of 55. The accompanying map shows how these temples are beginning to dot the earth more than ever before. Latter-day Saints still look forward to the fulfillment of prophecies by Brigham Young and others of the time when there will be thousands of temples worldwide bringing blessings to the living and the dead.

Richard O. Cowan, *Temples to Dot the Earth* (1989); Boyd K. Packer, *The Holy Temple* (1980); James E. Talmage, *The House of the Lord* (1980).

TEMPLES AROUND THE WORLD

Tokyo, Japan, 1980

Taipei, Taiwan, 1984

Manila, Philippines, 1984

New Zealand 1958

Sydney, Australia 1984

Seoul, South Korea 1985

Hong Kong

Stockholm, Sweden, 1985

Freiberg, Germany, 1985

Frankfurt, Germany, 1987

Switz., 1955

Preston, England, Area

London, 1958

Spain

Johannesburg, S. Africa, 1985

São Paulo, Brazil 1978

Buenos Aires, Argentina, 1986

Santiago, Chile, 1983

Lima, Peru, 1986

Bogotá, Colombia

Guayaquil, Ecuador

Mexico City, 1983

Guatemala City, 1984

Papeete, Tahiti, 1983

Apia, Samoa, 1983

Nuku'alofa, Tonga, 1983

Hawaii, 1919

Inset map (North America):

Hartford

Toronto, 1990

Kirtland, 1836 (no longer in use)

Washington, 1974

Atlanta, 1983

Orlando

Chicago, 1985

St. Louis

Nauvoo, 1846 (no longer stands)

Dallas, 1984

Denver, 1986

Alberta, 1923

Idaho Falls, 1945

Logan, 1884

Salt Lake, 1893

Provo, 1972

Manti, 1888

St. George, 1877

Arizona, 1927

Las Vegas, 1989

Los Angeles, 1956

Ogden, 1972

Bountiful

Jordan River, 1981

Mt. Timpanogos

Oakland, 1964

San Diego, 1993

Seattle, 1980

Portland, 1989

Boise, 1984

Legend:

• Temple in operation with date completed

o Temple announced or under construction

5,000 km

3,000 miles

BYU Geography Dept.

EMERGENCE OF MORMONISM ON THE AMERICAN LANDSCAPE (1950–1965)

Jan Shipps

For more than a century after the settlement of the Great Salt Lake Valley (1847), the great majority of Latter-day Saints lived in "Zion in the tops of the mountains," an area extending outward from Temple Square across all of the state of Utah, northward to Idaho and Wyoming, southward to Arizona, westward to Nevada, and eastward to Colorado. Known to geographers, historians, and other social scientists as the Mormon culture region, to the Saints the Intermountain West has always been Mormonism's center place; the remainder of the world, including the rest of the United States, was the mission field.

While nearly 20 percent of the membership of the LDS Church lived outside Zion as early as 1930, references to the Saints in both textbooks and the popular press continued for decades to picture Mormonism as a regional phenomenon, a faith community situated in the Intermountain West. This is not as surprising as one might think: with the exception of California and a few large metropolitan areas, branches of local Mormons outside the Intermountain West were nearly all associated with the geographical headquarters of regional LDS missions, which, for the most part, were housed in Victorian mansions or other substantial dwellings in residential areas. Although identified by signs as LDS mission headquarters, these structures did not resemble churches; therefore, they did not advertise the existence of local Mormon congregations. Moreover, despite the fact that a number of LDS ward houses had been built in southern California and in other Pacific states before 1941 and despite several substantial meetinghouses located in the larger urban areas of the nation, these buildings likewise failed to advertise the presence of LDS congregations effectively since they were not peculiarly Mormon from an architectural standpoint.

But this changed dramatically between 1945 and 1965 as LDS members from the Intermountain West, most of whom belonged to the Church's lay priesthood, settled with their families in many different areas of the United States. Joining branches of longtime Mountain Saints and the rapidly expanding cadre of LDS converts who had never gathered to Zion, these Utah Mormons provided the lay leadership critical to the organization of LDS stakes and wards all across the country. The formation of these basic congregational units of the Church called for the building of meetinghouses on an unprecedented scale.

In what turned out to be a brilliant decision from the standpoint of the maintenance of LDS identity in an altered situation, the Brethren at the head of the Church hierarchy decreed that the Church's standard building plans would be used for all these LDS structures. Their edict, which appears to have been made on practical and economic grounds, has been from an aesthetic point of view much maligned. But in view of the significance of place to the Saints, the sagacity of the decision that led the Saints to build structures that gave the impression of the appearance of a new religious enterprise is evident in retrospect.

Members of virtually all of these newly formed mission field stakes and wards included western Saints who had been born in the Church and reared in a distinctive Mormon culture. This culture was as firmly rooted in a sense of place (Zion in the tops of the mountains) as in the sense of unity and order implicit in a world whose structure rested on a coherent plan of salvation and a clearly defined system of ecclesiastical hierarchy that stretched from twelve-year-old boys ordained as deacons in the Aaronic Priesthood to the president of the Church, who was also its prophet, seer, and revelator. In many of these newly organized units there were also members who were lifelong Saints and longtime converts who had never moved west, but whose religious imagination as well as institutional life revolved around Salt Lake City, Mormonism's center place. In addition, the new LDS congregations included substantial and sometimes overwhelming proportions of Latter-day Saints whose conversion to this particular form of Christianity was only the first step in becoming Mormon; they needed a special place where the mormonizing process could go forward. No matter what their physical location, the neat utilitarian multifunctional structures that the local Saints built according to the Church's standard plan were distinctively Mormon places. The very fact that these clearly identifiable LDS structures could be found in town after town and suburb after suburb cultivated among the Saints what might be called a Zionic sense, making the very LDS meetinghouses themselves agents of assimilation and signals that wherever the Saints gather, there Zion is.

Martha Bradley, "The Church and Colonel Saunders: Mormon Standard Plan Architecture" (Master's thesis, Brigham Young University, 1981); Richard O. Cowan, *The Church in the Twentieth Century* (1985), especially Chapter 14; Tim B. Heaton, "Vital Statistics," in *Encyclopedia of Mormonism*, Daniel H. Ludlow, editor (1992) 4:1518–1537.

NEW BUILDINGS CONSTRUCTED ACCORDING TO LDS STANDARD BUILDING PLANS, 1950–1965

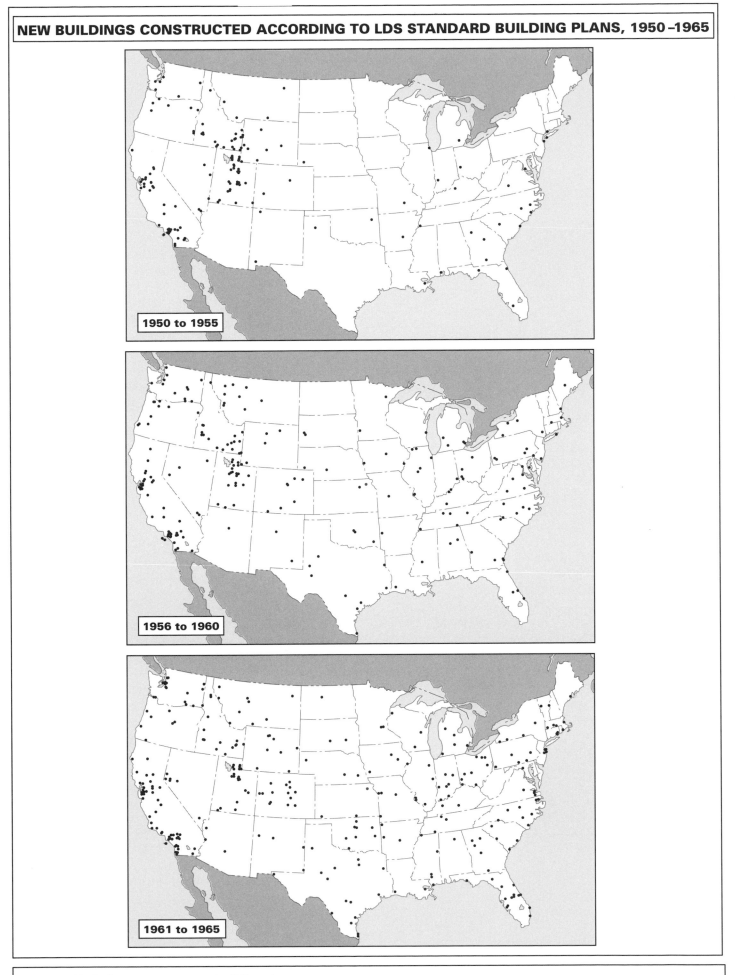

1950 to 1955

1956 to 1960

1961 to 1965

• Each dot represents one building site.

BYU Geography Department

APPENDIX

Eliza R. Snow's Travels, 1880–1881

March 1880

13	Tooele Stake
18	Salt Lake
19	Weber Stake

May 1880

4	19th Ward
26	South Cottonwood

June 1880

7	Box Elder Stake, Brigham City
14	Weber Stake, Ogden
18–19	Salt Lake Stake

July 1880

13	Draper
16	Bountiful
17	14th Ward

August 1880

3	Nephi
3	Fountain Green
4–5	Moroni
5	Mt. Pleasant, Fairview, Indianola
7	Mt. Pleasant
9	Spring City, Ephraim
10	Manti, Pettyville (Sterling), Mayfield
13	Gunnison, Fayette
14	Levan
15	Nephi
3–16	Mona [30 meetings in all]

September 1880

13	Batesville (Tooele Co.)
23	Sevier Stake, Richfield, "and other towns in Sevier County" [10 days, 20 meetings]

October 1880

24–25	Sevier Stake Conference, Richfield
27	Lehi

November 1880

9	Provo
10	Scipio
12	Holden
13	Fillmore
14	Meadow, Kanosh, Fillmore, Parowan

19	Washington, St. George
23	Washington
24	St. George
27	Santa Clara
29	St. George

December 1880

2	St. George
3–4	Pine Valley, Pinto, Hebron
14	Santa Clara
23	St. George
28	Santa Clara
31	Washington

January 1881

1	Began trip to Rio Virgin, Harrisburg, Leeds, Toquervill, Virgin City, Duncan's Retreat, Grafton, Rockville, Shonesburg
21	St. George

February 1881

5	Price
10–14	Kanab
15	Mt. Carmel
16–21	Orderville, Johnson
23–25	Kanab

March 1881

10–11	St. George
27	Parowan Stake
28	Beaver
30	Minersville
31	Snow and Young return to Salt Lake City

April 1881

[?]	Salt Lake City
23–25	Morgan

May 1881

17	21st Ward
20	10th Ward
22–23	Big Cottonwood
24	South Cottonwood
27	Provo (Utah County Conference)
30	Granite

June 1881

7	West Jordan
9–11	Weber Stake
12	Plain City, Harperville

14–15	Brigham City
16	Honeyville
17	West Portage
18–19	Malad City
20	Samaria, West Portage
21	"Indian Farm" (Washakie)
29	Sugarhouse

August 1881

17	20th Ward
27	12th Ward

September 1881

3–4	Cache Stake
5	Wellsville
8–10	Weber Stake
14	Tour of Sanpete Co., Nephi
16	Moroni
17	Fairview
18	Indianola, Fairview
19	Mt. Pleasant
20	Spring City
22	Manti
24	Fountain Green
25	Nephi

October 1881

21–25	Morgan

November 1881

5	14th Ward General Meeting
7	Provo, Spanish Fork, Santaquin
12	Goshen
14	Springville
15	Provo
19	14th Ward General Meeting
23	10th Ward

December 1881

5	South Jordan
10–12	Tooele Stake
16–17	Salt Lake Stake
27	10th Ward
	17th Ward

INDEX